RECOGNIZING THE

Recognizing the Non-Religious

Reimagining the Secular

LOIS LEE

OXFORD
UNIVERSITY PRESS

Great Clarendon Street, Oxford, OX2 6DP,
United Kingdom

Oxford University Press is a department of the University of Oxford.
It furthers the University's objective of excellence in research, scholarship,
and education by publishing worldwide. Oxford is a registered trade mark of
Oxford University Press in the UK and in certain other countries

© Lois Lee 2015

The moral rights of the author have been asserted

First published 2015
First published in paperback 2017

All rights reserved. No part of this publication may be reproduced, stored in
a retrieval system, or transmitted, in any form or by any means, without the
prior permission in writing of Oxford University Press, or as expressly permitted
by law, by licence or under terms agreed with the appropriate reprographics
rights organization. Enquiries concerning reproduction outside the scope of the
above should be sent to the Rights Department, Oxford University Press, at the
address above

You must not circulate this work in any other form
and you must impose this same condition on any acquirer

Published in the United States of America by Oxford University Press
198 Madison Avenue, New York, NY 10016, United States of America

British Library Cataloguing in Publication Data
Data available

Library of Congress Cataloging in Publication Data
Data available

ISBN 978-0-19-873684-4 (Hbk.)
ISBN 978-0-19-880853-4 (Pbk.)

Links to third party websites are provided by Oxford in good faith and
for information only. Oxford disclaims any responsibility for the materials
contained in any third party website referenced in this work.

*This book is dedicated, with love and gratitude,
to my parents*

Acknowledgements

This book would not have been possible without the people who gave their time, formally and informally, to discuss religion, non-religion, and secularity with me. Above all, I want to acknowledge their contribution and to thank them for their generosity with their time, hospitality, and stories.

I am also grateful to the following organizations for funding this work at various stages: the Economic and Social Research Council (ESRC) doctoral research funding scheme and the Sociology department at the University of Cambridge; Clare Hall, Cambridge; the Conway Hall Ethical Society, Rationalist Association, and British Humanist Association for supporting this project via the Blackham Fellowship; and the Religion and Political Theory Centre, UCL, and the European Research Council (ERC) Grant 283867, 'Is Religion Special? Secularism and Religion in Contemporary Legal and Political Theory', for supporting the project to its conclusion. I also benefited from the chance to develop this work as a visiting fellow at the Institut für die Wissenschaften vom Menschen (IWM), and am enormously grateful for the support of that institute as well as to the inspiring and wonderful people that I met there.

This work has been developed in conversation with many engaged and insightful audiences who have given their time to presentations of this research. There are too many to mention by name, but this book bears their mark in numerous ways. Material from some of the chapters has also appeared in different forms elsewhere, though extensively revised here. An earlier version of Chapter 1 appears as 'Talking About a Revolution: Terminology for the New Field of Non-religion Studies', in *Journal of Contemporary Religion* 27 (1), 129–39, 2012 and reprinted in *Secularity and Non-Religion*, edited by Elisabeth Arweck, Stephen Bullivant, and Lois Lee, London: Routledge, 2013. Sections of this chapter also build on my contributions to 'Irreligion', co-written with Colin Campbell and published in *The Vocabulary for the Study of Religion*, edited by Robert Segal and Kocku von Stuckrad, Leiden: BRILL. The analyses presented in Chapters 4 and 5 are developed from work appearing as 'Locating Nonreligion, in Mind, Body and Space: New Research Methods for a New Field', *Annual Review of the Sociology of Religion*, 3. Leiden: BRILL: 135–58, 2012;

and 'Vehicles of New Atheism: The Atheist Bus Campaign, Nonreligious Representations and Material Culture', in *New Atheism's Legacy: Critical Perspectives from Philosophy and the Social Sciences*, edited by Christopher R. Cotter and Philip Quadrio, Dordrecht: Springer, forthcoming. The arguments of this book have also been developed in 'Secular or Nonreligious? Investigating and Interpreting Generic "Not Religious" Categories and Populations', *Religion* 44 (3), 466–82, 2014; 'Ambivalent Atheist Identities: Power and Nonreligious Culture in Contemporary Britain', *Social Analysis*, 2015. 'Western Europe', in *The Oxford Handbook of Atheism*, edited by Stephen Bullivant and Michael Ruse, OUP, 586–600, 2013; 'From "Neutrality" to Dialogue: Constructing the Religious other in British Non-Religious Discourses', in *Modernities Revisited*, edited by Maren Behrensen, Lois Lee, and Ahmet S. Tekelioglu, IWM, 2011; and in my new introduction to Colin Campbell's *Toward a Sociology of Irreligion*, republished by Alcuin Academics in 2013.

I am enormously grateful to have received encouragement and mentorship from Patrick Baert, Brendan Burchell, Colin Campbell, Abby Day, Mia Gray, Kim Knott, David Lehmann, Cécile Laborde, Gordon Lynch, David Voas, and Linda Woodhead. My particular and deep thanks go Patrick Baert, Grace Davie, Kim Knott, David Lehmann, Anna Strhan, and Phil Zuckerman for their close readings and invaluable comments on earlier drafts of this book. At Oxford University Press, I am indebted to Tom Perridge and the anonymous reviewers of my manuscript for their supportive and insightful readings which greatly contributed to the development of the volume; and to everyone in the production team for their skill and support.

This investigation of the secular as an object of social scientific enquiry has been invigorated and enhanced by work with everyone involved with the Nonreligion and Secularity Research Network (NSRN). I am especially grateful to co-founder and frequent collaborator Stephen Bullivant, as well as to other co-directors past and present—Nicholas Gibson, Stacey Gutkowski, Johannes Quack, and Christopher R. Cotter—and to everyone on the NSRN Online and *Secularism and Nonreligion* editorial teams, with particular thanks to Ryan Cragun.

In addition to those already mentioned, I feel very privileged to have had conversations about this work (and other things) with the following people: Katie Aston, Aurelia Bardon, Peter Barry, Steph Berns, Andrew

Acknowledgements

Brown, Ole Birk Laursen, Matthew Engelke, Kira Erwin, Charlotte Faircloth, Carolyn Heitmeyer, Alexander Hensby, Maruta Herding, Barry Kosmin, Hettie Malcolmson, Ella McPherson, Lorna Mumford, David O'Brien, Frank L. Pasquale, Brian Pearce, David Pollack, Susannah Rigg, Shirin Shahrokni, Ruth Sheldon, Elitza Staneova, and Paul-Francois Tremlett, as well as with all of my esteemed colleagues at the Religion and Political Theory Centre at UCL.

This work could not have been completed without the company and support of the following people: Claire Cordier, Becky Hendry, Anna Jones Rodriguez, Keren Kossow, and Nevena Pecotic; the Gallaghers; my beloved grandparents; my family, Ginny Halley, Marcus, Ruby, Jodie, and Mae Lee, Rachel Hart, and Sam Richards; and Emily Berry and Katie Lee, who went the extra mile (or two, or three). Finally my thanks to Rob Gallagher, whose belief in this project—and me—has kept everything going and makes it all worthwhile.

Contents

Introduction: Revisiting the Secular 1

1. Contradistinctions in Terms: Vocabulary for the Study of Secularity and Non-Religion 21
2. The Insubstantial and the Substantial Seculars: Theories of Secularity and Non-Religion 49
3. The Unwaved Flag: Everyday and Banal Forms of Non-Religion 70
4. Out of the Shadows: Non-Religious and Secularist Bodies in Relief 86
5. Friends and 'Anti-Fennelists': Non-Religious Relationships and Solidarities 106
6. Disaffiliation and Misaffiliation: Identifying Non-Religion in Public Life 131
7. Beyond Unbelief: Non-Religion and Existential Culture 159

Conclusion: Reimagining the Secular 185

Appendices 201
   I. Glossary 203
   II. Interview Question Schedule 205
   III. Event Participation Questionnaire 209
   IV. Research Sample 211

Bibliography 215
Index 229

Introduction

Revisiting the Secular

So, after all, modernity may not be secular. 'Modernization'—that is, the developing of advanced industrial economies, media technologies, and their social effects—has been firmly associated with the marginalization of religion since at least the mid-nineteenth century, but many have come to see this link as irreparably flawed. Instead, that 'seat of secular modernity', the West, has experienced a pronounced reassertion of religion in public life, related in large part to processes of negotiating a few highly visible and highly controversial manifestations of religion: the less familiar religious cultures that travel with immigrant populations and which are conspicuous in their novelty; the small but dramatically violent forms that have come to prominence in global affairs; and the association of some familiar religious cultures with illiberalism and misconduct. In relation to these events and the generalized critiques of religion that they provoke, religious cultures have also been defended, reclaimed, and reformulated and, in academia, social theorists and social scientists have become more sensitive to the numerous forms of religion that have survived the emergence of modernity and even flourished within it. They have become interested also in the new forms of religion and spirituality that develop in these contexts, and in the emerging economies that have industrialized and expanded without experiencing any marked religious decline; of the BRIC economies (Brazil, Russia, India, and China), Brazil and India provide striking examples. These and other developments make it hard to see modernization as an intrinsically or straightforwardly secularizing force, and this has made it possible for some scholars to argue that secularization theory has become tenuous, if not totally defunct. The argument is far from a fait accompli (as it is sometimes presented), but it has nevertheless become necessary for scholars—and societies—to reflect more deeply on phenomena (secularity, secularism, secular modernity) and processes (secularization) that were for a long time taken for granted—a moment of critical reflection that is at least one thing that the 'post-secular' can be reasonably used to describe.[1]

All of this is true, and yet in many parts of the world the old story of secularization remains salient. In these places, traditional religiosity continues a steady decline and what is called 'subjective secularity'—unbelief and non-affiliation—continues to expand. Such populations have always been a part of the picture, recognized or not, but today the non-affiliated demand attention as the 'fourth largest religion' in the world (Zuckerman 2010c). Being 'secular' has become one of the most common things that a human being can be and living a life that is shaped only indirectly by religious cultures and beliefs is one of the most widespread.

The prevalence of secular or non-religious subjectivities is—or should be—an impressive fact therefore, but all too often it is lost in contemporary discussions that continue to treat religion as an unparalleled phenomenon of a profoundly singular nature. In fact, the scale of the secular population alone presents a great, perhaps the greatest, challenge to those who would argue that today we are witnessing not the secularization of the world but its desecularization; not the decline of religion but its transformation; not a secular or post-religious age but a post-secular one. The existence and vitality of this population should provide a forceful corrective to these accounts as well as to those critics of secularization who escalate their scepticism of secularization *theory* into a more comprehensive dismissal of the empirical processes that this theory has attempted to describe. Contemporary contributions are often guilty of this 'throwing the baby out with the bath water' and the literature concerning religion and contemporary society features an increasing number of publications that frame their work in terms of a so-called 'resurgence of religion', failing to take due account of secularization processes that are ongoing and, indeed, very advanced in many parts of the world. Though scholars may well question whether 'secularization' is the best way to conceptualize them, these are processes that they ought to account for.

---

[1] Thank you to Amy Levine for suggesting this point. See Beckford 2012 for an overview of the post-secular literature.

There are in fact several benefits that accrue from giving more attention to what it means to be secular. It helps round out our understanding of 'religion' in society, which is necessarily exclusive or incomplete if the secular is neglected: to focus solely on people's lived lives in relation to religion, or religious cultural diversity, or religious pluralism, is to discount those lives in which religion is conspicuously absent or conspicuously 'othered'. Taking proper account of these secular populations and experiences also provides a valuable check to runaway scepticism about secularization theory. It opens up new and fundamental questions for those seeking to understand contemporary societies and contemporary religion, such as what it is that really differentiates religious from secular populations—not as something we intuit or assume, but as an inevitably nuanced reality that we can only understand through detailed empirical research; or questions about how these populations shore up and destabilize different political and institutional relationships with religion. In addition, drawing similarities between the religious, spiritual, and secular, all potentially manifest in behaviours, identities, institutions, and spaces, forces us to admit that we are not as confident as we once were about why certain secular forms emerge when and where that they do. We are forced to admit that we have just as many questions about secular populations as we do about religious and spiritual ones—and maybe more, given that there is no tradition of research associated with the secular as there is for traditional and, more recently, alternative religions (Campbell 2013; Casanova 2011; Bullivant and Lee 2012; Baker and Smith 2009). We have to admit, as Charles Taylor (2009: xi) has argued, that we may not even be sure of what core terms such as 'secularity' really mean or of what we mean when we use them. If the significance of ongoing secularization processes and the experience of secular people are recognized, this provokes then, not the need for some 'post-secular' approach in which secularity is dismissed as a description of a bygone era, an undesirable norm or an outdated conceptual tool, but the need for a deeper, more critical engagement with it.

This book responds to this need by contributing to the new empirical study of 'secular' populations and culture, as a result of which it is, I argue, possible to disaggregate the secular into different parts and develop a new vocabulary, new theory, and a new methodology for the study of these parts. The book is part of a fast-growing area of research that builds on the theoretical debates mentioned above—relating to secularization, desecularization, religious change, individualization, and to the more ambiguous notion of post-secularity—by engaging with what it means to be without religious and spiritual experience as a lived and necessarily social reality. Other scholars have acknowledged the need for this kind of research (e.g. Campbell 2013; Asad 2003; Turner 2010; Baker and Smith 2009; Zuckerman 2008; 2010a; 2010b; 2012) but, perhaps because it is difficult to know where to start, perhaps because the idea of these populations' secularity as a hollow characteristic is so deeply entrenched, it is only very recently that empirical research has begun in earnest. The foundation in 2005 of the Institute for the Study of Secularism in Society and Culture (ISSSC) at Trinity College, Hartford, Connecticut by Barry Kosmin and Ariela Keysar marks a significant moment in this trajectory. So too does the emergence of the international Nonreligion and Secularity Research Network (NSRN), which I founded in 2008 in collaboration with Stephen Bullivant, Nicholas Gibson, and Stacey Gutkowksi and have since developed with many others (Bullivant and Lee 2012). This book not only draws on my own empirical work but also gathers insights from working with colleagues in the development of wider fields of non-religion studies and secularism research, in order to consolidate a theoretical framework, conceptual foundation, and agenda for future research.

    The central empirical question that this book engages with is whether people who are not religious are characterized and identifiable by their lack of engagement with religion, as secularization theorists anticipate, or whether they are, instead, shaped by experiencing or performing their difference from religious others. A related concern is the extent to which the rituals and practices used by secular people, but which also have religious equivalents or antecedents, should be understood independently of religion, or whether they are developed in contradistinction to religious cultures so that they are substantially and meaningfully irreligious or non-religious—rather than insubstantially areligious, post-religious, or secular. These questions rely on a distinction between the 'insubstantial secular' and the 'substantial secular'—or, as I suggest, between the 'secular' and the 'non-religious'. This introduction sets out this distinction and how we might move from an overly inclusive and vague notion of secularity that problematically combines both things—the insubstantial and the substantial secular—to a more specific set of concepts that help us unpack and understand secular life.

STARTING WITH THE SECULAR

My research into the secular began in 2006, arising from various signs that there might be something more to those empirical phenomena that are typically, if somewhat indeterminately, called 'secular', and a sense that being 'secular' might not only be a matter of being *without* religion but also a matter of being *with* something else. These indications include the number of people able to identify themselves as 'not religious' in survey research, combined with the fact that these people live their lives in various relationships with religious cultures. Identifying as 'not religious' is a small but extremely common example of non-religious practice, albeit one that takes place at the instigation of a social researcher. But identifying oneself in contradistinction from religion might plausibly take place outside these settings and be associated with more diverse forms of thought, action, and interaction, especially in religiously plural social contexts. In itself, the scale of this non-religious population and its location in culturally diverse and hyper-mediated societies suggests a high incidence of interaction between people who do and do not participate in religious cultures (Campbell 2013). Significantly, in these interactions the absence of religion necessarily becomes meaningful and concrete rather than irrelevant or insubstantial. What is more, we already have indications that people understand themselves in contradistinction to religion and that this positioning matters to them. So, for example, the 2008 British Social Attitudes survey found that 37 per cent of Britons were clearly non-religious, exactly the same percentage of people who said they were clearly religious (Voas and Ling 2010: 69). This survey also found that over two-thirds of those identifying with the non-religious category (26 per cent) said they were 'very or extremely' non-religious, with a further 11 per cent saying they were 'somewhat' non-religious. This actually contrasts with the religious group, three-quarters of whom said they were 'somewhat' religious (Voas and Ling 2010: 69). The meanings behind these identifications are unclear and the contexts of these data are complicated; these findings cannot, for example, be taken apart from a religio-secularist tradition that privatizes religion and is suspicious of extreme piety—a framework that places demands on religion that are not being placed on the non-religious. Nevertheless, they show that it is not only reasonable but demonstrable to reconceive of 'secularity' as something present in social life—something that acts in the world and is acted upon.

As well as being significant elsewhere, in so-called secular Europe 'atheists' (Siegers 2010) or the 'unreligious' (Voas and Ling 2010) equal or outnumber the religious in many national populations. The secular appear to be more numerous still if we include those who are more ambiguously unreligious: Siegers' (2010) work may imply that 'fuzzy religiosity', the category David Voas (2009a) suggests for those who are neither actively religious nor actively non-religious, is a form of indifference to religion and the same interpretation might be reasonable in relation to those who are only 'nominally religious', the category used by Abby Day (2011) to describe that common type of fuzziness in which the individual identifies with a religious culture but does not otherwise participate in it. Indeed, indifference to religion is possibly the modal form of 'religion' in Europe—equally significant, intriguingly, in countries that are otherwise mainly religious (as in Poland, for example) as it is in countries where the remainder is predominantly unreligious (as in Denmark) (Siegers 2010). Notably, the same effect is observed in relation to 'secular Europe' and 'religious America': in a recent study, the 'fuzzy faithful' numbered 36 and 24 per cent of British and US populations respectively, while these populations differed more widely in the size of their actively religious and actively non-religious populations (Voas and Ling 2010: 71). In fact, the contrasting distributions of these *actively* and *passively* non-religious populations presents a paradox that is itself good reason to investigate further, using empirical methods to grasp what emerge as quite complicated empirical realities.

Though these so-called secular populations are sizeable, then, it is also true that some of them are a relatively new feature of human life, decades rather than centuries old. It is therefore only quite recently that a broad and nuanced empirical engagement with secularity has become a real possibility. This means that scholars are able to re-engage with theories of secularity and secularization that were introduced by the founders of the social sciences and which have held these areas of study in their grasp ever since. The sociological theory of secularization is as old as sociology itself and, via the work of Max Weber and Émile Durkheim especially, central to its first two concerns: the nature of society and the nature of industrial modernity. The beginnings of the discipline were motivated by anxieties about social cohesion in Europe and religion was seen to be the exemplary means for achieving such cohesion. Adopting the non-theist rationalist perspective that was gathering force at the same time and which understood religion to be inconsistent with modern science and reason, Weber, Durkheim et al. thought that modernization and secularization would be coterminous. Thus, in its beginnings, sociology can be understood as an investigation of how societies can possibly achieve cohesion in the absence of religion. Yet, because these scholars worked in contexts rich with religious cultures and because their theories encouraged them to look for signs of the marginalization that they understood to be underway, their work tended to focus on processes of religious decline rather than the transformation of religion into new cultural formations. The general tradition of 'secularizationist' thought (to use a label Steve Bruce (2011) has recently provided) tends, therefore, to focus on the nature of industrial modernity as a real and existing social reality and context rather than on the nature of the secular, which is seen less as a concrete reality than a marker that flags where religion once stood. The emergence of actual secular realities, including the observation that these realities are rarely religion-free, opens all aspects of this framework to scrutiny. We may ask, precisely how is it that religion has diminished in the lives of 'secular moderns'? Is it a blanket effect or do particular aspects of religious practice and culture recede while others remain active and significant? Are 'secular moderns' more rational and more reasonable than other people? Are they less social? Are their cultural lives impoverished compared with those who participate in the religious cultures that we know to be so infinitely rich? Are they part of rationalized, bureaucratic social systems, living disenchanted lives, as Weber foretold?

The idea that industrial modernity involves some kind of reduced role for religion is, as we have seen, now contested along various fault lines, most of which focus on religion itself: whether and how religion can be defined; whether the emergence of new forms of spirituality imply that religion is not so much diminishing as altering; whether the compartmentalization of religion to its own sphere of social life is as clear-cut as secularization theory suggests; and, indeed, whether the significance of religion can be seen to be declining in any general terms. But, as scholars have become increasingly aware, the nature of the secular is the necessary other side to all of these coins and is a source of intrigue in its own right. Thus, the empirical study of what, if anything, characterizes this 'secularity' is an important way into vast, slippery debates that strike at the very heart of social theoretical traditions.

CONCEPTIONS OF THE SECULAR

Though dedicated studies of secular people remain comparatively rare, some ideas about what secularity might entail can be drawn out from literatures, such as they are, dealing with secularization, secularism, irreligion, and atheism, as well as theories of modernity. These literatures provide the possibilities that this book contends with. There are actually several concepts discussed in relation to secularity that might be considered in thinking about the nature of the secular: 'secularism', 'not religious', 'non-religious', 'the nones', 'post-religious', 'areligious', 'indifference to religion', 'atheism', 'non-theism', 'unbelief', 'agnosticism', 'godlessness', 'scientism', 'rationalism', 'rationality', 'spirituality', Bailey's (1997; see also 2001) 'implicit religion', Davie's (2007) 'vicarious religion', 'latent religiosity' and even, by Durkheimian sleights of hand, 'religiosity' itself. Some of these have been broken down into subsidiary concepts that provide yet more possibilities for thinking about the secular: atheism may be 'positive' or 'negative' (Martin 1990; Bullivant 2013); secularization may have many dimensions (Dobbelaere 1999); secularity may have different manifestations (Taylor 2007); and secularism and secularity may be seen as different aspects of the same thing (Kosmin 2007). There is also the possibility of being secular by degrees, as in Kosmin's (2007) 'hard' and 'soft' secularisms or Modood's (2010) 'moderate' and 'radical' forms.

These concepts do not provide simple ways of 'unpacking' the secular: they frequently elide; their usage varies across and even within disciplinary and theoretical traditions (and sometimes even within single pieces of work) (Lee 2012); their meanings are frequently treated as self-explanatory and left unarticulated and unscrutinized—especially the case with qualified terms such as 'anti-religious', 'post-religious', and 'areligious'; and nothing illustrates so well the need for reflexive and systematic conceptual work as the commonplace and illogical pairing of 'religion' with 'atheism' that occurs in academic as well as popular discourse (Lee 2012). Nevertheless, these terms do provide implicit and partial accounts of what secularity might mean: materialism perhaps, or hostility towards religion; the freeing of rationality from the yoke of religion, or simply the *belief* that rationality has been freed in this way; maybe secularity is religiosity experienced indirectly rather than directly, or maybe it occurs when dampeners are put on our naturally religious dispositions; and so on. Underlying this profusion of terms and meanings, though, are three core theories or assumptions about what secularity entails. These are as follows.

First, classic secularization theory uses adjectives such as 'areligious', 'post-religious', or 'indifferent to religion' to posit an idea of ideal-typical secularity as a non-entity or non-condition that solely involves the irrelevance of religion and the general ability for humans to live without it (e.g. Bruce 2002; Zuckerman 2008; Bagg and Voas 2010). The ontological claim about secularity made here is that it is nothing at all, the general absence of something concrete rather than the presence of something in particular. In short, there is not much to say about secularity. It really only exists in proxy, indicating everything that religion is not: if religion is seen to give way to modernity (e.g. Weber 2003; Gauchet 1997), then the secular *is* modernity; if religion is seen to give way to individualism, individualization, or social fragmentation, then the secular *is* individualism, individualization, or fragmentation (e.g. Beck and Beck-Gernsheim 2002; Turner 2010); if religion is seen to give way to scientific explanation and modes of reasoning (e.g. Durkheim 2001), then the secular *is* science or reason. This allows the secular to transform from being religion's other to a concept that encompasses, says Casanova (2011: 11), 'the whole of reality'.

On the other hand, recent work has focused on a substantive manifestation of the secular, in 'secularism' (e.g. Asad 2003; Levey and Modood 2010; Calhoun et al. 2011). In this work, the secular is associated with an outlook or ideology that constructs and constrains religion in ways that are typically—or necessarily—anti-religious. Secularism is a historical phenomenon in this view, particularly associated with Western modernity and bound up with political and institutional secularist regimes as well as with intellectual materialism and rationalism. The hypothesis arising from this body of work is, then, not only that the secular is substantial, but also that it is something specific, namely the constraining of religion according to an Enlightenment-derived modernist perspective that is typically anti-religious in intention or effect.

A third and final account of secularity comes from the study of irreligion, that is, the concrete ways in which people reject religion. The study of irreligion does not translate into a complete account of secularity: many scholars see irreligion as distinct from the secular, a step on the road towards it rather than its endpoint (e.g. Campbell 2013; Bruce 2002; Zuckerman 2008; Borer 2010) and accounts of irreligion and secularity are usually implicit and generally rare. Nevertheless, scholars have often approached irreligion and secularity together, expressing a notion that they are in some way tied to one another—and so claims about the former can inform investigations of the latter. The key claim about irreligion is that it is primarily an intellectual matter, involving the rejection of religious ideas on theoretical or moral grounds. Thus the rejection of theism plays a key role in these accounts and 'atheism' is a central motif.

These are, then, the three key notions of what it means to be secular: to be free from religion; to be modernistic and politically anti-religious; or to be intellectually irreligious. What is striking about these notions is that, though perhaps the latter two can be combined, it is not possible to be all three at the same time. This is a fundamental problem for existing theories and concepts of secularity.

APPROACHING THE SECULAR

This book presents research that used empirical, inductive methods in order to explore how people from a particular 'secular' population and context do, and do not, live their lives in relation to religion. The study used several methods of data collection. Formal and informal interviews investigated how non-affiliates in south-east England responded to various aspects of religion as it is locally or 'conventionally' understood (Towler 1984, in Knott 2005: 59). Formal conversations were semi-structured and took different courses, but they all dealt with key themes: religious, non-religious, and secularist identities; theistic and other typically religious beliefs; existential questions about meaning, purpose, life, and death; the use and experience of religious, non-religious, and civil life-cycle ceremonies; feelings about and experiences of religious and spiritual cultures; and, finally, the way in which religion, spirituality, non-religion, and areligion inform participants' social lives, focusing on their close personal network of family and friends. (The question schedule that guided these discussions is provided in Appendix II.)

Twelve initial interviews, acting as a pilot study for the larger project (Lee 2006), were conducted in Cambridge, before the main fieldwork in north London and surrounding areas between 2009 and 2011. Both regions have particularly high numbers of non-affiliates

(Voas and McAndrew 2012), as well as having significant religious components—current and historic—that non-affiliates frequently encounter. As a result, both regions are fertile locations in which to explore different faces of secularity—being without religion or being in contact with religion as its other. In order to investigate the potential parameters of a 'secular field', interview participants were chosen using a maximum variation sampling strategy (Schofield Clark 2003)—which is to say, interviewees were recruited according to different social networks and the overall sample included people with diverse demographic characteristics across categories of age, gender, sexuality, education, ethnicity, religious background, and political preference—all factors known to impact religiosity and its absence. A maximum of three people were recruited from each demographic 'location'. Despite much variety, the sample inevitably excluded people living and working in rural areas, a factor that may have a significant bearing on religion and secularity, and it also contained disproportionate numbers of people with higher levels of education, those identifying as 'white', and people aged between 20 and 40.[2] The sample did not aim to be representative and, as a qualitative study, the findings cannot be generalized to a larger population—in respect of which, I have avoided using numbers and other quantitative phrases ('the majority of' etcetera) in presenting this research.

Further ethnographic work situated these interview conversations in a wider cultural context. I lived and worked in Cambridge and then in Islington and Camden in north London for the duration of the fieldwork, and have drawn on innumerable informal conversations that took place over this period and subsequently. Ethnographic data were gathered in closed or private settings (the homes of interviewees and others; organized secularist and Atheist meet-up groups) and public ones (representations in national media; at larger-scale commercial events; and in the public spaces of Camden and Islington, both of which had a 'top ten' concentration of non-affiliates compared to other wards in England and Wales (Voas and McAndrew 2012)).

Analysis of this material considered both the degree to which and the ways in which the 'not religious' should be considered religious-

---

[2] The 20–30 age group is particularly large, but this reflects recruitment methods in the pilot phase using university networks and working largely with postgraduate students.

like or religion-related, rather than distant from religious cultures and post-religious in that sense. It considered how people in this category perceive and interact with the religiosity of people and things in their lives, as well as with substantively non-religious people and things. It considered also the role of overtly irreligious cultural threads—New Atheism, non-religious Humanism, and so on—as well as less explicit non-religious ones running through mainstream cultural contexts.

RECOGNIZING THE NON-RELIGIOUS

The development of this methodology followed my changing understanding of secularity. Typical of Western thinking, the pilot phase of this research approached secularity through the categories of atheism and agnosticism—according, that is, to what people think about God or gods. Even in the main fieldwork, I planned mainly to interview 'secular people', rather than considering other types of data. I went to events—activist ones organized by groups such as the National Secular Society and the British Humanist Association, and commercial ones such as the 'Nine Lessons and Carols for Godless People' show that has played in central London every year since 2008—but I did so not to explore these material and symbolic contexts nor with any more ambitious ethnographic project in mind. Rather, I went to recruit people for interview, in order to talk with them later about their thoughts and ideas and, through these events, to learn something about the intellectual and discursive contexts that might shape their ideas and vocabularies.

As this work proceeded, however, I began to notice that the people I met with engaged with religion and felt 'other than religious' in ways that extended far beyond their relationship with god(s) and claims about god(s)—and even beyond the intellectual altogether. These engagements were also emotional, social, cultural, and political. Instead of 'atheists' and 'agnostics', I started to talk and think about this group as the 'irreligious' and then, less narrowly, as the 'non-religious', and to question how comprehensively secular they really were, given the different ways that their lives were shaped in relation to and contradistinction from religion: the idea of non-religion encompasses more positive experiences of difference from religion alongside negative ones, and moves away from the problematic notion of 'indifference to religion',

Introduction 13

included in conventional definitions of irreligion (Campbell 2013), focusing instead on, as Day puts it, what it means to live *in* difference to religion (Day and Lee 2014).

The people I worked with also exhibited diverse attachments to theistic and spiritual cultures and it seems likely that most people have hybrid or multiple religious, spiritual and non-religious identities and experiences that cut across the 'religious-atheist' divide that dominates media portrayals. So it was that participants identified themselves as, for example, Atheist *and* C. of E. (a common abbreviation for the Church of England) at the same time, and did not necessarily see a contradiction in this. Alternatively, people might identify clearly as non-religious but also discuss the meaning they found in particular religious or spiritual cultures and their participation in certain ceremonies or rituals. Some of these cases are important to the arguments of this book, though others are not: some of these engagements with religion and spirituality are not discussed here, partly because they are not central concerns in this research design, and partly because they are the subjects of significant literatures in their own rights. Instead, the focus is on exploring the different things that anchor 'secular' experience, and on providing a critical account of this concept as a way of capturing these different aspects. Specifically, the book presents the notion of 'non-religion'—developed over the course of fieldwork to demarcate a set of social and cultural forms and experiences that are alternative to religion and framed as such. It proposes that new knowledge and new questions accrue if we recognize non-religion as distinct from the secular.

This book recounts, then, these two shifts in thinking—from the idea of non-religiosity, where it does exist, as a predominantly intellectual perspective to an appreciation of its richness and diversity; and from the idea of secularity and non-religion as closely related phenomena to a sense of their disconnection and even of the contradictions between them. Being 'secular', it appears, is given form by concrete views and values and by social and cultural investments that position the individual as other than religious. One of the central objectives of this book is to chart and bring to light some of the variety in the ways in which these investments are manifest in everyday lives, as well as to show why it is that we are not always aware of them. These manifestations are material, symbolic, and social. They affect our lives together and our interactions with one another, be it in professional and public life or in our most intimate relationships: with our partners, friends, and family. While the secularization paradigm was preoccupied with how far people and societies have moved away from their supposed religious pasts, then, this book shifts attention to the ways in which people and societies may move towards non-religious presents. It highlights the degree of assumption involved in aspects of secularization theory that see the endpoint of secularization processes in the achievement of hollow or insubstantial secularity, and see non-religious cultures as a temporary and incidental feature of that process; instead, this book suggests that we recognize the non-religious as a colourful participant in processes of religious change and open up the nature of that participation to empirical research. While they are now beginning to affect the social scientific study of religion more broadly, these shifts work against some of our most well-established and deeply entrenched ways of thinking about religion and society, as well as about secularity itself.

REIMAGINING THE SECULAR

So what then of the secular? If so much of what we have described as secular is better understood as substantively irreligious or non-religious, does this mean that we can put the concept to one side and forget it entirely? I argue that, on the contrary, distinguishing the non-religious from the secular gives rise to a more refined and more meaningful understanding of the latter, which can then be used to describe and explain the world with greater precision. Indeed, one of the most important consequences of recognizing the non-religious is exactly that it enables us to reimagine the secular. In particular, this new notion of 'secularity' replaces prior, sometimes gloriously commodious conceptualizations—captured well in Howard Becker's (1950, in Campbell 2013: 6) suggestion that the secular 'is not synonymous with the profane, infidel, godless, irreligious, heretical, unhallowed, faithless, or any similar term [but] subsumes them [and] includes a great deal more'. Instead, this book suggests that notions of 'non-religion' and 'irreligion' do much of the work that Becker and others put the concept of 'secularity' to, and argues that what remains is a concept that describes, specifically, any situation in which religious authorities and concerns—and, significantly, alternatively spiritual and non-religious ones too—are subordinate to other powers and interests, though they may still be important secondary considerations.

This account of secularity is therefore distinct from the notion of non-religion given above: religion is of intrinsic relevance to something developed in contradistinction from it, whereas this secularity concerns precisely the limited relevance or jurisdiction of both. This distinction is similar to one made in orthodox secularization theory, as I discuss—though this does not necessarily imply that the secularizationist view of how the two relate to one another is the correct one. Rather, the cultural firmaments of so-called secular life outlined in this book sharpen our attention to the ways that non-religiosity may sustain secularist ideologies (that is, theories allocating some domains and activities as religious, spiritual, and non-religious, and others as secular) and secular institutions. This calls into question the secularizationist idea that explicit non-religion is always and necessarily at odds with secular society, drawing out a tension in the literature that has received little attention. In fact, the secularizationist view of non-religion stands at odds with others: Campbell (2013), for example, also sees non-religious movements as temporary phenomena associated with the journey towards secularity rather than indicative of secularity itself, but he gives particular attention to how they catalyse and advance this transformation. And if non-religious actors bring secularity about, then this raises the possibility that some degree of non-religiosity may be necessary to *maintain* that secularity, even once it has been arrived at. Charles Taylor's (2007) recent updating of pluralist approaches to secularity makes non-religious actors more important still: for Taylor, the presence of 'unbelief' (the dimension of non-religion that he focuses on) as a viable option is integral to the emergence of secularity because it fundamentally changes the 'conditions of belief'. Insufficient scrutiny of non-religion has obscured the question of how it is distinct from and relates to secularity. In showing how the two might be distinguished, this book opens up the question of whether a secular society is one in which non-religious as well as religious cultures are irrelevant and invisible, or whether it is one in which non-religious cultures are firmly rooted, established, and visible in daily life.

This is to fundamentally call into question the efficacy of binary approaches, in which religion, non-religion, and secularity can be placed on a spectrum. In this, my observations share an affinity with recent work identifying alternative forms of spirituality and showing how they sit outside of and destabilize the traditional religion/secular binary used to understand 'religious landscapes' (e.g. Bender and Taves 2012: 3–9). Although active forms of non-religion are often called 'secular', they are not secular in the common senses of being either post-religious or entirely areligious because they take seriously both religion and, adjacently, the religious-like. As with alternative spirituality, therefore, the identification of meaningful and vibrant forms of non-religious culture and non-theistic experiences of transcendence needs to be located outside the religion/secular binary.

Instead of binaries and dualisms, a minimal notion of secularity of the sort proposed here accommodates and is sympathetic to typological approaches to secularism (sometimes referred to as 'secularity' by these authors), such as those of Tariq Modood (2010), Barry Kosmin (2007), Rajeev Bhargava (2009), and Monika Wohlrab-Sahr and Marian Burchardt (2012). It also encourages the typological approaches to the secular that are emerging especially in anthropological work—detailed and systematic accounts of the secularity that is brought into being through secularisms. Such accounts attend to dynamics between secularities and the specific religious, spiritual, and non-religious cultures involved in their formation and with which they continue to interact, as well as the influence of other cultures—social, political, and economic. The reality, as the growing scholarship on the secular attests to, is that there are many different ways in which it is possible for traditional religion, alternative spirituality, and non-religion to play a secondary role: they can be critiqued and excluded, or dismissed and neglected; they can be welcomed as enriching even in those secular domains to which they can only make a secondary contribution; and the ways in which this contribution is conceived will give rise to different kinds of secularity. Thus, there is more to be said once secularity—the mere fact that religion, spirituality, and non-religion are secondary matters—has been observed. Instead of limiting debates to what counts as 'true' secularity, this deliberately limited definition supports the widening of systemic empirical and theoretical work to consideration of what Wohlrab-Sahr and Burchardt (2012) call 'multiple secularities' and to multiple secularisms.

For these reasons, recognizing the non-religious enables us to rethink secularity in certain ways and also to imagine new possibilities and new questions.

THIS VOLUME

This volume opens with a chapter clarifying the core conceptual argument that has been introduced here and presenting the wider, relational vocabulary in which it is embedded. This vocabulary is bound up with the theoretical problems that the book investigates and with the conclusions that it comes to. This first chapter provides ways of thinking about secularity, non-religion, and non-theism that may be methodologically useful more generally, but which also provide the cornerstones for recognizing the non-religious and for re-imagining the secular in the ways that the book proposes.

Chapter 2 gives a more detailed account of the theoretical tensions this book highlights between notions of the secular as insubstantial and substantial. It also outlines the theoretical questions that recognizing the fundamental difference between these 'secularities' open up. This review of past approaches to secularity not only provides context and resources for approaching secularity and non-religion in research methodologies, but also makes a general argument for the more extensive research programme in conjunction with which my own work has been developed.

The following chapters provide more ethnographic detail about non-religion and secularity, considering different lived experiences of being 'not religious' in south-east England and drawing attention to the diverse ways in which people engage with religion as other and are therefore non-religious. All of these cases involve significant strains of non-religious cultural participation that go unnoticed—an empirical finding that is closely associated with and sheds light on academic confusions about the insubstantial secular. After all, these academic theories should be understood as part of the field of study and not outside it. Mimicking the ways in which social scientists have partly taken secularity for granted because they are, for the most part, 'secular' themselves (Campbell 2013), the people and cultures I encountered in fieldwork frequently failed to identify their own non-religious ideas, aesthetics, and communities. This is due to, I argue, their being experienced as embedded and ordinary.

Chapter 3 focuses on material and symbolic non-religious representations, calling attention to the banal forms that surround people in south-east England. These seem unremarkable and yet they establish and constantly reproduce non-religious as well as secularist norms. This taken-for-grantedness is perhaps especially powerful when it comes to material non-religion, not only because people in Western contexts are more attuned to intellectual statements of non-religion over other forms, but also because people often take the material world for granted. Recognizing the diversity of material forms of non-religion therefore opens up new ways of understanding these cultures beyond the intellectual and, in considering the mundaneness of these forms, shows how the ostensibly secular may have non-religious currents running beneath.

Chapter 4 continues this exploration of the material by focusing on the body. The idea of a secular body is a challenging and contested one (see Asad 2003; 2011; Hirschkind 2011; Connolly 2011). This chapter considers the different ways that non-religiosity, secularism, and secularity can be embodied, arguing that these conceptual distinctions help identify quite different modes of embodiment associated with being 'not religious'. In a continuing effort throughout this book to recognize forms of non-religiosity that have not yet been given extensive attention or even conceived of in some cases, this chapter highlights the ways in which people infer non-religiosity through different types of absence—the notable absence of religious modes of embodiment and dress, the combination of religious representations from which non-religious meaning is emergent, the objectified sense of freedom from obstacle between people sharing non-religious norms—the real presence of which is only visible when the normal equilibrium is disrupted in some way.

These expressions of non-religion are intrinsically social, but Chapter 5 focuses more explicitly on this dimension, investigating the ways in which non-religious engagements with religion structure social relations in both positive and negative ways. This chapter throws further weight behind the call to recognize the non-religious as part of so-called secular societies because it is particularly in discussion of social encounters that people's religious, spiritual, non-religious, and secularist knowledge and situated identities become visible. Building on the idea of everyday, banal non-religiosity, this chapter shows how non-religious cultures are shared between people at certain moments and, through these moments, build the tacit knowledge that informs their ongoing relationships. Despite notable growth in recent years, participating in organized non-religious activity remains relatively marginal, but this research shows that non-religiosity may particularly contribute to what Pahl and Spencer (2006) call the 'hidden solidarities' of everyday social relations and friendship. These solidarities are less visible than centralized and institutional ones, as are the cultural forms that mediate them. This adds another dimension to thinking about how substantial non-religious cultures might be rendered invisible and falsely cast as insignificant and insubstantial.

Chapter 6 is a case study of self-classification, looking at representations of the self as non-religious and secular, and the work that these representations do. It discusses how identifications relate to people's other non-religious practices but also argues that practices of self-classification can be treated as a significant form of social action in their own right. Methods of self-identification illustrate the ways in which people in so-called secular societies are required to conceive of themselves in relation to the religious people and cultures also present in these societies. It problematizes the idea of 'secularity' as a way to capture these empirical realities, but also shows how the idea of the insubstantial secular has infiltrated self-understandings and social relations, through the use of negative or inverted identities—'atheist', 'not religious', and 'indifferent to religion'. Despite appearances, however, such identifications express rich and discrete non-religious commitments and therefore compete with more explicitly positive identities such as 'Humanism'.

Having established the existence and array of visual, spatial, material, and embodied forms of non-religiosity, of the relationships and patterns of association informed by it, and of self-understandings and personal and political practices of self-classification and identification, Chapter 7 focuses on belief. This chapter points to the existential threads that run through and appear to determine non-religious cultures in significant ways. Maintaining the view that modes of non-religiosity cannot be reduced to the intellectual, either in theory or in practice, this chapter considers how existential positions are expressed, not only in belief, but in all of the possible manifestations discussed in this book—practices, social relations, and symbolic forms. In recognition of this, the chapter describes these positions not purely as existential *philosophies*, but as existential *cultures*. It shows how the philosophical gives form to these cultures, and outlines the three existential outlooks that are commonly proximal to non-religiosity, at least in this ethnographic context. It also proposes that existential cultures can be proximal to religious and spiritual ones in exactly the same way. Therefore, I argue, the notion of existential cultures may contribute to the development of inclusive approaches to the philosophy of religion.

All these chapters introduce ways of recognizing the non-religious in personal life and society as well as ways of rethinking our idea of secularity in light of this. Recognizing non-religion as something autonomous from the secular highlights long-standing but usually implicit questions about how two distinct sets of phenomena relate to one another. A deeper sense of both opens up many more hypotheses besides, and provides the opportunity to integrate the study of non-religious forms with the study of traditionally religious and alternatively spiritual ones in a deeper way than the study of secularity and secularization could ever accommodate. These shifts in thinking have immediate implications—empirical, methodological, theoretical, and political—and the conclusion to this volume considers several of these. But the conclusion is also, necessarily, full of questions, and recognizes that the concept of 'non-religion' is to some extent a temporary device, used to open up new avenues for research that will, in turn, take us beyond it. Recognizing the non-religious and reformulating the idea of secularity is, then, about new possibilities—new ways of distinguishing and imagining constellations of the religious, spiritual, non-religious, areligious, and secular—about which there will be a lot more to say.

1

Contradistinctions in Terms

Vocabulary for the Study of Secularity and Non-Religion

This volume argues that a deeper engagement with the secular pushes us to clarify the difference and relationship between two distinct faces of secularity: secularity as a relative disengagement from religious culture and authority; and secularity as a potentially powerful but dissenting form of engagement with religion. These two forms are discussed and illustrated in Chapter 2, while this chapter focuses on terminology, setting out a method for making this distinction in the language we use.

This discussion is situated in relation to the wider conceptual challenges facing any scholar or student in the field, and which extend beyond this single, albeit crucial issue of distinguishing substantial and insubstantial forms of 'secularity'. Terms used in this area frequently require qualification: 'and now I am talking about secularity in the sense of x, rather than in the sense of y or z'; indeed, Taylor (2007: 15) refers to secularities '1, 2, and 3'. There is also a strange disparity between the existence of several concepts relating to secularity—atheism, non-theism, Freethought, non-religious humanism, scepticism, areligion, unreligion, irreligion, non-religion, and so on—and a lack of sustained, theoretically and empirically informed accounts of these concepts. It is reasonable to suppose that these two situations are closely related to one another—that the lack of systematic and detailed conceptual work has facilitated the generation of more and more new terms as a quick fix for the problems and shortcomings that users inevitably encounter. A piecemeal approach like this may resolve immediate difficulties but it is also likely to introduce new overlaps and slipperinesses between terms, thus replacing old problems with new ones. Indeed studies of secularity and/or non-religion are filled with terms that are either imprecise or overly narrow and which are confused and combined with one another without consistency and often without reason. Some scholars (e.g. Campbell 2013: 18; Pasquale 2007: 760; see also Lee 2012) have gone so far as to argue that such terminological issues are responsible, at least in part, for inhibiting the study of the secular hitherto.

The objectives of this chapter are, then, as follows. First, it draws attention to the use of terms that are not only slippery in themselves but tend to elide with other core terms in this field of study; and, as a first defence, it encourages reflexivity on the part of anyone using them. Secondly, it draws out the distinction between the concepts of 'secularity' and 'non-religion' that I propose, and shows how this may improve on other attempts to distinguish between 'aspects' of secularity. It provides a definition of both concepts and demonstrates how we can thereby begin to navigate the field by organizing and clarifying existing terms rather than inventing new ones. Finally, these two core concepts are used to ground a more systematic approach to other key terms such as 'atheism', 'non-theism', 'humanism', 'secularism', and 'post-secularism'. This comprehensive and integrated conceptual framework will, I hope, be useful to others—whether they apply it, contest it, revise it, or do all three.

This discussion proceeds in four stages. Whether developing a conceptual framework at the beginning or, indeed, at any stage of a research programme, is feasible or useful is contested by scholars in many fields. Before presenting this framework I first engage with these critiques and the epistemic issues they raise in relation to categorization; I demonstrate why a conceptual framework is needed, much more in light of these critiques than in spite of them. The second section deals with the concept prior to secularity and non-religion: religion itself. The third section outlines the vocabulary I propose for talking about and beyond the secular. The final section presents some implications of this conceptual framework for empirical and theoretical work, as well as some of the immediate 'next questions' it provokes.

A glossary of terms is provided in Appendix I.

Contradistinctions in Terms 23

WHAT'S IN A NAME?

Researchers vary in their views on the value and validity of defining core concepts and providing conceptual guidance in social research. In the study of religion, this is particularly visible in recent constructionist and post-structural contributions that reject the idea that there is any distinctive substance that the term 'religion' can be used to denote. This work often advocates Foucauldian, genealogical approaches to the study of religion instead, recommending that, in order to learn about 'religion' in the social world, social scientists attend to the ways in which the category is used by people (including academics) to describe phenomena and examine speakers' objectives and the context in which they speak. Talal Asad (1993; 2003), James A. Beckford (2003), Timothy Fitzgerald (2000; 2007), and Russell McCutcheon (2007) have made important contributions to this literature in their distinctive ways. Scepticism about the value of doing extensive conceptual work has, however, a much longer history, and is visible in the sociology of religion from its inception. Max Weber, a founding contributor not only to sociology but to the sociology of religion, resisted the task of definition in his work. *The Sociology of Religion* collection opens with these words:

> To define 'religion,' to say what it *is*, is not possible at the start of a presentation such as this. Definition can be attempted, if at all, only at the conclusion of the study. The essence of religion is not even our concern, as we make it our task to study the conditions and effects of a particular type of social behaviour. (Weber 1993:1)

Weber's argument is that researchers do not necessarily need a working vocabulary to enter the field or to design an empirical study, and it is a view that still has extensive currency in the sub-discipline.

Such contributions provide important insights into the purpose and possibility of defining core terms. However, the difficulty for scholars working with secularity and non-religion is that, as researchers exploring the potential of a new field, it is not as easy as it is, say, for Weber to identify 'a particular *type* of social behaviour'; yet, at the same time, it is clear that there are behaviours afoot worth accounting for. In addition, 'secularity' is an analytical category that is not always used by the people or expressed in the objects and spaces that it is applied to. Linda Woodhead (2011) points out that discursive approaches are easiest to apply when the category of religion is central to the case in hand, but are problematic on the many occasions when this is not the case. What should we do, for example, when individuals prefer not to use the term themselves yet have a lot in common with other groups who self-describe as religious? Such concerns apply well to secular and non-religious populations: one of a few things we know about so-called secular people is that they do not always identify themselves explicitly in this or any other way that references religion. For example, while 18 per cent of Britons said they do not believe in God in the 2008 British Social Attitudes survey and a further 19 per cent said there was 'no way of finding out' if God exists (Voas and Ling 2010: 71), only 8 per cent identified themselves as 'atheist' in the same year (Bruce 2002: 193). Methodological issues with survey design provide a partial explanation of this phenomenon (Bruce 2002: 193), but a study of the secular needs to provide for the possibility that not all non-religious engagements with religion are represented in tangible, codified symbolic forms. The study of secularity therefore requires an analytical vocabulary at the outset, if only to enable empirically informed scrutiny of that vocabulary and its longer-term efficacy for understanding the social world.

In relation to religion, Woodhead's view is that stronger constructivist approaches pose insurmountable problems if researchers of religion are to identify a field in which to situate their work. Again, this issue is acute for scholars working with secularity because associating it with 'a suitable field of study' is such an open question. Weber's instruction for researchers 'to study the conditions and effects of a particular type of social behaviour' gives away how much he is able to take for granted when he tries to recognize cases of religion for his study; the researcher of secularity and/or non-religion, like the researcher of less traditional or more diffuse modes of religion, does not have this option. Indeed, when the entry-point to research is a theoretical one, then whether or not there is any particular type of social behaviour at hand is precisely the question. What is more, the study of secularity is not spoken for by an accumulated body of work or proven research tradition. As Campbell (2013: 17) says, '[t]he claim of the sociology of irreligion to be accepted as an important and viable sphere of study clearly cannot be admitted until its specific subject of investigation has been outlined'. Hence, he says, 'without even a provisional delineation a sociology of irreligion cannot exist'. For the researcher of secularity

Contradistinctions in Terms 25

and non-religion, therefore, neglecting the conceptual framework at the outset of a 'presentation such as this' not only risks excluding from that study relevant phenomena that do not clearly represent themselves as such but also provides the very real possibility that the field as a whole will be discounted.

'RELIGION' IN THE STUDY OF SECULARITY AND NON-RELIGION

The starting point of this investigation is the commonly used but under-researched idea of the 'secular'. In comparison with terms such as 'irreligion', 'non-religion', and 'atheism', the 'secular' is often perceived to be more independent from 'religion' and this autonomy is thought to be a great advantage. Presumably this sense arises from the term's having no explicit etymological relation to 'religion' or 'theism' as the other terms do. Yet 'secularity' is not independent of 'religion' at all but is rather only meaningful in relation to it. The idea of something being secular is simply unintelligible without an understanding of something else as religious and a view as to where the (moving) boundary between the two falls. 'Religion' and relational terms such as 'non-religion' are indeed 'semantically parasitic categories' and it is true to say that 'we cannot understand what we mean by [one] unless we put it into relation with [the other]' (Fitzgerald 2007: 54; in Cotter 2011b). Scholars such as Asad, Fitzgerald, and McCutcheon have established this point and go further still, arguing that the reverse is also true: 'religion' is a concept that has no meaning without the 'secular'. They argue that it is only once a notion of a secular domain is developed in contradistinction to a religious one that it became meaningful to describe something as 'religious'. Before that, they argue, beliefs and practices associated with religion ran through every aspect of human social and cultural life and were invisible, that is, implicit, as a result.

Anyone seeking to talk about secularity must, then, begin with an understanding of religion. And they must take responsibility, too, for participating in a conceptual framework that takes 'religion' as its core feature. Most, though not all, of the conceptual framework outlined within this chapter involves concepts made meaningful by their relation to 'religion'. It is therefore necessary to consider whether the discussion of secularity and non-religion reifies or provides a counterpoint to the exclusive notion of religion that critical and post-structural scholars critique, as well as to outline, more simply, what concept of religion scholars of secularity and non-religion should use, if the approach is found to be an acceptable one.

Taking the ethical issue first, I argue that there are two major reasons to explore phenomena that take 'religion' as a root term— one historical and one theoretical (Lee 2012). The historical case for working with 'religion' is that this concept has dominated Western thinking for some centuries and continues to do so at the point at which scholars of secularity and other relative-to-religion phenomena enter the discussion. Were this cultural history different, we might propose to make, say, spirituality our core concern and our relational vocabulary would reflect this: we would begin our studies by focusing on the 'non-spiritual', the 'aspiritual', the 'anti-spiritual', and so on. However, religion is the established centre; indeed, even the concept of 'spirituality' is often only made meaningful by being differentiated from 'religion', as in 'spiritual but not religious' survey categories, or the idea of '*alternative* spirituality' as a parallel to 'traditional religion'.

Secondly, the theoretical case is that using religion-related terms has some intrinsic value. One benefit of studying 'secularity' and 'non-religion' is that, while it inevitably means taking on the debates and controversies surrounding the definition of 'religion', it also means benefiting from the term's many achievements. Significant amongst these is its value as a general and helpfully amorphous concept: 'religion' is more inclusive and more pliable than narrower categories such as 'theism', and it is accommodating of diverse approaches such as the lived religion and material religion methodologies that have recently come to prominence in the study of religion.

Finally, it may not be necessary to defend the study of non-religion and secularity from critics who fear that it will reify the problematic notion of 'religion' because, in fact, the studies of both provide new vantage points from which to examine 'religion' as a cultural artefact. In so doing, they provide new, empirically grounded opportunities for critique. Fitzgerald (2000) and McCutcheon (2007) have argued that an idea of religion as a special, unparalleled, and distinctive feature of human life serves religious interests well, but has little analytical value. The study of populations that are excluded from this notion of religion provides, however, fresh opportunities to test and, if necessary, challenge these exclusive conceptions of religion. Thus, the historical and the theoretical arguments are closely bound together: if religion exists as a concept about which claims are made, so the study of phenomena that are contingent on it—the religion-related and the religious-like—is not only legitimate and necessary but also provides a way of interrogating the concept of 'religion' itself.

If scholars are going to work with religion-related concepts though, it is imperative that they are specific about what they mean by 'religion'. In some studies, a purely discursive approach, working with emic understandings, is sufficient: what do research *informants* mean when they talk about 'religion'; what do *they* consider to be religious-like; what phenomena do *they* consider to have no relation to religion at all? For other studies, this one included, *analytical* concepts are under scrutiny and this requires a deeper conceptual engagement with 'religion'.

In this work, I am interested in religion as a theoretical construct, particularly as it is used in the Western and local academic and popular discourses that the empirical study is situated in relation to. The study focuses on mainstream notions of religion in these settings and the ways in which it makes sense to describe 'not religious' populations as different to these religious ones. The notion of religion used in this project is therefore one that Knott (2005: 61) calls the 'common sense starting point' for research in Western contexts or, following Towler (1984, in Knott 2005: 59), 'conventional religion'. In Knott's (2005: 59) summation, conventional religion indicates religious institutions, their traditions, beliefs (which, in this context, certainly includes theism), and practices, and the people who adhere to them. Despite critique, this conventional definition still shapes the majority of what is said about religion in Western popular and academic discourses, whether in sociology, anthropology, politics, philosophy, history, or in the arts. Within social science, it is the understanding of religion adopted in most quantitative methodologies, including our large-scale surveys, and in many qualitative studies besides. Knott also points out that working with conventional notions of religion has the benefit of enabling access to a remarkable array of social—and, in her work, spatial—phenomena for study and, while it constrains this work in many ways, it also allows for exploration beyond the discursive.

A RELATIONAL VOCABULARY

The vocabulary presented in this book is relational, developed in order to explore the possibility that so-called secular populations engage with religion in a number of ways—some direct, and some mediated by academic and others' analytic categories. The vocabulary takes up Campbell's (2013: 20–1) approach in which the phenomena at hand are not defined substantively, but 'as a general form of response' or 'characteristic set of responses' to religion, or what Quack (2014) describes as a 'relational approach'. Many of the terms in this vocabulary are familiar and a few may even be self-explanatory. However, in order to resolve the terminological issues that have challenged this field, and to address an insidious problem with apparently self-evident meanings that are nothing of the sort, it is necessary to be thoughtful and specific about how we describe these relationships. Social scientists are increasingly sensitive to the substance and nuance of relations with religion (e.g. Asad 2003; Lee 2012; Quack 2014), a view that is congruent with the growing prominence of relational epistemologies in the social sciences in general.

The following sections present a vocabulary for the study of non-religion and secularity that attempts to describe relations with religion systematically and precisely.

RELIGION-RELATED TERMS

The first set of relations that this vocabulary describes takes 'religion' as its partner. The vocabulary then distinguishes between different ways of relating to that object, as follows.

Anti-Religion, Areligion, and Indifference

First, the term 'anti-religious' can be used to indicate an oppositional stance towards religion, be it disaffection or acute hostility. This is one of the few truly straightforward concepts in circulation in discourses relating to 'secularity'. Definitions of it are consistent (c.f. Campbell 2013; Lüchau 2010; Lee 2012) and it is used widely without clarification to mean the same thing. So far, so good.

'Areligion' is only slightly more complicated. It is used, sensibly, to indicate the state of being without religion, the prefix a- meaning 'without'. Whereas anti-religion implies an (antagonistic) engagement with religion, areligion indicates the absence of engagement entirely. Perfect areligion involves total ignorance of religion, a state that might be of interest for a number of reasons. The incidence and cause of areligion might, for example, be significant to anthropologists, historians, or social researchers working with communities that have not developed religious traditions or institutions and that are distant from (or even isolated within) communities that have. So, for example, in nineteenth-century Britain, the 1851 Church census (the first and last of its kind) revealed that large swathes of the population had no religious culture, not because they were opposed to it per se but because they had little contact with religious institutions (Kitson Clark 1965: 147–205). Cognitive researchers are also interested in areligion, in their work exploring how, and how much, the brain is implicated in the formation of religious practice and experience: cases in which these practices and experiences are absent provide crucial data for comparison.

This all seems straightforward again, but this understanding of 'areligion' is slightly different from another in circulation, in which a slightly broader definition is made that includes 'indifference to religion' (e.g. Lüchau 2010: 178). The issue here is the notion of indifference itself, which is used frequently in discussion of secularity, but is an ambiguous concept that requires deeper scrutiny. Indifference in fact sits some place *between* the state of being without religion and of rejecting religion (discussed below). It implies knowledge of a religious other as well as a dismissive stance towards that other. It can also imply religious and non-religious practice, so long as the practitioner remains somehow detached from that practice. The indifferent person might go along with a friend to church, for example, find it mildly diverting, and then forget all about it. His or her religious identity might switch frequently over their lifetime, as they dabble with different ideas and cultures without ever deeply caring or committing; thus, unpredictable and therefore apparently 'meaningless' religious practice may be a better indicator of indifference than signs of areligiosity (Siegers 2010). As is demonstrated in this volume, it is certainly the case that many people who think of themselves as indifferent to religion are actually committed to a sense of themselves as other than religious: they might, for example, dislike being misidentified as a religious person, and they might be quite unlikely to take up an invitation to visit a religious meeting place or participate in certain or any religious rituals. These ways of enacting 'otherness' may be subtle and undramatic, but are nevertheless concrete and influential as such.

The argument in this volume is not that indifference to religion does not exist. It is, rather, that it is a more nuanced and more interesting category in the study of religion than is often recognized and requires more careful attention. It should be interesting to study indifference *qua* weak levels of engagement with religious, spiritual, and/or non-religious culture—a quantitative distinction similar to Kosmin's (2007) notion of 'soft' and 'hard' 'secularisms', and one that might generate qualitative phenomena, too. Is indifference always a blanket experience, for example, or are people indifferent to religion in certain places and at certain times while engaging at other points? Are they indifferent to particular aspects of religion while continuing to engage with other dimensions, as discussed in Chapter 6 in relation to 'indifferentism'? Indeed, the concept of indifference begs the question, indifferent to *what*—what specifically? In terms of concepts and the research possibilities they engender, the difference between being without religion—areligion proper, in this vocabulary—and the more complicated phenomenon of indifference is therefore meaningful, relevant to very different research questions and calling for distinct research designs.

Post-Religion

Related to 'indifference' is the concept of 'post-religion', which may be used to describe something shaped historically but not contemporaneously by religion. A post-religious society is not necessarily one in which religion has become irrelevant per se, but one in which its effects are diffuse and indirect. It has a close affinity with secularization theory, both in its temporal aspect (secularization theory concerns the linear decline of religion over time), and in its idea of secularity as a state involving a profoundly reduced role for religion. It helps specify the 'secularity' of that theory, though it inevitably shares its limitations: both are religion-centred and discourage engagement with the rise and fall of alternatively spiritual and non-religious cultures; and both rely on a unilinear temporal approach and discourage awareness of movements in other directions, such as religious growth. Religious growth is, indeed, strangely undertheorized in the study of religion, so that scholars have not developed multidimensional models of 'religionization' as they have for secularization; the somewhat strange concept of 'desecularization' rather illustrates the point.

'Post-religion' can also be unhelpful if it is used to describe ongoing forms of religious influence that merely have their roots in past religious cultures, such as the use of religious ceremonies out of a sense of 'tradition' or in relation to national identities. Various scholars have shown that the significance of these modes of religiosity should not be dismissed, as they sometimes are (cf. Bellah's (1991) civil religion or Day's (2011) nominal religion), and that they may be as meaningful as doctrinal or philosophical ties to religious cultures. With these caveats, 'post-religion' can be used to describe a distinct relationship with religion and one that is central to important theoretical debates.

Irreligion and Non-Religion

In the seminal work of Colin Campbell (2013), the concept of 'irreligion' has had a central role in the burgeoning social scientific study of 'secularity'. First published in 1971, Campbell's *Toward a Sociology of Irreligion* took up the basic *Oxford English Dictionary* (*OED*) definition of the time, one which has changed little in the intervening years.[1] According to this, irreligion is a disposition towards religion involving hostility or indifference (or disengagement, in alternative phrasings). Ambiguities related to the notion of 'indifference' as well as problems attendant to discussing modes of (antagonistic) engagement and disengagement in the same breath raise concerns, however, about this definition. I follow Quack (2014) in salvaging 'irreligion' as a distinctive and useful term from 'non-religion', but suggest that the concept should be at once generalized and narrowed to indicate the *rejection* of religion—in whatever form this rejection might take and however acute it may be. As well as presenting the *OED*

---

[1] 'Irreligion, *n.*' *The Oxford English Dictionary*. 2nd edn (1989). *OED* Online. Oxford University Press. 11 October 2011 Available at <http://www.oed.com> (accessed 21 December 2011).

definition, Campbell also describes irreligion as the rejection of religion and this approach is generally consistent with the programme of study he outlines. But it is less arbitrary than the OED definition (why hostility and indifference, and not other forms of rejection?) and, by putting ambiguous notions of disengagement to one side, its meaning is not overly stretched.

Finally, and most significant to the argument I want to advance, is the concept of 'non-religion', broadened from the concept of irreligion with which I began this research. At that point, 'non-religion' was only used to indicate anything that someone wanted to describe, for whatever purposes, as 'not religious'. Non-religion is, in this sense, a very general concept and has no meaning outside its context: to describe, for example, a person as 'non-religious' can mean that they have no contact with religion at all (they are areligious), that they reject the claims of religion (they are irreligious), or that they are committed to philosophies and cultures developed in contradistinction from religious ones (they are non-religious, in my sense). Sometimes the meaning of 'non-religion' is apparent in the way it is framed; sometimes it is not. And because it has no independent meaning, it likewise has no dictionary or any other definition.

The sense of non-religion I propose is different. It is used to indicate not the absence of something (religion) but the presence of something (else), characterized, at least in the first place, by its relation to religion but nevertheless distinct from it. Non-religion is therefore any phenomenon—position, perspective, or practice—that is primarily understood in relation to religion but which is not itself considered to be religious.[2] Alternatively expressed, non-religion is a phenomenon understood in contradistinction to religion. Or, in Johannes Quack's (2014) Bourdieusian iteration, the non-religious describes a 'religion-related field', encompassing relationships between a religious field and phenomena that are located outside it. Thus, the 'non-' in non-religious describes a *meaningful* differentiation, as in the sense of 'non-violence', used in relation to phenomena that are frequently or typically violent rather than ones that are not, to take up a helpful analogy that my NSRN co-director Stacey Gutkowksi has offered. We speak of 'non-violent protest' and 'non-violent

---

[2] This phrasing of the definition is developed from earlier versions (Lee 'Glossary'; Lee 2011; Lee 2012) and in light of critique from Quack (2014) that draws attention to some ambiguities in past phrasing.

confrontation', but not of 'non-violent cooking' or 'non-violent exercise regimes', though these are equally violence-free and are accurately described as 'not violent'.

The most important point in this approach is that non-religion becomes a term used to identify a substantive characteristic, a quality that is real and existing in the world. Phenomena that are in some way non-religious may, in theory or in other contexts, be described by alternative means but, in the contexts at hand, are made meaningful by the ways in which they differ from religion. Contemporary understandings of 'materialism' capture this well: in principle at least, it is possible to think about materialism independently of religion; in practice, however, materialism is, in Western contexts at least, explicitly and implicitly understood in contradistinction to religion, frequently specified as or conflated with a non-theist orientation. And, in fact, the context is such that *failing* to identify materialism in relation to religion risks excluding it from several broader conversations, such that materialist approaches and ritual practices surrounding death, for example, had received scant attention in any area of sociology, anthropology, and other social sciences until researchers of non-religion started, very recently, to take it up. This concept of non-religion points us, then, to concrete phenomena and, alongside traditional and alternative forms of religion, it sits in contrast with 'areligion'—a distinction that forces scholars to take a view as to whether secularity (if that remains the best concept to focus on at all) entails high levels of non-religion or high levels of areligion, for it cannot entail both.

This concept of 'non-religion' is also more open and elastic than 'irreligion' in a way that will help scholars account for the unforeseen realities that will inevitably be encountered in charting a new field. It is highly influenced by Campbell's (2013) discussion of 'irreligion', with phrasing that echoes his.[3] But, by focusing on difference rather than rejection, non-religion can be used to describe additional experiences in which individuals and institutions feel different from but positively disposed towards the religion of others—interested in it perhaps, curious, or even thrilled. Taking up this approach, Steph Berns' (2014: 256) recent study of

---

[3] For example, my definition follows Campbell's in making primacy central: (2013: 17; emphasis added) writes, 'Since irreligion is defined *primarily* by religion, the notable lack of success in defining the latter term is a hardly a good omen for success in defining the former'.

'sacred entanglements' in the context of the British Museum finds that some people relate to religion not through a lens of rejection but through what she calls a 'lens of difference'. She describes a Scottish visitor to an exhibition of religious artefacts explaining:

> I think the interest that I have is more... What is it? Secular?... As I said, for somebody who doesn't [follow a religion] it's just fascinating and interesting... *I'm not religious so that adds to the fascination,* I think. It's such a *different* way of looking at things and certainly, it made me think this seems so unlikely and yet it creates such an intense belief for many people. (Berns 2014; emphasis added)

The idea of rejection does not sit well with this example, in which the sense of otherness is clear but so too is the way that this sense of otherness creates—incites and enhances—a way of engaging and an attempt to connect with religion.

A focus on difference rather than rejection also ties the study of non-religion in helpful ways to other strands of social theory and philosophy. It is, for example, more amenable to multiculturalist approaches, in which social integration is seen to rely on diversity and difference as much as cultural consensus (Kuper 1999: 234–5). Of course, some forms of non-religion involve the rejection—the dismissal, refusal, or casting off—of religious cultures and claims. The significance of these processes in contexts of religious decline is easy to see. But not all forms of non-religion reject religion per se, and the idea of non-religion is intended to accommodate both possibilities—pro- as well as anti-religious experiences of otherness. Where an exclusive focus on irreligion can be polarizing therefore, an interest in difference encourages the exploration of the complexity of non-religious as well as religious outlooks and subjectivities.

In the context of this study, which is interested in conventional Western notions of religion and understands non-religion in relation to that, examples of non-religion so defined include atheism and agnosticism.[4] The study engages with humanism and political secularism too, but not as forms of non-religion necessarily—both have religious versions—but as cultures that, *in the empirical setting at*

---

[4] This approach contrasts with scholars who employ other definitions of religion. E.g. Eller (2010a) includes atheist cultures such as (atheist) Buddhism within his understanding of religion and therefore does not include atheism within his study of non-religion.

hand, have strong non-religious components. British secularist discourses of the nineteenth, twentieth, and twenty-first centuries have frequently united and sometimes conflated non-religion and political secularism: for example, the National Secular Society (NSS) lobbies for secularist legal and political arrangements, but the culture of the society also has strong non-religious currents. Similarly, the British Humanist Association makes explicit and central reference to non-religion in its self-description (see Chapters 6 and 7 within this volume), while the US concept of 'secular humanism' is likewise used to identify an explicitly non-religious humanistic tradition. Similarly, despite a commonplace association with non-religiosity in some places, there are also important religious examples of rationalism and naturalism (Martin 1990). Thus, rationalism, humanism et al. are included in this discussion as artefacts of some of the non-religious cultures I encountered in the field, not because they are intrinsically non-religious. The distinction is this; humanism is not non-religious; many humanist organizations are.

This issue of application is necessary if we are to avoid essentializing categories according to their non-religious elements. Thinking of non-religiosity as a characteristic of an empirical phenomenon rather than a description of its fundamental nature is a helpful corrective to this. So, for example, in the UK, Humanist life-cycle ceremonies are developed as alternatives to religious ones and they not only involve but perform non-religiosity. This does not, however, imply that all aspects of such ceremonies are non-religious. Likewise, it is perfectly true that many Rationalist and Humanist groups are, in their discourses, self-understandings, and activities, extensively concerned with differentiating themselves from religion, but this does not mean that rationalism or humanism is, always and by definition, non-religious. Indeed, to the extent that they present ritual services not only in contradistinction from religious ones but also drawing on the languages and content of religious models, they may be seen to have religious dimensions. Yet the idea that they are 'really religious' is as crude as the idea that they are solely non-religious, because these religious practices are conducted in relation to significant non-religious ones and may be performed within a broader non-religious framework that inflects the meaning of religious elements. What is necessary is to recognize that empirical cases we take as our units of analysis are typically complicated, multifaceted, and, like all human cultural forms, perfectly capable of accommodating contradictions.

It is often, therefore, preferable to think of non-religion as an aspect of a phenomenon rather than a comprehensive description of it. So, for example, blasphemy, anti-clericalism, and anti-religion are all manifestations of non-religion—all irreligious too, in these cases—but they are often combined with religious observance and practice; and Stephen Bullivant (2008b) has coined the term 'irreligious experiences', after William James's (2008) 'religious experiences', to describe the role that doubt and other senses of difference and alienation from religion can play in religious as well as non-religious lives.

On the other hand, it can be useful to identify whole and (relatively) bounded phenomena—institutions, cultures, objects, people, populations—as non-religious, just as we might identify others of these as religious. This is simply shorthand for saying that the non-religious characteristics are dominant, or that they are dominating our interest, and not that the phenomenon at hand is purely or solely non-religious. In precisely the same way, we might describe the Church of England as a 'religious institution' because its primary or differentiating characteristic is its religiosity. We do not mean that all of its logics and actions relate to religious concerns and cultures at all times; nor do we mean that it has no secular interests or, indeed, has no non-religious aspects. To illustrate this last point, we might think of the way that alternatively spiritual groups often describe themselves in contradistinction to religion: 'New Age' cultures, for example, frequently see themselves as less bounded and less dogmatic than religious cultures, and, in view of this, reject the label 'religion'. This mode of distinction has informed the emergence of the 'spiritual but not religious' category in recent times. And yet, unless a group *generally* and *primarily* understands its alternative spirituality in contradistinction to religion, and not, as is usually the case, according to a distinctive set of principles, practices, and aesthetics, it is not meaningful to mainly identify that group as a non-religious one. Despite its non-religious *elements*, then, it is misleading and unhelpful to identify alternative spirituality or most churches as 'non-religious traditions', while it is quite reasonable and helpful to identify New Atheism as one. In the context of dualistic and polarized approaches to the religious and non-religious, or to the religious and secular, these specificities underlying certain, helpful shorthands are worth calling attention to.

Contradistinctions in Terms 37

The example of alternative spirituality is instructive in another way. It is a reminder that, though the concept of 'non-religion' appears to be part of a binary (religion/non-religion), it is, in fact, conceived of as one of several positions understood in relation to religion and should therefore unsettle binary approaches. Areligion, alternative spirituality, and non-religion each describe distinct positions in relation to religion; alongside religion itself, I tend to identify these four positions as part of a 'religious landscape'. The shortcomings of this approach are obvious, but it improves upon reductive binaries and provides opportunities for new studies which will, in time, give rise to much better ways of describing this landscape.

THEISM-RELATED TERMS

In contrast to 'non-religion', the notion of 'atheism' requires no introduction: it is understood, variously but widely, across the world. It does, however, have a range of meanings and applications (see Bullivant 2013) that mean it is also a more complicated concept than it may at first appear. For one thing, English-language prefixes are typically used quite differently in theism-related terms than they are in religion-related ones: whereas 'areligion' does not tend to stand for the rejection of religion only its absence, 'atheism' stands for both. As a result, it has been necessary for scholars to distinguish between 'negative atheism' and 'positive atheism' (Martin 1990; Bullivant 2013), or between 'non-theism' (denoting the absence of theism), and 'atheism' (denoting the rejection of theism). The vocabulary proposed in this book standardizes the use of prefixes, so 'atheism' indicates the absence of experiences of god(s) and 'non-theism' indicates something that is made meaningful by how it differs from theism. 'Anti-theist' stances are antagonistic modes of non-theism, just as anti-religious ones are antagonistic modes of non-religion.

Because of past inconsistencies in how language related to religion and theism is constructed, it takes some discipline to bring it into line. The pay-off is, however, increased precision, aided by an etymological logic to the prefixes applied: for example, the *a-* prefix means 'without', so the idea of 'positive atheism' is somewhat contradictory (and anyway redundant, if we have an alternative term); the *anti-* prefix is always used to indicate a negative relation; the *non-* prefix is always used to highlight or to create meaningful types of otherness. It might be argued that using 'atheism' to describe anti-theistic and other non-theistic positions is so entrenched that it ought to dictate how language is standardized in this growing field. In fact, the use and overuse of 'atheism' is a wider problem that calls for deeper reflection and reflexivity. The study of 'atheism' has dominated Western micro- and meso-level engagements with the secular, seen in the titles of collections such as *Atheism and Secularity* (Zuckerman 2010a; 2010b), *Religion and the New Atheism* (Amarasingam 2010), *The Cambridge Companion to Atheism* (2007a), and *The Oxford Handbook of Atheism* (Bullivant and Ruse 2013). The hold is such that 'religion' is paired with 'atheism' in academic as well as popular discussions, even though they are different phenomena entirely: so, for example, scholars have recently developed 'a scale measuring degrees of *religiosity* [combined with] a scale measuring gradual approaches to *strict atheism*' (Riis 2009: 231; emphasis added) and investigated why 'religion is natural, [and] atheism is not' (Geertz and Markússon 2010). Properly understood, however, atheism should account for only a part of the field of non-religion studies (where theism is understood as integral to religion). Thus, pairing religion and atheism in this way is a category error like comparing masculinity and feminism, for example, rather than femininity.

That 'atheism' is, implicitly, being used to identify much more than plain godlessness is actually noteworthy therefore: it reveals key assumptions in circulation about religion as well as its 'others'—that we think of rejecting religion as an intellectually driven matter, for example, or that, despite seeming to be increasingly sensitive to the practical, material, social, and other non-cognitive aspects of religion, scholars still understand religion primarily in terms of belief in God to some significant degree. Jesse Smith (2011) finds in his study of US non-religious identities that the non-religious describe themselves as 'atheist' in order to articulate and consolidate an identity in the face of a prior discursive norm that emphasizes theism. The wider and uncritical use of 'atheism' as an analytical concept to understand the 'not religious' follows a similar trajectory and may be accused of Western- and Protestant-centrism. Indeed, 'atheism' is much less salient for understanding non-religion in many Muslim contexts, such that Arabic, Urdu, and some Persian languages derive a range of terms from the Qur'an to describe different kinds of religious otherness rather than focusing on atheism exclusively (Schielke 2013: 638–9).

Thus, rather than merely disaggregating 'atheism' into types, as several scholars have done, providing a systematic, relational vocabulary for the study of 'the secular' encourages an approach to 'atheism' in which it is just one aspect of a much broader picture. While many detailed conceptual discussions of atheism are available (e.g. Martin 1990; Cliteur 2009; Eller 2010; Bullivant 2013), a general comment about the prevalence of the concept has been lacking. In short, whether the meaning of 'atheism' is exclusive or inclusive, negative or positive, whether it means a person who does not believe in God or a person without a belief in God (Martin 1990: 463–5)—whichever of these approaches is preferred, 'atheism' and 'non-theism' alway relate to experiences of god or gods and nothing more (Lee 2012). This does not mean that the topic is not important or relevant to the study of non-religion, but, just as affirmative relationships with god(s) have been recognized as only one aspect of religious studies and of religion, so non-affirmative relationships with god(s) must be recognized as just one aspect of any study of non-religion. Recognizing the non-religious in research is, then, partly suggested in contrast to new studies of atheism, while it builds on that work at the same time.

THE SECULAR

These different concepts—non-religion, irreligion, anti-religion, non-theism, atheism, and so on—distinguish between specific phenomena that might be implicated in an investigation of the secular. They do not cover so much ground, however, that the concept of the secular is left with no meaning. Rather, it is by divesting the 'secular' of its responsibility for describing such a wide range of relationships with religion that we can think about what it is that the concept uniquely adds. The significant and discrete meaning that remains when all this other work has been done pertains to the identification of *phenomena—objects, spaces, people, and practices—for which religion is no more than a secondary concern, reference point, or authority*. Given that religion is centrally relevant to non-religion, irreligion, and anti-religion, they are not secular. Thus secularity may be said to describe not only the limited relevance of religion, but also the limited relevance of non-religion, as well as the limited relevance of alternative religions or spirituality.

This understanding of 'secularity' is consistent with a number of others in circulation; indeed, it arguably highlights the common denominator of many approaches. It is consistent with early Christian models, in which monks moved from their 'religious' life into 'secular' spaces and time outside the monastery (Knott 2005; 2014; Taylor 2007). In so doing, these monks did not lose their religiosity, but they did distinguish their religious life from this alternative world that was not governed by religion in the same way; in this world, religion was present, but no longer central. This notion of secularity is also consistent with the idea of it as marginalized religion, as envisioned in secularization theory. It fits also with the secularity in liberal accounts, in which religions may be vital but also limited presences to the extent necessary to maintain cultural pluralism and peace. It is consistent, too, with the idea of a secular state set in contrast to a theocratic one.

It is not merely a common denominator conceptualization, though, arrived at by finding a quality that fits all existing applications, but instead arises from distinguishing between incommensurable phenomena associated with secularity and, from this, drawing out the one quality that cannot be described in other ways. This is the basis of its wide applicability, not as a human quality but in its application as an analytic concept. I concur with Wohlrab-Sahr and Burchardt (2012) in the view that post-colonial analyses of the roots of the 'secular' concept in Western, Protestant traditions do not evacuate it of all meaning: genealogies are a method of critique not of destruction, and what results from them is the possibility of refining our language and discourses by divesting them of faulty suppositions and connotations, and thereby improving their analytical validity. At the very least, distinguishing between aspects of the 'secular'—a process that is partly provoked by these post-colonial and post-structural interventions—gives rise to the specific notion of secularity qua the subordination of religion and the religious-like, and this can then be investigated cross-culturally. Scholars may wish to rename this characteristic; the important thing from my point of view is to keep it in view and to distinguish it from other phenomena.

Another way of clarifying this (or any) notion of secularity is to consider what its alternatives are. For all that religion is discussed in a binary with it, there are several ways in which the literature is deeply ambivalent about what the counterpart to secularity actually is. Part of the problem is that the religion/secularity binary is actually one of several overlapping binaries involving 'religion': religion and secularity, religion and secular*ism,* religion and irreligion, religion and atheism. More confusingly still, these binaries blend into closely related others. So, religion and the sacred are not always understood as synonymous, yet the secular is sometimes placed in binary relationships with each of these; at other times, the sacred is contrasted with the profane, and sometimes with the profane *and* the mundane (Lynch 2012b). Religion can, as we've seen, be contrasted with areligion and non-religion as much as it can with post-religious states. It is interesting that, in terms of processes, claims of 'resurgent religion', which have become a familiar opening gambit in recent publications, are infrequently described as 'religionization', as the religion/secular binary would seem to encourage. Less comprehensive or perhaps less sure-footed concepts such as 'sacralization', 'resacralization', 're-enchantment', and, perhaps most ambivalent of all, 'desecularization' are more common.

The conception of secularity given here has a specific counterpart: the primacy of religious and religious-like cultures or authorities. 'Religion' might be an acceptable shorthand for this state, but is problematic in several ways, not least due to the ambiguity between this manifestation of religion and the others described earlier. It is imprecise too: the opposite of secularity is not the having of a religious character but the having of a *predominant* or *determining* religious character. Terming this specific phenomenon 'religion' also revives the idea of a religious/secular binary or a spectrum between religion and secularity, which is at odds with the qualitative distinctions made here. The difference between a situation in which religion ectetera is dominant and one in which it is restricted is not one that can be measured quantitatively; it is an either/or distinction. It may be possible to describe phenomena as more or less secular according to the number of its parts that are secular, but it is not possible for a religion to be 'more secondary' in a single case than it is in another. Variation between this kind of secularity is better described by typologies than by degrees. Finally, describing 'religion' as secularity's other loses sight of alternative spirituality and substantive non-religion. Regardless of whether scholars agree with the way I have integrated them here, some attempt at including these different phenomena should be made.

The 'other' to secularity so defined is perhaps something along the lines of 'theocracy', the dominance of religious concerns. It is not wholly satisfactory: the term focuses on religion, rather than alternative religion and non-religion; and it focuses on power—on modes of governance, rule, or influence (*-cracy*)—and sits uncomfortably with cases in which we merely mean to describe the centrality of religious concerns: to describe a church as a 'theocratic building' or to describe what is called in the UK a 'faith school' as a 'theocratic school' demonstrates the problem. This is only the greater if we want to describe material and symbolic manifestations. The 'regular' life of a monk is not quite 'theocratic'. Given the deep problems attendant to thinking in terms of a religion/secular binary though, I suggest keeping theocracy in mind as a placeholder for the much better concept that will emerge from attending to these issues more closely. Doing so will also prevent the reaggregation of atheism, non-religion, and secularity that is encouraged by locating them all in binary relationships with a single concept, 'religion'. Given these issues, there may be good conceptual reasons to rename the secular and, with it, its other, as well as analytical and ethical ones to do with its embeddedness in Western traditions of thought. Identifying what it is we need these concepts for, however, is a constructive step in the longer-term process of reimagining the secular.

Secularity and Secularism

Following this conception of the secular, 'secularity' is easily understood as the state of being secular—akin to 'secularness' but less unwieldy. This idea of the secular or secularity solely as a condition—of time, space, thought ectetera—is consistent with the origins of the term, used to describe a space that is not primarily ordered according to religious rules and conceptions of time (Taylor 2007). On the other hand, it is sufficiently abstract for scholars to consider its applicability to non-Christian settings (Wohlrab-Sahr and Burchardt 2012). It also helps make sense of the term 'secularism', which has to be a theory or ideology (*-ism*) of *something*. 'Secularism' is therefore an account or ideology that demarcates something as secular, notably but not only one advocated by the state. As Knott puts it (2014: 37): 'If "secularity" is the condition or state of being secular (as in "locality" and "local"), then "secularism", in general terms, is its ideological or theoretical expression (as in "localism")'. With this concept, it is possible to attend not only to secular phenomena but to their 'social and discursive reproduction and representation' (Knott 2014) or to their creation via 'symbolic distinctions' (Wohlrab-Sahr and Burchardt 2012: 881). This means that more diffuse and taken-for-granted cultural determinants of how distinctions between the religious and the secular are made (Wohlrab-Sahr and Burchardt 2012: 876) need not be set apart from explicit ideologies, as Wohlrab-Sahr and Burchardt propose, while at the same time it encourages us to attend to the diverse secularisms that they draw attention to in their recognition of multiplicity.[5] It also suggests that we cannot assume that the secular is conceptually prior to secularism, as Asad (2003: 16) contends, given that the thrust of Asad's own argument is that making a distinction between a 'religious' and 'secular' domain is what brings both concepts into being. Rather, the relationship between secularity and secularism is opened up for fundamental theoretical debate akin to those that have explored and contested the causal relationship between nationalism and the nation-state.

This view of secularism is distinct from those that see it as a singular historic phenomenon, only manifest in one meaningful form: in Christian and post-Christian industrial and therefore economically differentiated societies. Instead, this conception of secularism is minimal and sufficiently abstract to produce typologies with variable notions of the depth and reach of the secular. In the similar model that Wohlrab-Sahr and Burchardt (2012) have developed, there is a fruitful analogy to be drawn between secularism (in the sense given here) and 'multiple modernities' (Eisenstadt 2000 in Wohlrab-Sahr and Burchardt 2012: 877), in which the idea of a single unifying concept ('secularism', 'modernity') can be maintained without the idea that it emerges via a single homogenous and homogenizing pathway. It is an approach that invites detailed and rich typological distinctions between secularist forms rather than differentiations by degree. Secularist ideologies may vary in numerous ways: according to the phenomena they see religion et al. as secondary to, according to the types of religious et al. cultures and practices that are marginalized, and according to the reasons they give for how these arrangements have come into being. Just as there is no such thing in this model as extreme secularity (an institution

---

[5] Wohlrab-Sahr and Burchardt (2012: 881) make the following distinction: 'For reasons of analytical clarity, in what follows we propose to reserve the concept of *secularism* for the ideological-philosophical program—hence, for the explicit *ideology* of separation—and related political practices, and the concept of *secularity*, by contrast, for the culturally and symbolically as well as institutionally anchored forms and arrangements of differentiation between religion and other social spheres.'

emptied out of religion is seen as equally secular as one in which religion provides a secondary organizing logic but is still given a significant and central role), so there is no such thing as secularism in the singular and no such thing as a perfect or ideal-typical form.

Non-Religion and Secularity

Having made a distinction between non-religion and secularity, it is no longer necessary to use 'secularity' and 'secularism' to describe different aspects or dimensions, as in Kosmin's (2007) and others' idea of personal 'secularity' and political 'secularism', or to qualify 'secularism' according to personal and political dimensions. This is to be welcomed, as such approaches engender tricky comparisons between 'religious secularists' and 'secular secularists', or 'secularist secularists'. These compounds are more than absurd: they imply that non-religiosity is more compatible with secularist views than religiosity is, an idea that is not only contentious but patently wrong. Indeed, the history of political secularism and secular liberalism is widely considered to be closely tied to religious pluralism—not the triumph of a new non-religious modernity but a pragmatic solution to religious diversity and conflict (Brahm Levey and Modood 2009b). Differentiating the non-religious and the secular resolves these issues, and facilitates the use of the terms 'secularity' and 'secularism' to describe another, also significant distinction between a general condition and an ideology.

This alternative approach also opens up the possibility of considering how non-religion, secularity, *and* secularism may have personal and political dimensions—something that past distinctions between 'personal secularism' and 'political secularism' make troublesome at best and obscure at worst. Instead, clearly distinguishing these phenomena calls attention to the personal and political dimensions of each. For example, in political spaces we can distinguish between secularist constitutions, which then imply that only some government agencies will have cause to develop or implement specifically secularist policies demarcating activities and spaces in which religious needs are paramount, while many others will simply be secular in nature, their action not determined according to religious, spiritual, or non-religious concerns. Both are part of the political landscape, and both demand scholarly attention, but for different reasons and as part of different methodologies. Elsewhere, we can think about how so-called 'political secularism' can be manifest in personal beliefs and practices. So, for example, political secularist distinctions between legitimate and illegitimate public spaces for religious practice are bound up with similar distinctions played out in domestic spaces and according to personal religious, spiritual, and non-religious cultures—in the spaces people allow and exclude the practice of prayer or performance of religious rituals in their own homes, for example. Likewise, personal non-religious views about the absence of an afterlife become political matters when treatment of the dying and deceased are negotiated in public institutions and the law. The organization of religion into certain spaces in public domains— the provision of prayer rooms, for example—can, in turn, be embodied in habits and emotional responses. In discussion of this research, people spoke of being uncomfortable with the presentation of religion in certain public spaces while they felt comfortable with it in others; some mentioned intuitively turning away from religious practices in certain public spaces, revealing an embodied sense of these as private. Steph Berns (2014: 188–96) recounts how a room used by the British Museum for prayer during its *Hajj: Journey to the heart of Islam* exhibition in 2012 was explored, tentatively, by visitors when it was unoccupied because the room's purpose was unclearly signed; but on occasions when the room was being used for prayer, they hovered uncertainly around an invisible threshold at the entranceway. Challenging distinctions between 'political' and 'personal' modes of secularism, these kinds of habits and attitudes travel with people as they move between 'public' and 'private' spaces and show how secularism is always, at once, 'a doctrine and a set of porous practices that embody and exceed it' (Connolly 2011: 648). Thus, this vocabulary aims to retain crucial distinctions that scholars have made, while ceasing to imagine any phenomena as intrinsically personal, intrinsically philosophical, or intrinsically political—again, and as always, with a view to expanding the reach of our methodologies and analysis.

Post-Secular

The post-secular involves a critical stance towards the concept or reality of secularity, in which 'secularity' is usually understood to mean areligiosity or anti-religiosity. The term can be problematic for those who do not define 'secularity' in this way, though it may still be used to indicate a reflexive stance towards it. According to this vocabulary, post-secularity indicates a concrete social reality, some kind of real and existing condition or state—although, it is, as James A. Beckford (2012) argues, difficult to imagine what 'post-secularity' might entail as an empirical phenomenon. 'Post-secularism', as a theoretical position, is more tangible, describing precisely this critical attitude towards modes of secularism and the secular spaces they create.

Secularization

According to this conceptual approach, 'secularization' is not a process in which religion declines absolutely but one in which it declines to some extent. Indeed, many secularization theorists understand secularization in this way, as a process of relative decline, though other advocates and critics focus see it as involving absolute decline. The problem is that the notion of decline itself encourages us to think in absolute terms, with a zero endpoint in view. Secularization can, however, be reconsidered, as a way of describing a transition from a religion-governed jurisdiction to one in which religion plays a secondary role—the marginalization of religion not to the zero point but to a subsidiary position. This notion of secularization is equally consistent with theories that distinguish between declining belief, societal differentiation, and the privatization of religion, because all of these transformations involve the overall marginalization of religion in society, whether that decline is seen to happen comprehensively or whether it is seen to be confined to particular domains.

Standing on different theoretical ground, genealogical approaches tend to see the secular as a singular historical phenomenon, emanating from a Western centre. So, for Asad (2003: 16), 'over time a variety of concepts, practices, and sensibilities have come together to form "the secular"'. The complex he has in mind is a configuration of political secularism, liberalism, modernism, individualism, and nationalism associated with the Western Enlightenment. On the other hand, the 'secular' encompasses a lot in this broad genealogical approach as it looks to ways 'religion' is constructed, to anti-religious assumptions and attitudes, and to what happens to politics, subjectivities, and bodies not only when they adopt 'secular' dispositions but also when they lose contact with religious ones, such as with what Asad sees as a religious attitude to suffering.

The argument I present in this volume is somewhat different. It suggests that, rather than conceptualizing 'the secular' as involving a 'great deal more' than individual forms of areligion and anti-religion, we stand to gain from reconceptualizing it as involving a great deal less. A reduced notion of secularity allows it to be untangled from sometimes historically related but distinctive phenomena—liberalism, individualism, nationalism—all of which can manifest with support from religious cultures too. The broader understanding of secularity does far too much: if we use the concept to capture everything that does not have an explicit religious basis, regardless of whether that something is totally unrelated to religion, an aberration from religion, a critique of religion, an attack on religion, or an alternative to it developed in some kind of contradistinction from religious forms, then everything is secular that is not overtly religious and, to the extent that religious actors are involved with all of these things, the space allocated to religion itself also becomes very limited. It is unclear what analytical work such a concept of the secular could ever do.

CONCLUSION

The reliance on prefixes and suffixes attached to a few root concepts reflects that this vocabulary is a typology of relationships. Its aim is to clarify these relationships and highlight their variety. As such, it complicates binary approaches to religion. Though 'non-religion' sounds like a single partner to 'religion', this relational model treats it as a concrete phenomenon that can be differentiated from alternative forms of religion (or alternative spirituality) as well as from areligion. To describe a religious landscape inclusively, then, is to attend to its traditionally religious, alternatively religious, and non-religious cultures as well as to its areligious or post-religious features in which all of these phenomena are marginal to some degree. To engage with the secular is to explore this delimitation in its different forms and locations, and in any number of combinations. A relational approach is therefore emphatic of heterogeneity.[6]

---

[6] Johannes Quack (2014), Monika Wohlrab-Sahr and Marian Burchardt (2012) develop similar approaches to my own, and variation between them, relatively slight though it often is, provides an opportunity to refine this approach further.

This typology of relationships is unlikely to be complete or exhaustive, nor helpful in the way it currently is indefinitely. But it is useful for now and as a concrete basis for revision. Meanwhile, this and other terminological discussions alleviate the daunting conceptual issues that have threatened this field of research. Scholars are right to suggest that research in this field has been inhibited by terminological confusion, but it is as much a problem that so many scholars use terms without reflection or explication. The problem of language is most acute when the problem itself is undetected—and this has been a particular challenge in this field. As Campbell says, there are particular difficulties for researchers 'confronted with a virgin area of territory to survey [but finding] the land covered with the signposts of explorers from other disciplines' (2013: 18). The contributions of theology and philosophy, for example, are likely to make the sociologist's task harder rather than easier (Campbell 2013: 18), something we see clearly in the overuse of 'atheism' and 'unbelief' as synonyms for all of non-religion. The terminological discussion and vocabulary offered here intends to make it much more difficult to fall back on established but unscrutinized concepts, as well as to make distinctions between phenomena that are frequently confused with one another though they are fundamentally different. The following chapter turns to the most significant of these differences: the distinction between insubstantial and substantial modes of 'secularity', or between the secular and the non-religious.

2

The Insubstantial and the Substantial Seculars

Theories of Secularity and Non-Religion

The premise of this book is that there is an important paradox in contemporary engagements with secularity. This is that, while 'the secular' is a familiar analytic concept and one attracting increasing attention, its meaning remains unclear. The question is not merely whether the term indicates this or that empirical substance—whether it refers, say, to institutional differentiation or to individual unbelief—but is much more fundamental: the question at stake is whether 'the secular' denotes any kind of substance at all.

This question is not often clearly stated, but emerges from a tension between accounts of the secular that take fundamentally different views of its ontology. Briefly put, some scholars treat the secular as insubstantial; some argue that secularity is a substance which emerges from religious diversity; while others, in making either unbelief or anti-religion central to their analyses, either imply that these concrete phenomena comprise the substance of secularity or make this claim explicitly. Recently, some aspects of these debates have crystallized; in particular, a conception of the secular as a (substantive) matrix of religious pluralism has been contrasted with a negative or 'subtractive' account (Taylor 2007) in which secularity is a situation in which religion is marginal or absent. Other aspects of the debate remain implicit, however, partly as a result of the conceptual confusion discussed in the last chapter. Notably, theorization of the relationship between secularity and substantive non-religiosity has either been ignored or impaired by a focus on one of the two at the expense of the other. In this, Taylor's *A Secular Age* is one of a few exceptional cases in that it makes clear space for non-religion (or, more specifically, unbelief) in its theory of secularity. Yet, even this account imbalances a sophisticated theorization of secularity with a much more conventional treatment of unbelief. Thus, the fundamental nature of the secular, as it is commonly understood, is very far from a closed question. As Taylor himself admits, contemporary scholarship has not yet achieved clarity on this, although he says it can be congratulated for having at least become aware of its own confusions—'a Socratic mode of wisdom that [scholars] stand in need of in this domain' (2009: xi).

Frequent use of the term 'secularity' contrasts with a scarcity of explicit and/or sustained empirical accounts in contemporary work. Nevertheless, these usages are revealing in that they contain ideas and instructive assumptions about the nature of secularity. This chapter reviews this literature, then, and draws out hypotheses from these senses of the secular. It also identifies a line of consensus running through this otherwise decentralized literature, which is its view of the secular as fundamentally insubstantial. Whether expressed in argument or assumption, this understanding is taken up in research and therefore shapes subsequent ways of thinking about the secular and methodologies for its study. Notions of a 'secularization paradigm' have been put forward, and this paradigm can be seen as partly culpable for the asymmetric treatment of religion as a substantial, cultural phenomenon while simultaneously failing to even imagine ways in which the 'secular' can be conceived of in similar terms. In this volume I treat this assumption as an empirical question and respond to it as such, but this chapter shows how merely recognizing the assumption and the breadth and force of its impact (even in emerging research dealing with non-religion and non-theism) broadens and otherwise transforms how we think about and approach 'the secular'.

THE INSUBSTANTIAL SECULAR

The idea of the insubstantial secular pervades social scientific research. It is visible in religion-centric methodologies, in which the secular is viewed as a context in which religion exists and is enacted. Here, the secular is the 'everything but' that surrounds and interacts with religion—the political, administrative, palliative, economic, domestic, and other domains that are distinguished from the religious one in differentiated societies. Despite mounting awareness of problems with 'subtraction' accounts of secularization (Taylor 2007) and, therefore, with the insubstantial secular, new work continues to follow this vein. Recent cognitive approaches to religion, for example, have tended to explore the neurological pathways that give rise to religious experience, with key works barely making mention of areligious, non-religious, atheistic, and non-theistic cases. Though the field is broadening, with new scholarship attending to 'religion's others' more closely (e.g. Lanman 2011; 2012; Geertz and Markússon 2010), it still bears the mark of its assumption that the secular is insubstantial.

Similarly, large-scale surveys have been particularly interested in traditional religiosity, measuring church attendance, religious affiliation, and theistic belief and, in more expansive surveys, asking about a larger number of beliefs that are nevertheless largely Abrahamic or Christian: belief in God or a higher power, the afterlife, heaven and hell, sin and the devil.[1] Surveys with fewer questions about religion, including national censuses, ask questions about 'religious affiliation', in which respondents are able to choose a confession and sometimes to elect an affiliation of their own description or to select a 'not religious' option. Such methods are not designed for the possibility that 'secular' experiences and identities might be heterogeneous (Campbell 2013: 10; Barker 2007: iii; Vernon 1968); it is not possible to organize absence into types. What is more, researchers are inconsistent in how they describe this 'secular' group on surveys—as the 'not religious', 'no religion' or 'none'; as 'atheist', 'agnostic', and even 'atheist/agnostic'; or a combination of categories from either approach. Yet we now know that people respond differently, even to slight differences such as 'no religion' and 'none' options (Bullivant 2008a; Day 2013; Lee 2014). All of these approaches are designed with religious cultures in mind and measure the secular as a residual category rather than according to precise, research-informed types. As a result, they often use insufficient sample sizes and non-random sampling to gather data on what has

---

[1] For examples and discussion, see Davie (1994), Halman and Moor (1994), Halman and Draulans (2006), Keysar and Kosmin (2007), Gill et al. (1998), and Voas and Crockett (2005). In addition, Voas and Day (2007) provide a useful and critical overview of current measures with reference to the British case in particular.

frequently been approached as a control group rather than one of central interest (Campbell 2013; Vernon 1968). Significantly, these surveys are developed to tell how far populations have moved from traditional religiosity rather than to explore what they might have moved towards.

This idea of the insubstantial secular is deeply embedded and unites scholars across deep divides—theoretical, methodological, geographical. The idea appears to be driven by secularization theory—hardly surprising when we remember that the common usage of 'the secular' derives in large part from the success of this thesis—but it appeals to those arguing against it or away from it, too. In fact, there is good reason to believe that the notion of the secular as insubstantial is as much religion-centric as it is secularization-centric, as critical religion scholars have proposed. But its wide use means that reflecting on the insubstantial secular is crucial to understanding how this notion has and continues to set the terms of debate.

Secularizationists

Paradoxically, secularization theory can be seen as taking up a religion-centric approach in its notion of secularity. It constantly implies that the secular itself is insubstantial, a sort of anti-state that does not itself involve any particular way of being but merely the disappearance of another, substantial mode: the religious. Secularization theory almost always refers to processes which result in the declining significance of religion. Notwithstanding some approaches that segregate the discussion according to the micro-, meso-, and macro-levels, secularization is normally split into two streams: the separation of 'church and state' (or religion and politics), and declining participation in traditional religion. Some scholars also emphasize the differentiation of religious and secular spheres and contrast differentiation with decline. Since they do not mean, however, that religion continues to play a vital though compartmentalized role in all of the spheres of social life that it did formally, but rather that religion ceases to play the same vital role in at least one and normally several of these newly compartmentalized spheres, a single notion of secularization using the concepts of decline, marginalization, diminishment, and decreasing significance is perfectly sufficient. Because it is a theory of decline, the secularization thesis conceives of the secular, not as an autonomous, distinct, substantial entity, but as a purely analytical form, used merely to measure the marginalization of the real and substantial entity of interest. In this model, then, the ideal typical secular condition is an areligious one, and the next best thing—given that once-religious societies that will inevitably commune in some way with their religious history—is the idea of the secular as post-religious. Secularization therefore measures quantitative rather than qualitative shifts, as Taylor's notion of it as a 'subtraction story' captures well.

Scholars explicating the 'secularizationist' (Bruce 2011) view of secularity include leading secularizationist Steve Bruce (2002; 2011) and the pioneering researcher of secularity and 'godlessness', Phil Zuckerman (2008). This idea of secularity is also widely diffused through the literature. For example, Bagg and Voas (2010) have recently used the idea of a 'triumph of indifference' to describe the advance of secularity of the UK, and the approach is exemplified in Norris and Inglehart's (2004) work. This takes the quasi-Marxist view that secularity is the default human state and is liberated by fortuitous economic conditions: they argue that conventional religiosity declines as 'existential security' increases, achieved through a combination of good welfare provision and a certain level of wealth, and they speculate that the reason for this correlation is that religion primarily operates as a source of comfort for those in precarious economic situations. Regardless of whether secularization is seen to give rise to post-religious populations that may maintain an idle curiosity about and even literacy in religious cultures, or to fundamentally areligious ones largely uninterested and illiterate when it comes to religion, the secular condition is always conceived of in negative terms, the only real qualitative feature of which is an attitude of equanimity towards religion. Bruce (2002: 42) gives the following summary of the insubstantial secular:

> In so far as I can imagine an endpoint [of secularization], it would not be self-conscious irreligion; you have to care too much about religion to be irreligious. It would be widespread indifference (what Weber called being religiously unmusical); no socially significant shared religion; and religious ideas being no more common than would be the case if all minds were wiped blank and people began from scratch to think about the world and their place in it. This is an important point, because the critics often assume that the secularization paradigm supposes the human default position to be instrumental, materialist atheism.

For Bruce (1996, in Bullivant 2010: 113), 'self-conscious atheism and agnosticism are features of religious cultures' and indifference is the key to secularity. It is a view taken up by the sociologist of secularity, Phil Zuckerman, in his innovative 2008 study of 'godless societies' in Scandinavia. For Zuckerman, indifference to religion is evidence that 'certain segments of Scandinavian society are about as secular as is sociologically possible' (Zuckerman 2008: 97). Likewise, Benjamin Beit-Hallahmi, a psychologist in the field of non-religion and secularity research, attempts to rebalance engagements with religion and religiosity in modern human sciences with new work '[a]ccounting for the *absence* of religious faith' (Beit-Hallahmi 2007, in Zuckerman 2008: 95). This is similar to Zuckerman's methodological concern with 'how to study the relative *absence* of something' (Zuckerman 2008: 76) and to 'describe and understand men and women as they go about living their *religion-less* lives' (Zuckerman 2008: 96; emphasis added). Such work is significant in its own right. Zuckerman, for example, takes on normative and highly critical accounts of what it means to be without religion—as unhealthy, dysfunctional, or a painful condition to be endured. In contrast to such received wisdoms, his accounts of, say, bereavement experiences in unreligious societies are concerned to show that people can and do manage in the absence of religion. Nevertheless, such work does not yet take on the task of detailing *how* they manage in the absence of religion. It does not think about what they do, rather than what they do not do. To that extent, approaches within the secularization paradigm take religion-centric thinking and methodologies on their own terms.

The secularizationist approach is significant because it is deeply entrenched in sociology. Canonical scholarship has typically understood secularity and secular modernity in this way: Anthony Giddens (1991), Ulrich Beck and Elisabeth Beck-Gernsheim (2002), and Zygmunt Bauman (2000) all discuss the dissolution of traditional structures, including religious ones, as a feature of modern life and are concerned to understand what happens to society, for good or ill, when this happens. In his exploration of the modern psyche, for example, Giddens (1991: 204) claims that rites of passage are entirely absent from modern life, meaning that 'individuals are left without structured ways of coping' with the business of living. Even though his modernization theory is more optimistic than others, secular modernity is still conceived of in terms of loss and the reconfigurations

The Insubstantial and the Substantial Seculars 55

that take place as a result of what moderns are left without. On the supposed absence of rites and rituals, he says:

> something more profound is lost together with traditional forms of ritual. *Rites de passage* place those concerned in touch with wider cosmic forces relating individual life to more encompassing existential issues. (Giddens 1991)

In this way, social theory has reinforced the subtraction story of secularization and, with it, the notion of secularity as insubstantial.

Critics of Secularization Theory

Critics of secularization theory have not typically questioned the idea of the insubstantial secular. This is illustrated in the arguments made by Bruce's long-term interlocutor, Rodney Stark, as well as by others involved in what is called the 'rational choice theory of religion'. Here, the critique targets not the proposed notion of secularity, but its stability over time. The rational choice approach applies economic metaphors to the study of religion with, for example, Stark and Bainbridge (1996) arguing that religions offer certain products for tender in religious markets. Key amongst these products is the promise of entry to a desirable afterlife. Given that this product cannot be delivered to consumers within their lifetimes, religions trade in proxies or 'compensators' (Stark and Bainbridge 1996). These are products, they argue, universal appeal—not under certain circumstances, as in Marx's view or Norris and Inglehart's, but under all circumstances, as a result of our human capacity to conceive of our own deaths. This means that demand for religious compensators is constant and decline in religious vitality is therefore a supply-side failure, say for example if there is insufficient competition and therefore unappealing products on offer (Lehmann 2010). Where other disputes concerning secularization theory focus on the extent to which that theory is backed up by evidence, the challenge posed by rational choice theorists is theoretical: it has to do with different ways of theorizing the insubstantial secular, as an absence that is felt (and hurts) as opposed to an absence that does not really matter. Significantly, because the absence of religion is painful, it can only ever be short-term—a view that undermines the idea of secularity as a meaningful state in its own right. The secular is merely a time or space in which religion has failed to reach its full potential or 'actualize'. It is a transitional or liminal condition, albeit one that might endure for some time or indefinitely even. Secularity has no form and involves no 'products' of its own. It is profoundly insubstantial.

Rational choice theorists have led the way in the 'reversal of consensus' surrounding secularization and its paradigmatic status (Lehmann 2010: 1870), but other critiques have focused on evidential rather than theoretical issues. So, concepts such as 'desecularization' (Berger 1999a; 1999b), 'resacralization' (Davie 2010), and 're-enchantment' (Gane 2002; Berman 1981) are used to dispute not the model but the direction of change. Elsewhere, scholars of religion and modernity have shifted attention to the growth of evangelical and fundamentalist movements, even within wider processes of decline (Lehmann 2010: 194). Again, this approach returns its attention to religion within secular contexts rather than focusing on the secular context itself. Finally, several scholars dispute whether any degree of secularization has ever occurred, an argument that naturally gives no attention to the concrete reality of secularity. In so-called secular Europe, somewhere between two-thirds and three-quarters of the population believe in a god or supernatural power despite not being religiously active (Davie 1994; Halman and Moor 1994; Voas and Crockett 2005; Stark and Finke 2000), suggesting that Europeans may be experiencing religious continuity or religious change rather than religious decline. Grace Davie (1994) famously called the phenomenon 'believing without belonging' and, in an argument that has some compatibilities with the economic approach, has recently said that religion has a dynamic but fundamentally unbroken history, which oscillates between times of 'believing without belonging' and times of 'believing *and* belonging' (2010). Davie has also provided a theory of 'vicarious religion' (2007), in which a largely inactive religious majority nevertheless have their religiosity fortified through contact with the religious activity of others: that is, the apparently secular are not themselves actively religious but they appreciate and feed off the religiosity in their environments. They are not so much secular, then, as they are religious in a new way. Edward Bailey's theory of 'implicit religion' (1997), in which apparently secular populations continue to find religious meaning in the world, works in a similar way, as does scholarship attending to the individualization of religion and alternative spirituality (e.g. Heelas and Woodhead 2005; Houtman and Mascini 2002; Houtman and Aupers 2007). All of these approaches focus on uncovering traditional or new stirrings of

The Insubstantial and the Substantial Seculars 57

religion beneath secular façades, rather than exploring the ways in which secular populations are actually or substantively secular.

Religious and Theological Approaches

I have focused on the secularization thesis or paradigm in terms of explaining the way social scientists have and, more importantly, have not approached 'the secular'. However, the same idea of the secular as insubstantial is found in approaches working outside that paradigm, including several theological ones. Indeed, the notion of either hollow or purely intellectual and irreligious modes of 'secularity' was set out before the popularization of secularization theory. So, for example, the religious 1851 response to British Church census findings discussed in Chapter 1 outlines these two ways of being unreligious:

> Apart from the religious portion, our population generally may be divided into two classes mainly. The one consisting of those who are given up to low sensual indulgence, the other, of those marked by a sceptical activity of mind, disposed to question everything. (*Congregational Year Book* 1851, in Kitson Clark 1965: 164)

Thus, 'religion's others' are cast as an intellectual—indeed, possibly an *over*-intellectual—disposition and as a more lowly unchurched experience. Though the language and moral implications may have changed over the intervening years, it is nevertheless quite striking how little our understanding of secular populations has evolved.

Critical approaches to religion and secularity call for genealogies of religion and the secular and show how a vacant notion of the secular has served not only 'secular' but also 'religious' authorities well. Religious powers can use their supposed singularity to set themselves apart in order to maintain the position of authority they had previously enjoyed when there was no competing secular authority; at the same time, secular authorities can claim to be 'neutral, rational, natural', and empowered to make 'authoritative statements about religion' on this basis (Fitzgerald 2007: 26). Thus, the religious have been constructed as special and 'non-modern' (Asad 1993: 23) through the same processes that saw the naturalization of the secular. In these intriguing accounts, both religious and unreligious actors are invested in the notion of the insubstantial secular—

something that might go some way to explaining the power and widespread of that idea.

THE SUBSTANTIAL SECULAR

Working against this tradition of treating the secular as an insubstantial condition, some contributions present the secular as a substantial form. This involves a fundamentally different ontological account, therefore, and includes alternative visions of what the substance of secularity might entail as well as evidence that methodologies attending to this substance may be worthwhile.

Secular in Relation

The first contribution of this sort is a body of work that takes a relational approach to ontology in general, in which the idea of a neutral relationship is viewed as a contradiction in terms and most probably a political strategy rather than a representation of reality. Applied to the secular, this argument implies that if a secular individual or population interacts with religion in any way it is therefore situated in a meaningful relation to it and is, in my sense, non-religious. So long as 'secular' actors *encounter* religion, that is, they must be involved in processes of position-taking and position-making, and these processes give secularity some substantive form. In a relational view, the idea of 'post-religion' fails to do credit to the particularity and meaning of everyday cultural encounters. Following Campbell (2013), this project is based on the relational premise that people interact with religion qua 'religion's other', and that an account of dispositions of 'otherness' is therefore necessary.

Post-colonial accounts, receiving a seminal statement in Talal Asad's (1993; 2003) work, also pay closer attention to how substances underlying secular positions are formed through engagements with religion. This work reconsiders the idea of secularism as a system in which institutions respond to religious diversity by taking a neutral stance towards all religions and highlights instead the ways in which secularism involves the management of religions. Secularism becomes something that people can believe in, a 'powerful idea' with, 'effects [that]—like the effects of some religious faiths—vary according to how far people believe in it and in which ways' (Cannell 2010: 86). This literature highlights the ideological nature of secularism and, because secularism has substance, it is seen to vary in quality and quantity. Most of this literature is focused on the state rather than so-called secular populations, and it has tended to be theoretical rather than empirical. In relation to related discussions of post-secularism, for example, Turner says that 'it has been philosophers and theologians—and not the sociologists—who have defined the parameters of [this] discussion' (Turner 2010: 649). Nevertheless, this theoretical shift has drawn attention to the ways in which secular actors are not minimally concerned with religious ones, but are rather engaged in substantive relations with them that accord to certain ideas about what it means to be religious and what it means to be secular, as well as to the investments and intentions that they mean these encounters to serve.

A focus on encounters between the religious and the unreligous draws attention to the structures that give rise to these encounters. In fact, in the globalized and highly mediated environments in which we live, such encounters are frequent and diverse in form. Even in places where religious identification and participation continue to decline, mediated contact with religious cultures and, indeed, with non-religious cultures is increasing (Knott, Poole, and Teemu 2013). In 1971, it was Colin Campbell's (2013: 24) view that millions of non-religious encounters would be taking place every *day*. Though personal religiosity may have declined in some places since that time, social diversity and increased mediation mean that the number of these encounters is likely to have increased. The hold of the idea of the insubstantial secular is such that the way in which these encounters must necessarily produce non-religious others is often lost from view. Researchers and policy makers have, for example, been interested in 'inter-faith' and 'multi-faith' engagements and neglected or struggled to find ways to involve 'non-faith' participants. The concepts of 'inter-faith' and 'multi-faith' themselves exclude those whose positions have been described in the negative. Recent attempts have been made to welcome 'people of all faiths and none', but this clumsy and inflexible phrase demonstrates the problem. Yet such interventions do attempt to overturn long-standing asymmetries in how we think about the religious and the secular, and try to imagine the latter as people with interests and views that may be meaningful in relation to religious ones.

The Anti-Religious Secular

A second theory of the secular as substantial comes from an increasing focus on anti-religious perspectives. This work contends—often with normative, reforming intentions—not only that secular populations participate in *some* form of position-taking, but that this position-taking is specifically anti-religious in nature. Thus, while this approach accepts the view that secularization has advanced, it does not accept that the resulting secular population is areligious or post-religious in nature. Berger, Davie, and Fokas (2008: 61–3) provide a useful summary of this post-secular 'turn' (McLennan 2010) and the arguments of two of its most prominent advocates, José Casanova and Jürgen Habermas. They highlight Casanova's contention that, 'Europe should become, as rapidly as possible, post-secular', as only then will it be possible, 'to counter the secularist assumptions of many (if not all) social and political commentators, who necessarily "turn religion into a problem"' (Berger et al. 2008: 62). It is because of this, Casanova says, that religious citizens have been unfairly burdened in secular contexts:

> In the name of freedom, individual autonomy, tolerance, and cultural pluralism, religious people—Christian, Jewish, and Muslim—are being asked to keep their religious beliefs, identities and norms 'private' so that they do not disturb the project of a modern, secular, enlightened Europe. (Casanova 2006, in Berger et al. 2008: 62)

Berger et al. draw attention to the deep similarities between this and Habermas's view, which they summarize as demanding that:

> secular citizens ... must learn, sooner rather than later, to live in a post-secular society. In so doing, they will be following the example of religious citizens, who have already come to terms with the ethical expectations of democratic citizenship, in the sense that they have adopted appropriate epistemic attitudes toward their secular environment. (Berger et al. 2008: 62)

They call attention to Habermas's idea (2005, in Berger et al. 2008: 62) of an 'asymmetric distribution of cognitive burdens', between religious and secular citizens, and 'the duty of the more secular citizen to overcome his or her narrowly secularist consciousness in order to engage with religion' in terms of Rawlsian 'reasonable disagreement' (Berger et al. 2008: 61–3).

So, from this literature we have a picture of the 'secular consciousness' which is 'narrow' in its secularity and conceives of religion in relation to an Enlightenment and modernizing project. The result is an anti-religious stance, which necessarily 'views religion as a problem' and demands, therefore, that it be excluded from public life. For themselves, the secularist demands free rein, taking on little of the 'cognitive burden' involved in religious–secular interactions and negotiations. Thus, we have one clear and categorical conception of what the secular person 'brings to the table'—namely, antagonism towards religion—an attitude that is thought to be pervasive, shared by 'many (if not all) social and political commentators'.

Sociologists in particular (Bruce 2011; Lee 2011; Wohlrab-Sahr and Burchardt 2012) have drawn attention to the simplification of the so-called secular outlook that this account involves. As Wohlrab-Sahr and Burchardt (2012: 879) note:

> The critique of secularization theory has certainly increased the sensitivity to cultural differences and unjustified generalizations. However, there is now a danger of an essentialism of historically and culturally 'unique' constellations and undue generalizations about the ideological power of Western secularism.

However, though it is at risk of reducing what is, after all, the world's 'fourth largest religion' to a single outlook, this work does pose a real and innovative challenge to the idea of secularity as insubstantial.

That said, the insubstantial secular creeps back into these accounts. This is because these accounts are critical, and make the removal of secularist views—that is, the instatement of the insubstantial secular—their goal. Because the secular or secularist outlook is seen as antireligious, these authors seek to eradicate it. In this way, the cultural content of 'secularity' is viewed as a problem—an aberration from the proper or better state of affairs in which secularity does not intervene in religious life. In general, these critics do not treat religion and non-religious secularism in equal terms. They suggest that the non-religious reflect on their narrow view of religion, while at the same time maintaining a substantive but very narrow sense of what the non-religious attitude entails. In relation to this, this work has yet to develop rich and empirically informed accounts of non-religious cultural life. Additional concerns include McLennan's (2010:4) argument that contemporary critiques of secularism offer an intra-secularist rather than anti-secularist argument which should be regarded as part of the 'secularization of secularism' itself. In short, this scholarship has provided an ontologically significant, though somewhat limited account of the secular as substantial.

The Non-Religious Secular

While the relationship between the secular and the non-religious is unclear, several kinds of closeness between them is often assumed or implied. This is especially the case in non-specialist research and popular discussion in which 'militant atheism' and other explicit and forceful statements of non-religiosity are presented as expressions of secular society. These descriptions basically conflate secularity and non-religion, that is. As a result, conceptions of non-religion provide further ideas about what the substantial secular might entail.

Dedicated accounts of non-religion are relatively few and far between (Bullivant and Lee 2012), but there are still several references to non-religion in the scholarship from which to derive hypotheses about the nature of secularity. Chief amongst these is the view that non-religion is fundamentally intellectual in character—a sense that is well established and widespread. The intellectualization of non-religiosity is seen in the attempt to make the category of 'religion' inclusive of secular populations by extending it to 'religion and philosophy' or 'religion and ethics'. The tendency to pair 'religion and atheism', as discussed in the last chapter, is another clear example of the intellectualized view of non-religion, in which atheism contrasts with a more expansive notion of religion. The employment of this pairing, even by those researchers who have worked hard to overturn theistic- and belief-based approaches to religion and emphasize its practical and cultural aspects, illustrates how deep-seated this view of non-religion is. In this way, an uncritical focus on 'atheism' reveals the continued popularity of belief-based notions of religion, running contrary to the one or several 'cultural turns' that the sociology of religion has experienced (Lynch 2012a) and a move in sociology to emphasize the role of material forms.

In practice, too, research into non-religion has focused disproportionately on 'atheism', 'unbelief', and other cognitive and codified forms of non-religion. Theological and philosophical treatments, which dominated the field until recently, naturally focus on ideas and beliefs. Rather than taking social approaches, many histories of secularization also focus on scientific cultures involved in that process, highlighting the importance of evolutionary theory, the archaeology of religion, and the role of public intellectuals who became the well-known faces of non-theist and secularist discourses, such as Charles Darwin, T. H. Huxley, and Leslie Stephen. But in the social sciences, too, most accounts centre on non-religion as an intellectual phenomenon. Early contributions focused on 'unbelief': to take an important example, the Vatican, hosting the first academic conference in the field, made its subject 'the culture of unbelief' (Corporale and Grumelli 1971). The framing of Susan Budd's (1977) early contribution is similar, in a volume called *Varieties of Unbelief: Atheists and Agnostics in English Society, 1850–1960*. Even Campbell's 'sociology of irreligion', which advocates a wide-ranging approach to this study and particularly emphasizes the need for attention to irreligious action and emotion (2013: 22–3), focuses on well-defined atheist, agnostic, secularist, and humanist intellectual movements. This emphasis on ideas and politics continues in the contemporary fixation with public anti-theist cultures and with New Atheism in particular, and with non-theism in general (e.g. Hunsberger and Altemeyer 2006; Bradley and Tate 2010; Beattie 2007; Zuckerman 2010a; 2010b; Amarasingam 2010; Martin 2007; Stephen Bullivant and Michael Ruse 2013).

Researchers are also disproportionately interested in people with clear non-religious identities—and especially with those who participate in non-religious or secularist meet-up groups—as compared with those who have more vague or more general self-understandings as 'not religious'. Analytic methods likewise focus on the cognitive and the discursive, treating meet-up groups more like 'epistemic communities', people brought together by a common codified goal—rather than as 'communities of practice', brought together by shared practices and locations in time and space in which ideas are emergent rather than structuring (Lave and Wenger 1991). Discussions of New Atheism have focused on its output—the work of the so-called 'four horsemen', Richard Dawkins, Sam Harris, Daniel Dennett, and Christopher Hitchens—rather than reception studies and other audience-based research about its actual effects.

As well as being primarily intellectual, another hypothesis concerning non-religion is that it is focused on and glorifies science and is humanistic. This view emerges in intellectualist accounts of how and why people lose their religion, that is, as a result of scientific education and scientific knowledge—an argument even peddled by social scientists, who sometimes ignore more controversial and overtly problematic correlations between non-religion and, in many Western contexts, whiteness, maleness, and youth, while drawing attention to the correlations with another sign of privilege, namely education levels. Likewise, post-structural critiques of secularist ideologies tend to focus on the way in which religion is seen to pose a threat to peaceful society and the concomitant belief that reason and logic are its guardians. Thus, the anti-religious form of secularism which post-secularists focus on is also one with a particular ideological and epistemological focus—on non-theistic rationalism and scientism.

Non-religious actors are themselves involved in the construction of non-religion as a matter of ideas and humanist epistemologies. This idea of non-religiosity as a matter of scientific awareness is seen in the kinds of representations taken up by non-religious people today and in the recent past, such as 'scepticism', 'rationalism', and 'free thought'. Though they are probably wrong to reduce unreligious perspectives to a single form, post-colonial critics are correct to identify a modernist form of secularism in which religiosity is viewed as irrational and unscientific as well as threatening and inclined to violence. By implication, the unreligious person is rational and scientific, and therefore moderate in their engagement with others—that is, characterized by their superiority of mind. This characterization of the non-religious is, says Campbell (2013), pervasive within the social sciences and goes some way to explaining social scientists' lack of interest in the study of irreligion before now.

While these literatures are useful in several ways, they rely on a great number of assumptions about what it means to be unreligious. On the one hand, the idea that non-religion is primarily intellectual, scientistic, and/or anti-religious in nature has not been subject to wide empirical scrutiny. On the other hand, such notions of the non-religious have encouraged what empirical work there has been to follow certain methodologies, focusing on the very few highly codified examples of non-religion at the expense of more diffuse cultural threads and fuzzier forms. This is despite the fact that the latter appear to outnumber explicit and proactive forms of non-religion by some margin. By working with self-representing non-theists mainly, the study of non-religion is dominated by works posing as 'case studies' for a larger population that they may not be at all representative of or even closely related to.

The Insubstantial and the Substantial Seculars

HYPOTHESES FOR RESEARCH

In short, while past work provides some ideas about what it means to be secular, a much wider empirical engagement is required. There are big challenges here and Baker and Smith (2009: 730) are right to say that 'creativity and determination' are needed to develop tools for the task. This is not only because the population is so large but because it is so novel to social research and our theories about its nature are so underdeveloped. Because of this, it can be challenging even to identify hypotheses for research. Focusing on unbelief, Grace Davie (2013: 262–3) wonders, open-endedly, what an 'experiential atheism [might] look like and how might this be expressed?' 'The answer', she says, 'is not immediately clear':

> At one level, it is true that atheists, just like believers, respond to what are called 'peak experiences'. At another, the fact that the criticisms that unbelievers direct towards religion are so often based on the primacy of reason must surely favour the rational over the expressive. A third point is worth pondering: believers are very often exposed to the experiential in the course of worship. It is built into the liturgy and becomes an essentially shared activity. Is there an equivalent for unbelievers, who— by definition—do not engage in such activities?

Davie gets at one of the core issues facing non-religion researchers: given a focus on reason and rationality, partly real, partly perceived, how should we begin to *imagine* substantive, social, and ritual non-religion in order to research it? Under such circumstances, where and how should scholars begin?

My suggestion is this. It may be fruitful for scholars to redraw these challenges as hypotheses. Thus the possibility that non-religion is essentially intellectual and anti-religious and not at all social and symbolic become the first questions for research. In addition, as 'religion's other', anything seen to be characteristic of religion can be converted into a hypothesis concerning the unreligious: if theism is characteristic of religion, the hypothesis is that non-theism and atheism should be characteristic of non-religion, and so on. Central concepts of religion include:

- Religion involves theism and/or supernatural belief
- Religion is communitarian and concerns the preservation of tradition
- Religion involves ritual and rites of passage ceremony

- Religion is concerned with answering existential, metaphysical, or 'ultimate' questions
- Religion involves a degree of *active* engagement in a religious culture
- Religion is the primary source of ethics or morality
- Religion concerns a universal desire for immortality.

All of these conceptions of religion provide, in turn, ways of thinking about so-called secular populations: as non-theist, atomistic, lacking rites of passage and life-cycle ceremonies, and so on. Each can be transformed into a hypothesis and tested by investigating the extent to which they are present in these populations and, if found to be, whether they are present in familiar forms and therefore evidence of latent or alternative religiosity, or present in alternative forms and therefore evidence of non-religiosity.

Given the proposed affinity between secularity and industrial modernity, another set of hypotheses can be derived from theories pertaining to the latter. An example of particular significance relates to patterns and practices of association. While religion is seen to be highly social, secular modernity is often associated with social fragmentation. One way of testing this proposition is to investigate the extent to which non-religious cultural forms are community-building or tend towards individualism. In fact, the nature of the social in modernity is contested and often discussed in nuanced terms, raising yet more possibilities for the study of non-religion. There is not only the collectivist and the individualist, but the individuali*z*ed (Beck and Beck-Gernsheim 2002), the possibility of looser forms of solidarity associated with network models (e.g. Castells 2010) and Durkheim's notion of 'organic solidarity' (Durkheim 1984). There is the possibility of more informal modes of solidarity, as in Spencer and Pahl's notion of 'hidden solidarity', and the idea that specific relationships, especially long-term romantic partnerships, become an increasingly relied upon social resource (Bauman 2000; Giddens 1992 in Pahl and Spencer 2004). Alternatively, we might consider Bryan Turner's argument that 'the social in the modern world is fragile and fragmented and [that] the erosion of the social has significant sociological implications for the survival of "the sacred"' (2010: 663). Following Maffesoli's argument in *The Time of Tribes: The Decline of Individualism in Mass Society* (1996 in Turner 2010), Turner (2010: 664) suggests that the religious landscape is, like others, increasingly dominated by micro-groups 'who share a common, but shallow and transitory culture'. The questions this suggests to the sociology of 'secularity' include whether the rise of non-religious forms such as New Atheism are examples of these 'new but fragmented and ephemeral forms of association' (Turner 2000: 665) and the extent to which this is indicative of non-religious culture in general.

Mounting critique of the idea of secular neutrality is challenging for the idea of the insubstantial secular, and the relational view advocated by Campbell and in contemporary sociology adds fuel to the fire. It remains unclear, however, whether 'secular' people are non-religious only to the extent that they experience religion around them, or whether they also have personal commitments and are part of communities that are, for now at least, best described as religious-like. Attending to the ways that people respond to religion and understand what it is that motivates these responses is one way to investigate this question. As well as various social, political, and economic concerns that give rise to non-religious responses, the discussion of this chapter provides further theories and hypotheses concerning 'secularity'. These can be summarized as follows:

Hypothesis 1. Unreligious people engage little or not at all with religious themes, questions, and practice (secularization theory); they have ceased to care about religion and are *'indifferent to religion'/post-religious*, or have ceased to be knowledgeable about religion and are *areligious*.

Hypothesis 2. Unreligious people are concerned about religious themes, questions, and practice, but this engagement is in some sense deactivated or repressed (rational choice theory, 'believing without belonging'). They have an unfulfilled or dormant religiosity and are *latently religious* or *vicariously religious*.

Hypothesis 3. Unreligious people are interested in religious themes, questions, and practice, but have resolved or mobilized them via some alternative spiritual and/or religious means (individualization of religion thesis; spiritualization of society thesis). They have become religious in new and possibly modern ways and are involved in *individualized religion*, or *alternative spirituality* or *alternative religion*.

Hypothesis 4. Unreligious people respond to religious themes, questions, and practices via rationalist, scientific, and atheistic modes of thought, and their engagements with religious people and objects are informed by this stance and normally critical or antagonistic towards religion (post-secularism). They have rejected religion and are *anti-religious*.

To complete the picture, a fifth hypothesis, not yet developed in social science literature, is:

> Hypothesis 5. Unreligious people respond to religious themes, questions, and practices in ways that are similar to but markedly distinct from religious or spiritual responses, but which are not primarily anti-religious, nor necessarily rationalist, scientistic, or even non-theistic; these responses shape their engagements with religious people and objects. They are *non-religious* in ways we need to newly conceive of.

Methodologically, these possibilities can be explored by working with unreligious people and considering their relationship with religious and spiritual people and cultural forms. What are the different ways that the so-called secular engage with theistic and supernatural beliefs? How are theism (and non-theism) and belief (and unbelief) in supernatural phenomena connected in their minds? How do they engage with and create moral discourses? Do they do so with reference to religion or to something else? How do those outside religious and spiritual traditions perceive and engage with those traditions? Do they participate in these traditions? If so, do they experience this participation differently from religious or spiritual people? Do they participate in alternative rituals and rites of passage ceremonies, or do they disengage from such practices in general? In all of these questions, we can also ask whether those who do not engage with religion and spiritual cultures—or engage as outsiders—experience a sense of absence, of something lacking or something alienating, as a result? Is their being without religion a source of pain or trauma?

As well as these cultural questions, there are more expressly social ones to consider, too. How do the 'not religious' perceive and engage with religious and spiritual people? How do they perceive and engage with other unreligious people? What ways of being without religion take social form—can non-religiosity or even areligiosity bring people together and help form cohesive communities? Is being without religion only social in the minimal sense of excluding religiosity from shared environments or does it bring people together in more meaningful ways? If being unreligious structures relationships, are the resulting social structures close, communal, and stable; loose,

The Insubstantial and the Substantial Seculars 69

networked, and fluid; or individualistic, individualized, or atomized? Are non-religious symbolic cultures particularly suited to giving form to one or other of these types of associational structure? How is 'secularity' cultural in this sense of being socially mediating?

Finally, all these possibilities can be considered in terms of their significance. Are any or all of these aspects of being 'not religious' strongly impactful on other areas of thought, culture, and society, and how does their influence compare with other concerns and conditioning factors? Even if being unreligious contains substantial, non-religious aspects, it may still be the case that these aspects are relatively insignificant, emerging only briefly perhaps in order to negotiate religion in social life and otherwise irrelevant to everyday life. Such questions open up space to think about the relationship between the substantially non-religious and the insubstantially secular, and thereby to scrutinize three rival claims about how the two relate to one another that is implicit in the literature. One approach views non-religion as a feature of established and stable secular societies, as in historical and particularist accounts of the rise of cultures of unbelief. In direct opposition to this, scholars within the secularization paradigm take the view that non-religion is only significant in the process of *establishing* a secular society—it is a transitory phenomenon that signals a developmental and unstable state of secularity rather than its achievement. A third perspective, most associated with recently prominent post-secularist (re)visions of a perceived secularist past, is that non-religion is a fundamentally uncivil and unnecessary aspect of secular society. In this view, a non-religious—and especially anti-religious—dimension to secularity can be explained by historical and political contexts, and this process of identification and explanation allows us to recognize and do away with anti-religious biases. As discussed in the previous chapter, the relationship between non-religion and secularity is a core theoretical question for social scientists to engage with, but it is one that we can only engage with once we recognize the fundamental dissimilarity between the two—between the substantial and insubstantial 'secular'.

The rest of this volume explores the questions set out here, but this chapter sets out one of the core contentions of the book: that these questions are worth asking. Just asking them means taking seriously the possibility of a substantial aspect to 'secularity'. Just asking them reforms one of the most taken-for-granted ideas about secularity—its insubstantial nature—into a question that can be explored both theoretically and empirically.

3

The Unwaved Flag

Everyday and Banal Forms of Non-Religion

In research presentations, scholars raising the prospect of 'material non-religion' are often met with a plain question: what kinds of material non-religion can there possibly be? This chapter is engaged in the task of making some of these material possibilities visible, introducing the range of images and objects that I became increasingly aware of as my fieldwork proceeded. The unimagined nature of material non-religion is itself significant: it reflects a striking feature of these forms, which is precisely that they go unnoticed. This might seem to confirm the secularizationist view: if people do not even notice the non-religious images and slogans around them, does this not suggest that they are fundamentally indifferent to them and that these don't really matter? This chapter explores an alternative view: perhaps the fact that people do not notice these forms demonstrates their embeddness and significance.

In this, I draw on Michael Billig's notion of 'banality' (1995) to think about the power of unremarkable material expressions of cultural forms. Billig's groundbreaking idea of 'banal nationalism' argued against focusing solely on nationalism as unusual, exotic, and impressive social movements—the kind of nationalism that 'only comes in small sizes and bright colours' (1995: 6). Instead, he says, established nation-states are founded on and fortified by small, daily reminders of citizens' status as nationals. The focus of this argument is not materiality, but the everyday. In practice, though, the material and the everyday are closely bound up with one another, and Billig's exemplary case is a material symbolic form—the national flag—and its relationship to social and material contexts: 'The metonymic image of banal

The Unwaved Flag

nationalism is not a flag which is being consciously waved with fervent passion; it is the flag hanging unnoticed on the public building' (Billig 1995: 8). This unwaved flag goes unrecognized yet, Billig argues, it powerfully shapes the cultural environment—ever-present, failing to disrupt our consciousness precisely because it is normal, deeply enshrined in the familiar places where we live and understand ourselves. Although the banal can be discursive, the example of the unwaved flag highlights the importance of material forms and environments in taken-for-granted cultures. Striking statements of New Atheist culture—the Atheist buses, Richard Dawkins provocative broadcasts—or of Islamophobia provoke our interest, with good reason, and have prompted social researchers to undertake discourse analyses to understand their motivations and effects.[1] But these discourses represent the exotic and explicit in the field of non-religion: they are non-religion in its 'small sizes and bright colours'. These are distinctive and visible precisely because they are unfamiliar, novel, and sometimes violent. By contrast, other expressions of non-religion are like the dusty, unnoticed flag: they excite little attention and yet may be the more profound influence on contemporary culture. Hence, the idea of the unwaved flag brings together the two streams of this chapter: it provides a precedent for shifting attention from more obvious ideational expressions of non-religion to less codified symbolic manifestations, as well as a powerful illustration of how such symbolic forms may plausibly be interpreted as vital means through which non-religious society produces and reproduces itself.

FOREGROUNDING NON-RELIGIOUS BACKGROUNDS

The most literal equivalent to Billig's unwaved flag—the dusty banners fixed to public buildings that have been there for as long as

---

[1] The 'Atheist Bus Campaign' began as a series of advertisements, run on the side of London buses in 2009, supported by members of the public, Richard Dawkins, and by the British Humanist Association. The adverts read: 'There Is Probably No God. Now Stop Worrying And Enjoy Your Life'. The campaign received much media attention and was extended to other places in the UK. Similar campaigns were launched in a number of cities around the world.

anyone can remember and have become unnoticed backdrops to the stages in which people move and act—are mundane visual representations of non-religion. With a limited formal symbolic language and no flag to speak of, non-religious banners typically involve a non-religious message or slogan. However, their impact is, as we shall see, only partly accounted for by the content of those slogans. Rather, their significance emerges not only or primarily through intellectual or political engagement, but also through the way these slogans fail to break through the mundane. Following Billig, they therefore participate in the reproduction of non-religious cultural norms by acting as quiet but daily reminders of these norms. Therefore, while non-religious images in the 'background' do not ostensibly structure everyday lives, in failing to disrupt them, they also reveal themselves as part of the ordinary cultural contexts within which we live and with which we are complicit.

Domestic Non-Religion

Banal non-religious banners are visible in both 'private' and 'public' spaces. In the former, non-religious sentiment is expressed in images around the home—postcards and other pictures 'light-heartedly' ridiculing religion, for example, and fixed to bedroom walls or with magnets to the front of fridges. This research did not involve a systematic review of such images, but I began to notice these neglected artefacts in the homes and workplaces of research participants and of friends and colleagues I visited during the course of fieldwork. From this, I gathered sufficient material to suggest that it might be useful for social researchers to account for these in some way.

Several of these non-religious symbolic forms were comic rather than activist in tone, something that may reflect the particular role of comedy in British non-religious discourses.[2] Examples include images on greetings cards with casual and dismissive references to religious ideas and images—'Jesus is Coming. Look Busy', beside an image of Jesus intended to be kitsch—as well as more acutely anti-religious slogans. At social and activist meetings, non-religious ephemera were exhibited deliberately, with explicit intentions; by contrast, these greetings cards, postcards, and newspaper cuttings

---

[2] I am indebted to Lorna Mumford and Patrick McKearney for discussion of their work concerning the importance of comedy in British non-religious culture.

were shown more casually—often part of sprawling displays of pictures of mixed subject matter. These displays have aesthetic qualities as well as being tied up with processes of identity formation and representation. They may be deliberate creations or built up organically over longer periods. Yet these displays are not ostentatious and may be left untouched for relatively long periods of time, transforming from foregrounds into the backgrounds that we cease to be aware of. They are also relatively informal: these are not overt ideological statements but rather a complicated and gradual layering of symbols and meanings that form into an integrated but dynamic expression of a person or group of people's experience and outlook. Like Billig's unwaved flag, these casual and sometimes forgotten displays become embedded in the fabric of the domestic space, no longer visible to those who most frequently make use of the space—though, significantly, they may be striking to visitors who are less familiar with them.

Non-religious culture might infiltrate domestic spaces in other ways. The presence of books associated with non-religious cultures is another example, something that was particularly relevant over the time frame of this research in which New Atheist volumes were bestsellers (Bullivant 2010). As these texts move to household bookshelves, their impact shifts from being merely intellectual to being symbolic and aesthetic, communicating cultural tastes and identities, alone and in combination with other artefacts in the home. Another example of banal non-religion in domestic settings, and one that was particularly striking in this research, was the incorporation of non-theist slogans into the packaging for toiletries products. One example is an item from a mainstream brand of British toiletries called 'Soap and Glory'—a name that is itself a play on the phrase 'Hope and Glory', associated with Elgar's British patriotic song, 'Land of Hope and Glory', which allies country with an implicitly Christian God. Alongside this implicit reference to Christianity is, however, an overt reference to non-theism: the packaging design includes a range of light-hearted, intentionally kitsch phrases and mottos, such as, 'Yes, You Can Have It All . . . Soft, Smooth Sexy Skin Whenever You Want It', and one of these reads, 'Cleanliness Is Essential When Godliness Is Improbable'. This motto, displayed in quotation marks as though a common saying, refers to a familiar religious one: 'Cleanliness Is Next To Godliness'. This phrase is well known in the British-Christian context that the nostalgic design of the Soap and Glory bottle makes references to, not only in its name but also in its imagery and design: in addition to the brand name, the bottle also features a 1950s-style black and white photographic image of a white-skinned, blonde woman, clothed in underwear from that era. If we consider that it is inconceivable that a casual non-theistic statement of this sort might have appeared in the branding of a similar, mainstream product in the 1950s—and how much controversy it would have caused had it been—the significance of the banality of this slogan becomes clear. The packaging does not seem to have been at all controversial or provoked any complaints; Soap and Glory continue to use the slogan on its shower gel bottles today, now some five years since I first became aware of it. In a nostalgic packaging design that draws heavily on a certain construction of British national culture, the non-religious has been incorporated—alongside elements of Christian religion, and both become part of a narrative of Britishness. In the secularizationist view, what is significant is the fact that people do not notice and do not complain about these representations: they don't care. However, the convergence of gendered, nationalist, and ethnic representations with religious and non-religious ones in this image makes connections with traditions in cultural studies and cultural sociology that take very seriously 'background' images in terms of how they produce and reproduce norms. In this light, it becomes strange, if not complacent, to neglect the religious—and non-religious—dimension in such examples. In fact, the image reflects a mainstream culture in which both Christian and non-religious cultures dominate: most people in the UK identify as Christian or 'not religious', as we have seen, and they operate in and contribute to intellectual and discursive contexts in which non-religion is understood to be a matter of unbelief. The close fit between the nostalgic image presented on this soap bottle and wider cultural contexts deepens the sense of their interrelation and significance.

Public Non-Religion

Distinctions between private and public domains have been central to discussions of religion throughout and in relation to the modern period, and play a key role in contemporary debates concerning secularism. Feminist scholarship has undermined the notion of the domestic as a private space and, indeed, the above examples of domestic non-religion are also public in several ways. One of the more subtle instances of this is a result of the role of such displays in identity construction, which is then performed and shared in social interactions outside the home. Within the home too, collections of images, books, toiletries, and other artefacts are visible to the various people who share and visit it. What is more, these artefacts have a life outside domestic settings: over the course of fieldwork, I saw the same greetings cards and toiletries I had seen in people's homes on display in shops where they were available for sale. Indeed, in open public spaces, banal forms of non-religion, like banal forms of religion, can be more widely visible than explicit forms precisely because they are not classified as non-religious and set apart with other non-religious items. For example, whereas British booksellers locate religious texts in sections devoted to 'mind, body, spirit' (Woodhead 2012b) and place non-religious texts alongside popular science texts (a categorization that is itself interesting), non-religious greetings cards are displayed in high-street shops mingled in with secular and areligious ones. In the same way, Soap and Glory soap bottles are stocked in high-street chemists, not in an 'atheist' section, of course, but with other toiletry products. This makes these non-religious expressions visible to a much wider audience.

Another possible form of 'public non-religion' emerges from the co-option of religious images and symbols to non-religious ends—a form of non-religious material culture that is, yet again, indirect and diffuse. In my fieldwork, I wondered what to make of the way that popular high-street shops sold clothes and jewellery bearing images from different religions side by side. I photographed bracelets featuring Catholic and Hindu images, displayed together in a chain store selling clothes and accessories. The commercialization of these products suggested to me a certain irreverence. These bracelets are similar to those sold outside many pilgrimage sites but their meaning seemed altered by this different context.

More research is needed to know how images and objects such as these are 'made meaningful by [their] viewers' (Pink 2006: 29), and researchers of non-religion should heed Knott's (2005) warning against the dangers of over-attributing religious meaning to religious symbols and clothing: the same could be true of non-religious artefacts and meanings. Without systematic research, we do not know whether such examples are a sign of real pluralism or of non-religious normativity. Yet these examples—and a sensitivity to non-religious perspectives in general—opens up new analytical possibilities beyond the assumption that religious images are solely or necessarily vehicles of religious meaning. Scholars of popular and commercialized religious cultural forms might, for example, broaden their sense of how these forms not only promote, inhibit, inscribe, and refigure 'authentic religiosity' but non-religiosity, too.

Outside of domestic settings, the urban environment is marked by other non-religious representations that form part of a public non-religion, and these can be positive and affirmative as well as critical and antagonistic. Over the course of fieldwork (and since), I frequently encountered graffiti bearing non-theist, anti-religious, or non-religious slogans and images. A particularly attention-grabbing example appeared around 2012 in the London borough of Hackney, made by a graffiti artist, Stik, whose work has become well known in recent years. Stik is known for his stylized stick figures, outlined in black and coloured in white. The detail on the figures is minimal and they are gendered in a conventional way, familiar from public signs used around the world, in which the male is a plain figure, the female clothed in a stylized dress. The works are positive in tone: the figures are friendly looking and often portrayed in companionable groups. The 2012 example was typical, portraying two stick figures—a man and a woman—in a companionable pose, holding hands. The male was shown in the normal way, basic and unadorned, but the female was different: Stik departed from his white palette, clothing the female figure in a black niqab.

The image appears to be positive, in intention and form, depicting a warm relationship across a religious divide. But it is also representative of a cultural context in which the secular individual is normalized and naturalized—unadorned and unmarked by any cultural markers—while religion, especially but not only Islam, is presented as a conspicuous other. That the figures are holding hands also shows a cultural bias in its expression of fellowship, given that holding a man's hand would be problematic for many wearers of the niqab. Nevertheless, it would be a gross simplification to describe an image like this one as anti-religious. Instead, it illustrates the complicated intended and unintended messages such images communicate. Moreover, while it may be tempting to focus entirely on the construction of religiosity in such images, it is equally important to recognize the

The Unwaved Flag

ways in which the non-religious person is portrayed—depicted here as male, acultural, normal.

A focus on banal forms of public non-religion is not to deny the significance of more consciously constructed forms, found, for example, at organized non-religious events, explored in new research by Katie Aston (e.g. 2012) and Matthew Engelke (e.g. 2012b) as well as my own work. Here, scientific aesthetics (concepts, formulae, diagrams, and so on) are central, images of Charles Darwin, constructed as figurehead and hero. In addition, natural forms—animals and trees—are motifs. Such images and icons commonly appear in other public and domestic spaces and are rendered in commercial products. Though their association with non-religious cultures is frequently difficult to assess outside overtly non-religious contexts, recognizing that they may be bound up with everyday non-religious cultures opens up new possibilities for researching and describing 'secular' socio-cultural environments.

Material Non-Religion

The materiality of such non-religious representations is crucial to understanding their effects and the ways in which they relate to the social and cultural contexts in which they are located. So, for example, the message, 'Jesus does not exist', etched into an official notice posted on a north London public library wall communicates something different from the same words uttered in a conversation or debate. This includes the banality that is emergent from the relationship between medium and message. The graffiti has remained intact over several years; it is still there as this book goes to press, though it has become so worn over time that the text has become less and less legible. A contrasting case is seen in the vestiges of a bold, newly inked Islamophobic message, written on the glass of an advertisement panel at a north London bus stop. Some of the words had been hastily obscured, even by the time I saw it, which must have been a matter of days or hours after it had been written: someone had attempted to remove an expletive used in relation to Allah by scratching into the glass to obscure the writing. It is likely that this graffiti would have been removed quickly by authorities, because of the offensive language and the sensitivity of the subject matter in a context in which Islam has become a common target of racist and anti-religious abuse. But the message could not be removed soon enough for one person who encountered it.

The words are important here, but so too are the material trajectories, which follow different courses and tell us something about contemporary non-religious cultures. Both items of graffiti are irreligious and blasphemous, and both are visible in the public sphere and shape its contours; recognizing this is one way of recognizing the impact of non-religiosity. But, while acutely anti-religious discourses have been rightly given attention by researchers of religion, I want to call attention to the possible significance of less controversial cases, illustrated here by the anti-Christian graffiti, apparently viewed as too unremarkable to warrant attention. The case reminds us that the non-controversial are present and therefore have effects. Because the message appears to have been considered insufficiently disruptive (or not disruptive at all) to be concerned about, so the graffiti has been allowed to remain intact for a much longer period— to become dusty with age. It has participated in the public domain for years, acting as a quiet reminder of both Christian and anti-Christian aspects in local cultural life. One implication is that this anti-Christian view is acceptable, in a way that the anti-Islamic slogan is not. In this way, the banal, like the controversial, helps produce the contours of social life. The two might matter in different ways, but they both matter. Attending to the presence of non-religion in material environments and to the specificity of each case is one way to bring the effects of the banal to light.

Irreverence and Indifference

Most of the examples given so far in this chapter express overt anti-religious sentiments, non-religious self-understandings, or non-religious culture more widely. There is at least one exception: it is not clear whether the slogan, 'Jesus is coming. Look busy' expresses a casual form of religiosity or is dismissive of it. This ambiguity illustrates why reception studies have become so crucial to the study of media forms, revealing meanings that cannot be guessed at. On the other hand, images are a potentially significant form of banal non-religion for the following reason. While the light treatment of religious cultures might appear to be post-religious, the display of such images *performs* this 'post-religiosity'—and a performance of post-

The Unwaved Flag

religiosity is a contradiction in terms, similar to the paradox of expressing 'indifference to religion' as a social identity, discussed in Chapter 7 in this volume. It is a commonplace one, too. 'Retro' Christian images with a comic caption of this sort are popular in British greeting cards and other areas of design. Another greetings card, seen in a high-street gift shop, depicts an image of Jesus being presented with loaves and fishes, an illustration of the sort that were commonplace in early twentieth-century Britain; the caption reads, 'No. Mine was the herb-crusted cod with a rocket and parmesan salad' (Simon Spicer). When I presented this research at a conference in Antwerp, I saw a t-shirt for sale with a familiar image of Jesus and the Sacred Heart with the slogan, 'Football Is My Religion', the Sacred Heart replaced by a football. The aesthetic was similar to the greetings card, but the non-religious positioning more overt—identifying the wearer not only as an unreligious person, but as someone dismissive of the claim of religious culture to be treated as distinct from any other cultural form.

In the UK today, such images turn up with relative frequency and excite little attention. They are banal. As with so many cases in this book, its significance only becomes visible in relief—by observing the contrast between responses to these and other forms. In 2011, for example, an advert using similar Catholic imagery provoked a number of complaints and was banned by the British Advertising Standards Authority (ASA). The advert was for a mobile phone dealer, Phones 4U, and also depicted Jesus Christ and the Sacred Heart, the image doctored in this case so that Jesus is winking and giving a thumbs-up sign. The ASA upheld the complaints, saying that the advert appeared to 'mock and belittle core Christian beliefs and was likely to cause serious offence'. In response, Phones 4U acknowledged the casual tone, but denied any anti-religious feeling: the advert was not, they said, intended to show disrespect but only to show 'a light-hearted, positive, and contemporary image of Christianity' (BBC News 2011). The different ways that similar images are interpreted illustrates their ambiguous meaning, as well as the way in which 'light-heartedness' should not be seen as the absence of a stance, but as a real and concrete position that sits at odds with other ones. Such apparently harmless images can jar with the views and experience of others and cause offence. That several such expressions do not excite controversy is not because they are intrinsically inoffensive, but because the norms that they communicate are salient to the people who enjoy them or pay them little attention.

There is nuance, too, to the specific way that religion is constructed in these images: in this line of material culture, the visual language of religious traditions is taken up in distinctive ways. Familiar Protestant and Catholic images are pervasive and they tend to be older images, styled in a nostalgic way. Such images produce and reproduce a sense of especially Christian heritage, combined with an irreverence that communicates contemporary non-religious norms. There may also be secularist norms operating here, in which religious piety is treated with suspicion and monitored (while non-religious piety is not). This normative context may encourage religious people themselves to be irreverent about their beliefs, something that is easier for those in the mainstream to manage than for those of minority groups. Such representations of (some) religions can obscure multicultural histories and religious presents, and may foster an unreflexive, flippant approach to religious cultures, the more dangerous side of which can be seen in public discourses relating to irreverent representations of Muhammad in Western media. In these discourses, Islamophobia is commonly cloaked in liberal rhetorics about freedom of speech (Brahm Levey and Modood 2009c), expressed as an aggressive demand for 'light-heartedness' and for a certain mode of religiosity in which the religious are required to laugh at themselves. What is not always recognized is the extent to which there is a double standard at play in that non-religious cultures, diffuse and invisible, do not themselves experience the same demands—although at the same time non-religious cultures are not identified as sources of meaning and solidarity that might also be worthy of respect.

Here as elsewhere then, recognizing non-religious currents that flow unseen has political as well as empirical and theoretical implications. Framed in relation to theoretical work that shows how hiddenness can be caused by embeddedness, and by drawing to light the qualitative differences between images that do and do not excite our attention, the impact of these 'backgrounds' raise significant problems for the idea that 'secular society' is areligious, involving no meaningful contact with religion, or post-religious, involving superficial contact with religion as a curiosity relating to past or distant cultures. By contrast, spontaneous local expressions of religious-like and religion-related imagery and the production of commercialized forms indicate an active field of social life. What is more, drawing banal forms of non-religion to the foreground calls attention to ambiguities about what counts as non-religious and blasphemous rather than pluralist and multi-faith. Such distinctions are normally made through analysis of unusual and controversial occasions of non-religious, religious, and secularist 'flag-waving'—in response to the Salman Rushdie/*Satanic Verses* affair in the late 1980s, for example, or the Danish cartoon affair in 2005 (see Knott 2005, and Levey and Modood 2009c). In contrast to these dramatic events, attention to implicit forms of non-religion alert us to the ways in which it penetrates deep into the ordinary and prosaic, constituting and reconstituting a non-religious culture which is then called to the fore at these more acute moments of tension. Just as Billig argues that it is important for us to shift our analytical focus away from extreme or explicit forms of nationalism and towards inclusion of more everyday taken-for-granted experiences, so these cases reveal the possible significance of non-religion that is produced and reproduced in the everyday as well as in the more vociferous non-religious and secularist movements that come more readily to mind and receive disproportionate attention in the study of secularism and in the emerging study of non-religious culture.

Official Non-Religion

The previous examples have focused on the range of ways that non-religion can be expressed in everyday settings. It is also, however, important to attend to the ways in which more explicit forms of non-religion may be expressed in similarly non-intellectual or partially intellectual ways. A few examples should show that, even in research, wishing to focus on more explicit and highly codified forms of non-religion, it might be important to broaden the focus to include more than ideational trajectories only—something that new anthropological work from scholars such as Matthew Engelke and Katie Aston is beginning to do. One example that occurred in the course of my research and which achieved a high degree of visibility is the 'atheist bus campaign', mentioned earlier in this chapter. This campaign saw various individuals (comedian and journalist Ariane Sherine and Richard Dawkins) and organizations (the British Humanist Association) organizing and funding a non-theist advertisement on the side of several London buses for some weeks in 2009. The advert read, 'There's Probably No God. Now Stop Worrying and Enjoy Your

Life', and was a protest against an advertising campaign run by a religious organization, JesusSaid.org, also on London buses.[3] It is easy and, indeed, helpful to take a purely discursive approach to analysing this phenomenon, focusing on the advert's messages and to the intellectual responses it excited. In addition, however, we can attend to the ways in which this event became the starting point for various, often subtle, cultural trajectories.

In the first place, the non-theist advert worked in purely aesthetic terms to do a number of things. For one, its graphic design was striking and has been taken up in subsequent British Humanist Association (BHA) campaigns. Some participants in my research indicated that they found it easier to follow the visual thread than the intellectual one: in passing one of the BHA's later campaigns, dealing with the 2011 Census for England and Wales (BHA 2011b), one woman asked me what these 'atheist' adverts were all about. From the general aesthetics of the advert, this woman derived a general sense of a cultural movement associated with the advert, maybe even of the particular organization, and associated both with non-religiosity rather than with secularism. In this way, the design contributed to some kind of 'brand recognition', making audiences aware of a generalized non-religious content. The text was transformed into an aesthetic aspect of place. Thus, this unusual and 'brightly coloured' non-religious representation became banal—part of the urban environment, familiar and half-noticed, engaged with in indirect ways.

A second way in which the bus advert communicated itself non-ideationally was via its relationship to the object of the bus itself. And not just any bus but the red double decker bus that is iconic of London and of the UK as a whole. An interesting analysis can be made here concerning the relationship between non-religious and regional and national identifications—and, indeed, the possibility of developing a notion of 'civil *non*-religion' in parallel to Bellah's civil religion (1991; Bellah and Tipton 2006). Such connections also reaffirm the aptness of Billig's 'banal nationalism' as a model via which to explore non-religious culture.

---

[3] This advert displayed a quote from the Bible and a link to the organization's website, which quoted from Matthew 25:41 to warn that those who do not follow Jesus' teaching would be '"condemned to everlasting separation from God and [. . .] spend all eternity in torment in hell"' (Sherine 2008a: n.p.). See Atheist Bus Campaign (2011) for an overview of the campaign, and Lee forthcoming for a longer discussion.

Research methodologies might also consider the dynamic and spatial aspect of the 'atheist bus', as it was often referred to, which moved through the city and became part of rather than merely a backdrop to its activity. A sense of shared space is given by campaign organizer Sherine in her initial objection to the Jesussaid.org advert:

> Yesterday I walked to work and saw not one, but two London buses with the question: 'When the son of man comes, will he find faith on the earth?' (Luke 18:8). It seems you wait ages for a bus with an unsettling Bible quote, then two come along at once (Sherine 2008a: n.p.).

Sherine locates the experience in her daily activity of 'walking to work'—an experience that is then replicated in the non-theist advert. And, again, in imagining the impact the religious bus might have, she writes:

> Imagine you've had a really bad day, and it's only 8.30 am. [...] You stumble out of the tube, and are confronted with the number 168 bus. It tells you that, along with your boss, a man with a beardy face is going to be upset with you, for ever [sic], because you've refused to acknowledge his existence, despite the fact that he's too antisocial to come down here and say hi. You promptly throw yourself under the number 168 bus. (Sherine 2008a: n.p.)

The medium here is important. The bus is part of everyday life, and it is also something that people participate in and identify with. Transport is something you use ('You stumble out of the tube') and agree to use ('You promptly throw yourself under the number 168 bus'), but it is also part of the 'background' or context in which you move. This makes these contexts all the more important: you cannot escape. It is for this reason that we need to notice that 'textual objects [...] not only mediate through written language but also take on a distinctive material form which situates them as objects within a culture' (Dant 1999: 165).

A final example worth mentioning shows how media expressions are translated into other media forms. This digital example relates to a freely available web-based tool that enables users to rewrite any or all of the text for the bus campaign and see it imaged, in the format of that advert, on the side of a London bus (<rultheweb.co.uk/b3ta/bus/> [accessed 21 February 2011]). I encountered this by chance while using a social networking site which circulates snapshots of people with whom you have a mutual contact. One 'friend of a friend' had used the image as his 'profile picture', having doctored the advert so that only the word 'god' was removed, replaced with his own name: it now read, 'There Probably Is No [John Smith]. Now Stop Worrying And Enjoy Your Life'. In this case, any explicit non-religious meaning is obscure: it is unclear whether the individual is identifying with the non-theist sentiment or just making a joke. What it does show, however, is how non-religious *artefacts* can be abstracted from non-religious *principles*. It also demonstrates how the visual and material forms of the message can be appropriated in diverse ways and how, therefore, a cultural sociology of non-religion might be quite a broad endeavour. This is particularly so given the use of 'digital hypermedia', with its particular facility for complex combinations of 'written and visual representations [which create] multilinear, multimedia and interactive texts that communicate theoretically, in institutional language and ethnographically' (Pink 2006: 127).

The example is also illustrative of the interactive or dialogical aspects of non-religious material culture, which is not only received by audiences but interpreted and developed by them. This is true not only of digital media, with its marked capacity for interaction, but also in more traditional formats. For example, the Alpha course ran a billboard campaign in response to the 'atheist bus campaign', presenting a multiple-choice question, 'Does God exist?' and tick boxes for the options, 'Yes', 'No', 'Probably', mocking the use of the word 'probably' included in the original campaign. As my bus travelled home through north London one evening, I saw a billboard bearing this advert and noticed, too, that someone had completed the rhetorical survey, a black tick placed in the 'No' box. This was an unexceptional act of graffiti, apparently spontaneous and without artistry, but it was also one that altered a corporate advertisement into a visible public dialogue. With the Alpha course 'reply' itself appropriating the format of the BHA advert for its own purposes, the example illustrates the complicated and everyday dialogues and dialectics between British religious and non-religious individuals, organizations, and symbolic cultures.

CONCLUSION

This chapter discusses a number of ways in which engagements with religion-as-other, that is, non-religious engagements, are expressed in material forms and, in so doing, are emphatic of an expanded, more inclusive understanding of non-religiosity. By focusing on banal forms, however, it also contributes to the overarching question of this book, about the nature of secularity, and the extent to which it is a non-religious, areligious, or post-religious condition. For Bruce (2002: 240), the primary cause of secularity, that is, indifference to religion, is 'the lack of religious socialization and the lack of constant background affirmation of beliefs'. This chapter suggests that secular societies may involve processes of *non-religious* socialization, and the presence of constant background affirmations of non-religious beliefs and cultures—a fundamentally different way of understanding secularity.[4]

In general, the material world receives less attention than the ideal, but this taken-for-grantedness makes it significant in particular ways. Its mode of influence is echoed in the idea of banality, in which the unnoticed is the noteworthy and in which the ideas, images, and objects that surround us and are part of our routine existence express deeply ingrained cultural norms. Billig's approach provides a critique of work that is distracted by the loud and colourful and ignores these immediate empirical realities. He takes issue with postmodern scholars who observe a decline of the nation-state even while they live and reify their nationalities. Similar observations can be made in the study of non-religion about the problems of being distracted by showy anti-religious cultures and failing to recognize more mundane non-religious positionings that are enacted in daily life. In southeast England, people encounter religion every day, through direct encounters with people and artefacts that are identified as religious and through mediated representations; against the idea of an exclusive religious domain or field that some are not only located outside of but entirely disconnected from, we need to recognize that every one of these small encounters requires even those who see themselves as outsiders to locate and relocate themselves in relation to religion.

The twist in the tale is this: according to Billig's theory, the apparently post-religious is transformed, from an expression of emptiness and shallowness into a expression of deep embeddedness. Instances of 'indifference to religion' are recast as cases of non-religious attachment and normativity. The suggestion is, then, that the 'secular' might be much more substantively non-religious than supposed, not despite its manifesting in ways that seem superficial, but because of it.

---

[4] See also Lanman's (2012) discussion of religious displays and belief acquisition; and Merino (2012) on non-religious socialization processes.

4

Out of the Shadows

Non-Religious and Secularist Bodies in Relief

Versions of the pithy remark, 'most people would rather die than think; most do so', are attributed to Bertrand Russell and rehearsed by A. C. Grayling, a philosopher closely associated with New Atheism and a frequent participant in events associated with it. I encountered Grayling a few times over the course of this fieldwork, at formal events but also by accident, in the area of central north London dominated by several of the universities of London; indeed, one research interview, with a postgraduate student, was conducted while Grayling sat at a neighbouring table in a Bloomsbury café. At events, I heard Grayling tell the Russell joke, more than once, in order to identify and characterize the 'unthinking' religious. At another event, I heard Richard Dawkins make a similar characterization of the religious mind. He talked about a research student working with a world-leading geneticist who was forced, he said, to renounce either his and his family's Christian beliefs or his life's work in genetics after confronting the mass of contradictions he finds between the Bible and his biological knowledge. Holding the Bible and the thesis before the fire, the student has to make a decision: which one will he cast to the flames? The answer is surely obvious, Dawkins implied—and yet, this young researcher chose to throw away the *thesis*—and with it his promising scientific career and service to knowledge. Here, Dawkins gestured as if to say, how can we hope to make sense of this irrationality? What can you do in the face of those who understand science yet willfully turn their back on it? What can you do with people who would rather do something else than think?

These kinds of non-religious narratives are a single but significant and highly visible strand in popular British non-religious culture.

They are embedded in many organized non-religious cultures, to the extent that one ethnographer has identified 'stupidity' as one of the central motifs of the particular non-religious discourses that he was working with (Engelke 2012b). My work has also drawn attention to the 'othering' of religious people as 'stupid', 'insane', or as having some kind of brain malfunction, and the way in which this represents a particular, rationalistic, and humanistic strand in non-religious thought (Lee 2006; 2011; see also Chapter 7 within this volume). Though different in content, such concepts function in much the same way as religious strategies of 'othering' via ideas such as 'sinfulness' or 'heresy', which are used to describe and build boundaries between legitimate and illegitimate forms of thought and behaviour. The focus on knowledge and understanding in non-religious cultures has roots in intellectual approaches to religion and non-religion, which scholars associate with Protestantism as well as with non-theistic, scientific traditions. Whatever its roots in religious rationalist cultures, though, in these discourses religion has come to be seen as grounded in emotion, ritual, and society, while intellectual ability and rigour is associated with unbelief and the secular life. In this new dualism, therefore, non-religion is located in the mind while religion is located in the body.

Building on the exploration of material non-religion developed in the previous chapter, this chapter addresses these dualisms by focusing on the human body. It engages with a debate explored in anthropological work, particularly in a special issue of *Cultural Anthropology* (2011) dedicated to the question, 'is there a secular body?'. Charles Hirschkind (2010; 2011) poses this question as a way of interrogating the emerging anthropology of the secular and secularism (e.g. Asad 2003; Cannell 2010)—and his response is a sceptical one. Following the attempt in this volume to disentangle different aspects of the 'secular', this chapter considers Hirschkind's question in light of a disaggregated notion of the secular in which the substantial non-religious, the adminstratively secularist, and the insubstantial secular are distinguished from one another. These distinctions give rise to different conceptions of how the body might be 'secular'—the different contours of the non-religious and secularist body and the more ghostly form of the insubstantial secular. The chapter discusses non-religious and secularist symbols that are 'written' or projected onto the body and explores how the bodily expression of ideas changes their nature, embedding them in our lives in

88 *Recognizing the Non-Religious*

intimate ways and also, especially, by structuring relationships between people. It also addresses the ways in which non-religion and secularism may be embodied more fundamentally, through attitudes, behaviours, and emotional responses. For both cases, the discussion considers both overt forms of embodiment and more subtle forms that emerge from particular configurations of religious and non-religious embodied attitudes and modes of expression. Hirshkind draws attention to Asad's caution that, because we in the West are so close to the 'secular', we are more likely to get a sense of it by looking for it in and through the shadows (Asad 2003: 16; Hirchskind 2010; 2011), an idea that resonates with the search for forms of non-religion that may be hidden away in the banal. As well as noticing explicit forms of non-religiosity, then, this chapter considers what else we can learn about non-religious bodies from the shadows they cast, seeking out these shadows as a method of investigating 'secular' bodies. So many of these non-religiosities are only visible through contrasting them with other bodies and embodiments—a method of observing non-religion in relief.

STATEMENT CLOTHING

The most explicit way in which humans use the body to enact social and cultural positions is through the things that they wear. The presentation of the body in clothing and other accoutrements is, perhaps, the most intimate and forceful of our symbolic expressions because, as Dant (1999: 85) says, 'apart perhaps from things that we eat, clothes are the material objects that are most consistently part of our individual and our social lives', and 'they are so close to our bodies for so much of the time they become like an extension of that body, an outer layer or shell with which we confront the social world'. Established codes of dress make our clothing, ornaments, make-up, and coiffures expressive of the groups we are or desire to be associated with. Hence, the study of dress has an established role in class analysis and other types of social research. Different ways of decorating the body have also played a central role in the study of religion: codes of dress, ranging from the general and commonplace (covering the head in religious spaces and elsewhere), to the specific and exclusive practices that are associated with more bounded, 'enclave' religious groups and which clearly demarcate insiders from outsiders; the altering of the body through temporary body paintings and permanent tattoos; rules about the management and arrangement of hair—all of these are familiar aspects of religious life and play an important role in the practice and public recognition of religion. By contrast, it can be hard even to imagine what non-religious preparations of the body there might be. New research in the study of non-religion—including findings from this research—show, however, several ways in which non-religiosity can be expressed in dress and other presentations of the body.

Most obviously, non-religious dress includes the wearing and display of clothing with slogans and images from non-religious cultures. Scholars working with organized forms of non-religion and non-religious secularism document, for example, the popularity of wearing t-shirts with non-religious slogans by participants of these meetings, and Engelke (2011) notices a particular focus on identifying science and rational thought positioned in contrast to religion. These explicit statements blur into the implicit, through the use of images rather than written statements—pictures of natural forms, scientific illustrations and graphics, non-religious logos such as the British Humanist Association's 'Happy Human'[1] or the 'Darwin fish', and aesthetic traditions such as John Worth's graphic design for the 'atheist bus' and subsequent campaigns (Aston 2012; Engelke 2011; Lee forthcoming). As well as being emblazoned on t-shirts, these images might also be carried with the body—in the design of notebooks, diaries, pens, or lunchboxes—or applied to it, in the non-religious tattoos that Engelke (2012b) describes.

As well as these quasi-corporate messages, non-religious slogans express other kinds of viewpoint. The example of the 'atheist shoe' is a case in point (see Aston 2012 for a longer discussion). These fashionable shoes have the word 'atheist' inscribed on the sole, and are much more a matter of identifying oneself positively as non-religious and with a particular non-religious socio-cultural group than of expressing hostility towards religion. The designers responsible for the shoe are a collective working between the cosmopolitan

---

[1] The 'happy human' symbol has been associated with organized Humanism since 1965. The British Humanist Association website (BHA 2011a) provides a history of its development.

centres of Berlin, London, Porto, and San Francisco. In the history they provide of their company and of the 'atheist shoe', they capture a contradiction seen in mainstream non-religious cultures: they say that they do not care about their non-theism and see it as an absurd notion and aesthetic, while they also devote considerable time and energy to their non-religious interests. The designers provide a website with pages outlining why 'We Don't Believe in Any God' and a page detailing what an 'Atheist is Not...', the latter setting out a sort of anti-manifesto about what it means to be an 'atheist': 'atheist' is not, for example, 'trying to upset people' or 'trying to recruit new atheists'. They explain:

> We are an incredulity of atheists, living in Berlin, London, Porto, and San Francisco, and furiously dedicating our days to not believing in god. Ok, that's not true; we barely ever think about god, let alone about being atheists [...] But, when one of us had the peculiar idea to create a handmade 'atheist shoe', we thought that sounded rather endearing and fun [...] We were excited—not only about the novelty of such an outspoken shoe, a powerful yet understated way for heathens to be more open about their godlessness. But the design was something special—the bauhausy, 1930s minimalism felt classic and original at the same time, and the shoe's comfort was a phenomenal surprise. Could this be an antidote to all the cheap, samey designs belched out by big sneaker corporations? We hoped so [...] Whether you're an atheist looking to tickle the world with a foot-first declaration of godlessness, or someone who's just keen on the aesthetics and craftsmanship of what we do, we really do hope you'll give our shoes a go.
> The ATHEIST Team[2]

In this, they exhibit the 'indifferentism' I discuss in Chapter 6, in which people imagine themselves as indifferent while displaying a range of commitments—seen here in contradictory claims about 'barely thinking' about atheism while also enjoying developing a more 'outspoken' form of non-theist identity. In the same way, the 'atheist shoe' is designed to appeal to those who understand themselves as casually non-religious, yet are clearly committed at the same time:

> We enjoy happy, full lives without god(s) and we don't often think about religion. But, when we do, we find it a bit weird and depressing; like a silly game of make-believe that's gone too far, threatening the

---

[2] <http://www.atheistberlin.com/atheist>, accessed 17 October 2014.

things we hold most dear, like independence, reason and love [...]
The number of atheists is rapidly growing, yet we're often passive or isolated, facing 'god' with just an apathetic shrug, while religion is organized, in your face...with symbols, rituals, community...all of which give it more power to make more of a mess. We'd love it if more atheists were to 'come out' and to find each other. Maybe our shoes will make it easier to spot the sexy, free-thinking people you like to hang with? No more hours wasted chatting up a pretty stranger only to discover they believe some invisible, magical sky-daddy is looking down and holding a view on whether they should sleep with you or not.

This website discussion gives an insight into the ways in which people who do not participate in organized non-religious movements and whose presentation of the self as non-religious may appear to be casual may nevertheless have strong ideological commitments. Throughout these webpages, the designers say that the shoe is an absurdist project, driven by secular issues of style and design; they argue that they are motivated by fashion and fun, and that people who are not 'atheists' can wear the shoes too. But these more expansive discussions tell another story. Like the 'football is my religion' t-shirt discussed in Chapter 3, then, the 'atheist shoe' seeks to make a positive non-religious identity statement rather than an antagonistic one and, though the products are marketed to wider audiences, it is clear from this website that the designers, and presumably many wearers, use the shoes to express deep-seated but clearly held non-religious views and identifications.

Because such items may be understood as secular or entirely areligious, driven by aesthetic tastes and fashion rather then strong philosophical feeling or socio-cultural commitments, they may be far less likely to provoke reaction than more overtly ideological expressions of non-religion. As such, they are further examples of the banal non-religion I have outlined. In the last chapter, some modes of dress—a t-shirt announcing football as the wearer's 'religion', bracelets bearing Christian and Hindu imagery—to which we might add the Christian crosses widely available in high-street clothes stores in the UK—were discussed as part of the material environments in which people move and act, but such objects take on new meanings when these items are worn on the body. Their value is local and everyday, more of a 'lived' form of non-religion but, as religion scholars have discussed, no less significant for that (McGuire 2008).

UNDERSTATEMENT CLOTHING

Non-religious statements may also be more subtle—emergent rather than overt. An instructive example was described to me by Jean,[3] a young woman in her mid-twenties who had, as a university student some years earlier, involved friends and family in a project to gather together pendants symbolizing different religious traditions which she wanted to compile into a multi-religious necklace. She had collected some pendants easily and cheaply but struggled to find others, and she eventually abandoned the project.

Jean's necklace is illuminating because no expressly non-religious images were included, yet Jean was interested in expressing secular values and doing so non-religiously, that is, positioning herself apart from the religious traditions that she also felt some sympathy for. Jean identified her own orientation as non-religious rather than religious, with 'possibly a passive religious upbringing' ('quite a lot of my "nurture" has been Christian'), and the intention of the necklace had been, she recalled, to recognize the principles she identified as common to all religions: 'be good to each other and life will be good'. She felt that, with capitalism, 'money and greed' had undermined the happy coexistence of religions and the necklace was a call to return to a core value: 'religion as nothing more than the first stirrings of socialism; religious symbols as nothing more than tribe postal addresses'. Jean felt she shared core values with religious people, but at the same time saw religion as anachronistic in contemporary contexts—an orientation much better described as non-religious than anti- or irreligious. In using religious symbols and framing them non-religiously in order to express particular moral and economic commitments, Jean's necklace also embodies the secular—issues beyond the religious, spiritual, and non-religious. What is more, the necklace project appears to have been undertaken somewhat casually and was easily disposable, suggesting that Jean's ideological commitment was not deep. Nevertheless the project had been, for a time, active and engaged and it expressed a distinct, considered ideological position that Jean may continue to hold and which may still relate to religious and non-religious cultures in her mind. Her ideas about the necklace clearly contrast with those associated with similar

---

[3] Pseudonyms are used throughout this book to preserve participants' anonymity.

multi-religious necklaces that can be bought ready-made: though Jean did not appear to be aware of them, I discovered many products of this sort available for sale via the Internet. Websites selling them associated the necklaces with religious tolerance and religious pluralism, or with alternatively spiritual cultures, or associated them with theologies that see religious cultures as sharing a single, common theistic truth. All of these meanings are intra-religious and contrast clearly with Jean's interests and intentions.

The example also highlights how meaning emerges in relation—arising here not from the religious symbols themselves but from the relationship between them. Forms of relational meaning are multiple. They include not only the meaning that arises from particular symbolic configurations, but also from relations between the wearer and the people who encounter these symbolic forms. What meaning do the latter attribute to these accoutrements? Is the wearer aware of these meanings? Analysts should, as Knott (2005) says, be wary of over-attributing religious significance to the wearing of religious symbols, but they can also make the attributing—and misattributing—of meaning an object of study in its own right, as an important social practice that structures social life. In social contexts in which representations influence the world not only according to the intentions of the producer but to the perceptions of others, the ambiguity of these displays, open to identification as religious, non-religious, or secular, means that their possible impacts are various. The difference between multiple intentions and multiple perceptions that Knott (2005) draws attention to complicated analytical possibilities in which interests and objects are configured in multiple ways to multiple effects. Symbolic forms 'speak' for themselves but they do so in many voices, any and all of which may be significant. Meaning is, then, not intrinsic but emergent, so that the same object might be identified as sacred or sacrilegious—meaning that can only be understood in relation to the broader context and network of relations in which it is situated.

The examples discussed in this chapter so far also raise issues about *under*-attributing religious—or non-religious—meaning in popular and academic accounts of dress precisely because so much of this meaning is only intelligible in context—in relation, or in relief. A tattoo of a tree, described by Matthew Engelke (2011b) in relation to his ethnographic work with the British Humanist Association, is not ostensibly non-religious even within an explicitly non-religious social setting; the non-religious aspect to Jean's necklace is even more veiled. It is possible therefore that, in contrast to religious images, we are in more danger of discounting expressions of non-religion than we are of giving them too much attention. Concepts such as vicarious religion (Davie 2007) and implicit religion (Bailey 1997) shine a spotlight on the religious commitments that exist in the shadows. Recognition of non-religious ones enables us to build on these approaches in consideration of new possibilities: implicit forms of non-religion and vicarious connections to more active forms of non-religious culture that might look like secular detachment. Similarly, recognizing the possibility of non-religious meaning encourages studies of popular culture that attend to the way that religious imagery—as well as non-religious and areligious imagery—may be appropriated in performances of non-religion or 'secular indifference'.

NON-RELIGIOUS DRESS IN RELIEF

The idea that non-religious representations may emerge in context or in relief has wider utility for identifying ways in which non-religion is expressed via the body in modes of dress. The Stik cartoon discussed in the previous chapter is illustrative. In it, the burka-wearing woman is contrasted with an unmarked male 'other'. This male may be religious or non-religious—we don't know—and whether he is othered from a particular form of Islamic culture or from religiosity in general is open to interpretation; both are types of non-religious positioning. What is significant though is the way that this generic, non-religious other is normalized in a way that the religious figure is not. By naturalizing not only non-religious thought but non-religious dress, embodied displays of mainstream norms may subsequently be constructed and construed as a kind of non-religious symbolism.

As well as identifying non-religion in the adoption of mainstream dispositions and modes of dress as a result of these processes of cultural naturalization, non-religion can also be communicated via more specific forms of expression and embodiment. In Chapter 6 I discuss a London journalist's portrayal of himself and people like himself as, at once, middle class, white, and atheist but this is also an embodied reality expressed through spatial and other bodily practices: cycling about socially segregated areas of the city and consuming luxury foods. Such intersectional socio-cultural roles are not only embodied in these habits and attitudes, but also in the styles of dress associated with this position. Thus, seemingly secular modes of embodiment that primarily express socio-economic positions may also indicate non-religious ones, especially in local contexts where non-religion is commonplace and established, as in the parts of north-east London where this research was conducted and which the journalist discusses. Similarly, to the extent that non-religious and non-religious secularist groups have distinct demographic and cultural profiles, they are associated with conventions of dress that locate them in socio-cultural space in particular ways. The embodiment of intersectional identities therefore contributes to making the non-religious visible.

While it might sound absurd to say that it is possible to tell if someone is non-religious just by looking at them, there is therefore a kernel of truth in this. Being 'secular'—or non-religious—is not a matter of ideas and beliefs that exist apart from the socio-cultural situations in which they occur. Thus, to infer religious and non-religious positions is as feasible (and as complicated) as inferring class positions from habits of taste (Bourdieu 1986). Read in particular contexts, the presentation of the self—in dress, in physical comportment, in movements around space—may express non-religiosity in just the same way.

Another way that non-religious dress emerges 'in relief' is through specific approaches to *religious* dress or its conspicuous absence. This is particular visible in ceremonial dress. In her recent work, Linda Woodhead (2014) argues that new norms for rites of passage ceremonies have been crystallizing in the UK, even as traditional religion declines, and that many people, religious and otherwise, draw on religious symbols to create an appropriate context for these ceremonies. Hence, expensive white wedding dresses have been reconstructed as 'traditional'. Such modes of dress have an ambiguous relationship with religiosity: on the one hand, they are a development and reconfiguring of religious practices which necessarily change over time; on the other hand, their use is sometimes bound up with the individual's wider secular or non-religious life and expresses these commitments.

Civil and Humanist ceremonies are also on the increase and their use often expresses non-religious positionings. Such ceremonies involve their own aesthetic languages, including modes of dress, one example of which is the deliberate avoidance of white dresses. This is an exemplary case of non-religious meaning that only arises in contradistinction to religious norms: wearing a non-white dress is only meaningful in relation to the practice and cultural associations surrounding wearing a white dress. Again, the boundaries between religious and non-religious cultures can be porous, with non-religious services drawing on religious symbols and tropes at the same time as they reject others—but there should be no assumption that participation in these ceremonies is somehow less embodied or less expressive than would be the case in religious ones.

Thinking of the clothing that people avoid as a type of embodied practice sensitizes us to other possibilities. In a truly secular society marked by indifference to religious and non-religious cultures there would be little to inhibit easy cultural exchange between religious and secular people when they come into contact with one another. This is sometimes the case, as with the popularity of a crucifix as a fashion accessory, which may be an indicator of wider secularity. But other items of dress have not made this transition and suggest underlying investments in particular religious and non-religious traditions.

All of these forms of 'non-religion in relief' are inherently ambiguous and call for the use of careful, innovative methodologies in future research. But recognizing the non-religious dimension as a possibility also provides new ways of exploring religion, non-religion, and secularity in society and new ways of thinking about material forms explored in the study of popular religious culture.

THE NON-RELIGIOUS BODY

Non-religion may also be embodied more fundamentally, in our physical bodies. Indeed, Copeman and Quack (forthcoming) see the requests people make about what will happen with their body after they die as the exemplary form of material non-religion. They discuss how these wishes rely not only on conceptions of what happens to the body and the mind after death, but are also shaped in religious, spiritual, and non-religious cultural contexts. These cultural contexts mean that people may have particular and often strong feelings about the cultures they participate in, even after death, as well as irreligious feelings concerning the cultures they do *not* want to participate in or support.

Another way that irreligion can be expressed is in the 'undisciplined body'—in physical reactions against forms of religious embodiment. In this research, many people identified particular bodily practices as non-religious or as secular. Some described, for example, a powerful and physical sense of resistance against bowing the head in Christian prayer. One woman said that she did not mind attending and listening to religious ceremonies, but found this kind of bodily participation difficult and strange. Being non-religious is, as Campbell (2013) says, contingent on religious, as well as non-religious and other cultures. Thus, embodied feelings of otherness may be as varied as modes of embodied religious practice itself. This echoes what Davie (2013: 260) has said with regard to cognitive dimensions of non-religious life—that some non-religious people 'know a great deal about the God in which they do not believe'. In the same way undisciplining the body and the emotional experiences associated with that follow prior forms of disciplining.

Embodied irreligious experience may also depend on particular understandings of the body in relation to religious and non-religious practice. For people who view religion in rationalist terms, embodied practice can be more appealing than cognitive participation. Cat, a charity worker in her twenties who described herself as a humanist and an atheist, said that she 'wouldn't not go' to religious ceremonies involving friends and family, but also said that she, 'probably wouldn't partake in the praying aspect of it'. On the other hand, more expressive and embodied modes would be fine: 'I might [partake] in the singing aspect of it just because I quite like singing and I don't really think, you know, I don't think you have to believe in the words that you're singing in order to do it'. For Cat, words thought in private prayer require belief, whereas performing those words in song divests them of their power as truth claims and makes them into another sort of practice entirely—one that she not find inconsistent with her own non-religious outlook. A distinction between how the mind and the body relate to non-religion plays a role here.

Another specificity of non-religious embodiment can be seen through comparing it with a *secularist* mode. Secularist modes incarnate differentiation between religious (and possibly also non-religious) domains and secular ones and might include, for example, the embodied understanding of religion as private witnessed by Steph Berns (2014) in the British Museum and described in Chapter 1 in this volume. Notably, secularist embodied understandings of the domains in which religion is legitimately practised can be experienced by religious people as by the non-religious.

Affect is integral to all experiences and emotional engagement was a type of embodiment that was frequently presented by participants in this research, extending far beyond irreligious experience (to use Bullivant's (2008b) phrase). Analytically, emotion was crucial to identifying non-religious (and/or religious or spiritual) engagements within ostensibly secular populations. Examples were numerous and diverse, and include feelings of discomfort and anger as well as joy and delight. Many of the discussions presented in this book have important emotional dimensions: irritation with religious, spiritual, and non-religious others; acute feelings of fear and sadness in relation to illness and death that were either consoled or exacerbated by non-religious as well as religious cultures; joyful responses to non-religious experiences or ideas; frustration with how religious and non-religious demands are handled in the workplace, in politics, or by friends; and on and on. Emotional responses were sometimes reported in interview and other conversation; at other times they arose in the course of those conversations.

In either case, they helped bring to light attachments that people were not fully conscious of or able to articulate. Emotions were therefore a significant methodological tool: not only were they bound up with people's attempts to express or understand themselves, but they were central to the analysis, too, providing insight into when and how a sense of otherness with religiosity matters. Riis and Woodhead (2010) have recently emphasized the importance of emotions in the sociological study of religion, and this approach is likely to be very helpful for the task of uncovering non-religious attachments, too, especially the 'banal' and 'hidden' forms discussed throughout this volume. Similarly, new work can draw on a growing literature on religious embodiment—and contribute to it by providing 'religious-like' cases that throw light on what makes modes of embodiment 'religious'. Philip A. Mellor and Chris Shilling, leading scholars in the study of embodiment in general and of religious embodiment in particular (Shilling 2008; Shilling and Mellor 2007; Mellor and Shilling 1997; 2010), argue that the study of religion in sociology is situated in opposition to rationalization processes (2010:

217) and they propose the notion of 'religious habitus' to recognize and understand the ways in which religion becomes an embodied reality. This habitus is described as relating to 'existential reassurances and anxieties reflective of human frailty, the stimulation and regulation of emotions relative to the sacred, and the development of rituals, techniques and pedagogics with the aim of stimulating a particular form of consciousness and experience, including those related to transcendence and immanence' (Mellor and Shilling 2010: 217). So conceived, this notion of religious habitus accommodates embodied modes of non-religious cultures alongside religious ones, complicating the idea of it as religious habitus per se. In this area as in so many others, the social scientific study of non-religious and secular forms provides a useful method of interrogating important theories of religion.

Badges, Barriers, and Shadows

Another way in which the body emerged as significant is as a medium through which social differences are imagined and experienced. A clear example of this emerged in informal discussion of my work with Cara, a Londoner in her mid-twenties whose primary identification was against strongly antagonistic modes of both religion or irreligion. She was generally non-religious, but positioned herself as untouched and unthreatened by the religiosity and non-religiosity of others. Our discussion, however, prompted Cara to reflect on religious and non-religious identities and, after some time, she tried to put something into words, seemingly for the first time. Once you knew that someone was religious, she said, it was as though they were wearing a badge with this information on it. To describe this, she gestured towards the top of the shoulder or just above it: the location of this marker. The idea that had occurred to her was that, although it was not good or bad per se—something she emphasized—nevertheless this marker was somehow present.

I found Cara's use of the body interesting. She gestured with her body to describe this form of religious identification, and the body was implicated in the bearing of this marker, albeit an imagined one. In this, Cara showed how non-religion might be related to the body in quite subtle ways, something in between the use of the body for expression and the more physical modes of embodiment discussed above. Religiosity was, here, mediated by the body and anchored in it. Contrasting with the idea that the secular world involves the compartmentalization of social activities and the privatization of religion, Cara indicated that religious otherness was something always present—as consistently present as the body itself. The sense of selves and others as non-religious and religious is not, here, something that emerges on particular occasions when it is overtly relevant and comes to the fore; rather, it appears as diffusely woven into everyday, embodied social relations. Again, this is 'non-religion in the relief': the 'badge' that Cara talks about is not a symbolic representation of non-religiosity, but of difference. It is the shadow of her own embodied non-religiosity that has fallen on the other.

The codification of religion as a physical marker was echoed in other interviewees' sense of inhibition between people as a result of their religious or non-religious orientations. The idea of there being a 'barrier' was communicated, using a physical metaphor to describe and perform social relationships across difference. One young woman, Claire, told me that she might, in some circumstances, be displeased if someone thought she was religious because:

> It's just something that's so alien to me. Like, I find it—if I'm friends with someone and I suddenly find out that they're religious, that's kind of shocking. That very rarely happens, but...

When I asked her if she could think of an example of this happening, she said:

> I don't *think* so, but there's some people that are in your friendship group, where they are religious, but you sort of forget about it and then occasionally it comes up. Like say with [my friend Katie:] she's not like a close friend or something, but if you're in your kind of normal *mode* of how you would be in your own sort of circle of friends, it would be totally acceptable among *us* to sort of just be like, 'Oh, crazy religious people!' or something, and if someone's there that you're like, 'Oh shit, I can't say that' or something... So that's always a bit, kind of hard to... It's kind of a barrier, I suppose, to being like, 'that's a normal person that I can be friends with', or something.

Claire's struggle to articulate what she means is consistent with her suggestion that these issues normally exist beneath the surface in her social life and may be something 'you sort of forget'. When it becomes relevant, however, the presence of a religious other disrupts otherwise non-religious norms, and this is felt as a difficulty so marked that it is experienced as a 'shock'. Claire's account provides an insight into the symbolic marker that Cara discusses. Claire has a stronger sense of otherness than Cara expresses and the metaphor she uses reflects that: a 'barrier' rather than Cara's 'badge'. But both are physical markers, expressing the embodied nature of social relations and the embodied way in which people experience someone as 'other'. Moreover, both examples show how religious and non-religious knowledge is often present only tacitly in social settings, entwined with knowledge and assumptions about people that are refracted through intersectional identities expressed in the body as well as in the things that people talk about.

Both cases also demonstrate how absence may be conceived of as a positive presence. In Cara's 'badge', difference is objectified, but the absence of this badge also has a presence of its own and a concrete influence on the conduct of social relationships between people identified as having a similar outlook. In Claire's account, the absence of religiosity is also the presence of a sense that, 'that's a normal person that I can be friends with'. I asked Cara whether she would experience something similar in interactions with non-religious people: would that also be information that she had in mind when she spent time with them? Would they have a badge of the same sort? Cara answered that, no, she did not think that there would be a badge in that case. Necessarily, shared non-religiosity was knowledge she carried with her in these interactions, but it is expressed in the absence of an imagined cultural marker. It is perhaps an exemplary case of banal non-religion—with non-religion in the background, taken for granted, exciting little attention or emotional response, but ever-present.

Stacey Gutkowski (2012) has used Bourdieu's idea of habitus to describe particular modernist modes of non-religiosity that she sees as established in the dispositions, bodily habits, and responses of British political and security elites. Her work calls attention to the way that the formation of habitus precisely involves making positions in socio-cultural space invisible (Gutkowski 2012: 88–9). The formation of the habitus, says Bourdieu (in Gutkowski 2012: 88), is a process through which attachments are 'internalized as second nature and forgotten as history'. Thus, embodying the non-religious may be seen as a process of drawing that non-religiosity 'into the shadows'.

THE SECULAR BODY?

This chapter conceives of a non-religious body and, more briefly, a secularist one, too. Where does this leave the secular body? According to the distinction made in this volume between secularity, secularism, and non-religion, the secular body is one marked by its remoteness from religious, spiritual, and non-religious cultures, which cannot but be a ghostly form of embodiment. The notion of a secular body is, then, truly a tricky one. Talal Asad's (2003; 2011) rich studies of the 'secular body' attend to humanist conceptions and experiences of pain and suffering in contrast with religious conceptions, but these studies are therefore not secular in my sense. Asad's idea of the secular body relies on a thick understanding of secularity as a modernist humanist disposition, but consequently the body in question is really modernist or humanist, rather than secular. As Hirschkind (2011: 644) says, 'to assimilate the secular to the modern [...] tells us very little about a key constitutive dimension of modernity'.

According to the conceptual framework presented here, secularity is insubstantial, a purely analytic device used by scholars and in everyday discourses to describe the subordination of religious and related concerns. It is, in a sense, all shadow. Or maybe it is, as Hirschkind (2011) concludes, not so much a shadow as it is a phenomenon shrouded in darkness: despite increasingly good understanding, he says, of 'how the doctrine of political secularism [...] has impacted the conceptual and practical development of religious life in many contexts [...], we have little sense of the social ontology of the secular, and the kinds of practices, sensibilities, and knowledges that it opens up'. In giving rise to a more specific concept of secularity—by stripping it down to the subordination of religion, spirituality, and non-religion—the vocabulary developed in this book opens up concrete questions of precisely the sort Hirschkind encourages. We may ask whether the subordination of religious, spiritual, and non-religious cultures is something that can be embodied. Even a narrow conception of the secular body may still be empirically significant, if, for example, the subordination of religious, spiritual, and non-religious cultures inflates the importance of others in the body. In another vein, active religious, spiritual, and non-religious cultures have sometimes been associated with equally good mental and other health outcomes in contrast to 'indifferent', areligious, or doubtful experiences. In that case, it may be that the body is severely marked by its secularity, and that the question is therefore a pressing one.

CONCLUSION

This analysis contributes towards our understanding of the nature of the so-called secular and of the non-religious currents that sometimes run beneath secular façades. It enriches the sense of non-religiosity as something not solely or necessarily a matter of thought, and runs counter to rationalist emic accounts as well as intellectualist analytic ones, both of which neglect the cultural ties and the embodied fixities of non-religiosity. Awareness of potential forms of embodied non-religion therefore helps counter the tendency to transpose mind/body dualisms on to secular/religious ones.

This work also adds further weight to the idea proposed in the previous chapter that the banality of non-religious norms makes them less visible, though nonetheless influential for that. The expression of non-religion in and on the body, in physical practices and dress, may be seen as examples of banal non-religion par excellence, especially when these modes of embodiment occur in everyday settings, diffusing the impact of images and slogans by drawing them into the mundane and making them familiar through repeated contact. This may be especially true when modes of embodiment are emergent, visible through reading 'in between' the explicitly present: the non-religiosity that is expressed through multi-layered, intersectional cultural codes; the non-religiosity that may be expressed through casual, pluralist, and other representations of religion which subvert religious meaning to other ends; the non-religiosity that may be expressed through the conspicuous absence of religious forms—be it a white wedding dress or an 'imagined otherness' that is experienced in embodied social relations. These are emergent presences that require drawing out from the shadows; Cara volunteered the idea of a religious 'badge', but I had to ask her if there was an equivalent non-religious one.

This work raises an interesting, counter-intuitive possibility of charting the ways in which religion, spirituality, and non-religion may be meaningfully 'absent'. The removal of religious objects has long been thought of as an analytic marker of secularization processes, but this discussion suggests the usefulness of attending to them ethnographically—as cultural forms that not only express absences but new presences, too. Such 'absences' may be visible indicators both of social processes of change and of new cultural contexts, and they may be politically, symbolically, socially, and emotionally powerful as such. Thinking again about the material contexts discussed in the previous chapter, such forms of emergent non-religion might, for example, be charted in terms of where and how religious buildings are appropriated to areligious and non-religious ends, with attention paid to how people respond to their reuse. In southeast England, church buildings are transformed into cafes, art galleries, performance spaces of various sorts (for poetry, music, film), housing, and supermarkets. In Islington, the Sunday Assembly, dubbed 'the atheist church' in the media, has sometimes used church buildings for its meetings (BBC, 4 February 2013).[4] Though explicit non-religious use may be more striking, in fact both developments juxtapose religious pasts with new interests, aesthetics, and embodied behaviours. Because changed use draws attention to the types of activity that are no longer going on within them, these contexts may encourage users to reflect more deeply than they otherwise would on the new practices and values enacted within them. These cases initially seem profoundly post-religious, yet they are not so much beyond meaning as they are expressions of new meanings, providing subtle daily reminders of new cultural contexts and thereby contributing to the production and reproduction of a sense of non-religiosity as normal.

Here, the secular appears to be bound up with the non-religious in significant ways. In turn, this provides new opportunities for adjudicating between rival theories of how non-religion and secularity relate to one another. Counter to the secularizationist view that, in secular societies, religion becomes irrelevant, these cases show how emergent non-religion is socially present and may be part of and influential in

---

[4] <http://www.bbc.co.uk/news/magazine-21319945>.

the world. This provides fuel for the view that non-religion is a vehicle for secularization (Campbell 2013; Borer 2010), but it also demonstrates that secularization can be a vehicle for 'non-religionization', too. This is because the removal of religious forms from material environments and the notable absence of religious embodiment is itself expressive. Searching for non-religion in relief points to the long shadows cast by historical forms and people's ongoing and creative relations with socio-cultural histories in the present. In these ways, recognizing and concretizing a notion of the non-religious as a substantial form of positioning in relation to religion, and of secularism as an arrangement of religion and the religious-like in relation to other forms, opens up new ways of imagining and investigating embodiments that an undifferentiated notion of the 'secular body' obscures.

5

Friends and 'Anti-Fennelists'

Non-Religious Relationships and Solidarities

The dominance of the idea of the insubstantial secular and the characterization of non-religion as intellectual discourage a sense of secularity as a social phenomenon and condition. British comedian Marcus Brigstocke makes a comparison beween being non-theistic and not liking fennel in order to show that both concern the absence of experience and meaning: 'I mean, I don't like fennel [but] I don't hang out with other "anti-fennelists" at the weekends' (*Something for the Weekend* 2010). For Brigstocke, it is absurd to think that being non-religious might structure social life. Academic perspectives appear to concur. The important exception to this rule is in the understanding of non-religion and non-religious secularism as anti-religious, which describes social relations, albeit hostile ones, between the non-religious and real or imagined religious 'others'. Secularism has also been recognized as relational in its effects: in critiques of modernist secularism, scholars argue that, even when the intention is benign, secularist actors perform their anti-religious secularism through the construction and thereby constraint of religious actors. This is another recognized impact of the 'secular' individual on social life, though again it is antisocial in nature.

Recently, however, scholars have begun to attend to the more constructive forms of association that can emerge in relation to non-religion, particularly through organized forms: Atheist, Humanist, and Secularist meet-up groups, student societies, and activist organizations. This work, much of it focusing on the US, shows the support that non-religious people give one another, particularly in contexts in which they are marginalized (e.g. Cotter 2011a; Smith 2011; Cimino and Smith 2007). This palliative form of association is somewhat ambiguous, in that it may be construed as a reaction to the impact of religion in society rather than an autonomous and self-sustaining form of social life, but it nevertheless indicates positive types of non-religious relationship that post-secularist and critical accounts of 'secular' people have not yet paid sufficient attention to—the social aspects of 'secular life' that are affirmative and encouraging rather than merely disruptive and antagonistic.

The material discussed in the previous two chapters builds on this work, showing how 'secularity' may be associated with the social in that material and symbolic non-religious forms necessarily mediate relationships and make those relationships possible. Though some of these forms are collected in relation to organized non-religious groups, most are widely dispersed through their social contexts. Whether non-religious symbols provide general information or warning signs—whether they act as badges or barriers, noticed or unnoticed—they are, we have seen, present within social life in diverse forms and likely to facilitate and inhibit social relationships in similarly complicated ways. This chapter focuses on these social aspects of non-religious life in more detail, considering the different ways in which non-religiosity shapes social life. It outlines different possibilities: the way that non-religion can work to bring people identifying as non-religious together and to set them apart from those identifying as religious and spiritual; the way it can facilitate relationships *between* these people despite their sense of difference; or give rise to tensions between people with common non-religious viewpoints. In contrast with many accounts, then, this chapter seeks to recognize the several ways in which non-religiosity is social while at the same time highlighting its complicated and ambivalent nature.

The chapter also considers whether there are types of association that the non-religious is more likely to manifest in and shows how this investigation provides a means of interrogating rival theories of the nature of social life in modern or late-modern contexts. Some scholars have argued that, despite increasing fluidity in the movement of people and symbolic forms across time and space, communal forms of association and religion persist in globalized industrial societies, albeit it in new forms (e.g. Wood 2007). Others argue that modern society and modern forms of religiosity are individualistic (e.g. Putnam 2000) or individualized (e.g. Beck and Beck-Gernsheim 2002; Beck 2010; Heelas and Woodhead 2005), or that they are fragmented, only sometimes reforming in intense, brief 'tribal' groupings that disband as quickly as they form (Bauman 2000; Turner 2010). Some scholars give substance to Durkheim's notion of 'organic solidarity' (1984), arguing that modern society involves new kinds of associational structure of a network model (e.g. Castells 2010), or in the diffuse, informal, or hidden solidarities epitomized in modern modes of friendship (Pahl and Spencer 2004; Spencer and Pahl 2006). This chapter argues that, in theory, non-religious cultures may manifest in any of these forms. It shows also, however, that, network models of 'hidden solidarity' are useful for understanding the dominant mode of non-religious association encountered in this fieldwork. It draws attention to the ways that this hiddenness means that non-religious solidarities require careful and creative attention to identify, and how this hiddenness triangulates with the sense of the non-religious as banal, taken-for-granted, and otherwise disguised that this book aims to throw light on.

REVEALING HIDDEN SOLIDARITIES

Tacit Knowledge and Friendship

Many participants in this research could position people in their personal networks according to religious, spiritual, and non-religious cultures. This sits at odds with the pervasive idea that secular people are post-religious. In contrast to that view, it appeared that religion-related cultural knowledge was relevant to these relationships in some way. Even when people struggled to position people in these terms, they might express a shared distaste for talking about religious and non-religious issues or cultures with their friends. For example, James, a 24-year-old journalist from Cambridge, explained that he did not know anything about the religious orientations of his friends precisely because they were his friends: whereas religion and non-religion might be relevant to family life, these topics were, by common consent it seemed, not the kind of subject matter deemed appropriate to be shared by and mediated between friends. In this way, the apparent absence of social knowledge was recast as a form of secularist normative structure, involving a tacit agreement to steer clear of these themes in certain social settings.

Asking interview participants to identify how their close friends and families would describe themselves in relation to religion, if they could,[1] also prompted recollections of connections and interactions that had not been discussed earlier in the interview. Marianne, a writer in her mid-thirties who preferred to identify as an 'atheist' or sometimes as 'C of E', observed that she rarely talked with friends about their religious and non-religious beliefs and practices. However, when she considered how it was that she had a clear sense of several of her friends' outlooks, she recalled, for example, regularly talking late into the night with one friend on these and other topics throughout their university years. Though these conversations had taken place years ago, through them she and her friends had developed self-understandings intersubjectively, while at the same time building and consolidating the friendship itself. Via these youthful conversations, it seemed, they had established certain understandings of one another that still informed those friendships as tacit knowledge years later. This example illustrates a common experience, in which people struggled to identify the source of their knowledge about friends and family's views about religion, even when they had some degree of confidence in those views. Another common reference point was friends and family's use of religious, spiritual, or non-religious rites of passage ceremonies. This draws attention to the ways that institutionalization codifies cultural positions and makes them tangible. But it is striking that non-institutionalized religious, spiritual, and non-religious cultures may still be communicated between people and structure their relationships in relation to religious, non-religious, and civil ritual practice.

Discussing the non-religion, religion, and spirituality of friends and family also proved to be a useful method for learning more about the interviewee's own position, illustrating how deeply individual identities are bound up with the socio-cultural worlds that they inhabit. Natalie, a young woman in her mid-twenties, described herself as nominally Christian. She went on to identify the diverse religious, spiritual, and non-religious orientations of her friends and

---

[1] In interviews, participants were also encouraged to say if they were not sure about how friends and family would describe themselves. They were advised that this lack of knowledge was also valuable information, and the discussion surrounding this exercise focused on how confident they felt in the answers they gave as well as the evidence they had for their views.

family and, in describing these orientations, articulated her own interest in exploring these cultures and a shared 'questing' orientation, in which exploring and seeking are their own spiritual ends. Rather than identify herself or friends as 'spiritual', as sociologists of religion might have done, Natalie drew on a range of mainstream categories and it was especially by talking through the different ideas that she discussed with friends and family and the books and films that they recommended to each other that her socially grounded alter-religious orientation emerged.

Intimacy and Religion

Issues relating to religious and non-religious outlooks were, on a number of occasions, identified as particularly important in long-term romantic relationships. This was even the case when people claimed to be largely indifferent to issues relating to religion or non-religion. Matthew, a retired academic in his seventies, described himself as 'areligious' and as 'uninvolved' in religious matters, but was clear and confident about his wife's orientation. I asked him how she would describe herself: did he know? Matthew replied:

MATTHEW: Same as me—well, not Unitarian but non-religious, yes.
LOIS: You say that confidently?
MATTHEW: Yeah, we see eye to eye on this.
LOIS: Okay, so this is something you've discussed or just—
MATTHEW: Taken for granted, yeah. We were always on the same wavelength on these matters.

As in Marianne's story, there is a sense of tacit knowledge, but an allusion, too, to explicit knowledge that has been long established: 'We were always on the same wavelength'. Having described friendships with people who hold diverse views—and the different enjoyments and tensions that this could throw up—Matthew spoke briefly and affirmatively of the outlook he shared with his wife. Moreover, this shared understanding appeared as a firm feature of their relationship, with Matthew referring at other times in the interview to their shared outlook in describing his own. Other people made more overt statements about the importance of a common outlook in romantic relationships, while some interviewees revealed that differences of view—intra-non-religious as well as religious–non-religious—could cause tensions in relationships.

Non-Religious Socialization

Further evidence that socio-cultural moorings are significant to religious, spiritual, and non-religious beliefs came from more general discussion of people's biographies. Particularly illustrative were those cases in which the individual had left a religious community quite suddenly, following a sudden change in outlook or having been expelled by a religious community. In such cases, people talked about experiences of trauma and ongoing emotional disturbance as they attempted to bring their beliefs and sense of self in line with the new socio-cultural environments in which they found themselves (see also Zuckerman 2012). Emotional disturbance might be exacerbated by finding that, in these new non-religious and secular contexts, friends and other acquaintances were not always inclined or able to understand their religious pasts. Alfie, a young man in his early twenties, talked about the assumptions that his non-religious friends had held about the religious community he had moved away from in his late teens, as well as their lack of interest in talking seriously about his religiosity. Instead, they tended to joke with Alfie about his religious life, little realizing the depth of emotion that he was experiencing over this period. On the other hand, people discussing such transitions sometimes took on these secular and/or non-religious norms so that they had no expectation that their experiences might be treated more sensitively and supportively. For some, participating in non-religious and secularist meet-up groups or activism was a way of coping with this predicament. Experiences like this complicate the idea of religious privatization and the suggestion that restricting belief to certain domains is a burden that religious people disproportionately have to bear in modern secular settings (e.g. Habermas 2006; Casanova 2006). Alfie's and others' stories show how non-religious experiences, superficial and profound, may also be excluded from or constrained according to the contours of certain social spaces.

Alfie's story is also suggestive of the way in which non-religious as well as religious commitments have social underpinnings. Now describing himself as an 'atheist', Alfie identified his father as an 'atheist' and his mother as a religious woman, very active in the religious community of which he had been a part. Alfie had experienced these two cultures side by side but described various clashes between them. In his childhood, he had been an active church member, participating in door-to-door proselytizing and attending a school for religious instruction every morning before going to his secular state school. Thus, Alfie's experience involves an unusual mix of influences: participation in a very active and pious religious community, participation in a secular school (where his friends were non-religious, often teasing him—in good humour, he said—about his religious practice), and a family who varied significantly in their perspectives. As a result, he said, of being confronted with sophisticated philosophical objections to his beliefs, Alfie came to question his faith and ultimately left the church in his late teenage years. He understood his movement between religious and non-religious cultures as voluntary and fundamentally related to this intellectual experience. Yet, the intellectual process was also bound up with the two social environments that he was a part of and attempting to negotiate.

Moreover, the experience of becoming a non-theist had been traumatic for Alfie partly for social reasons. First, the bounded nature of the religious community he had been a member of meant that he was forced to break with it wholly and suddenly. The trauma incurred through this was exacerbated by relying on non-religious people for support, who tended, like Alfie, to treat the issue as an intellectual problem rather than an emotional and social one. Yet even Alfie's experience of God had been social. When I likened the emotions he was describing to an experience of bereavement he said he could relate to this depiction and that, in many ways, God had not only been a friend but the closest friend that he had had. He described the depression that accompanied losing his belief in God and this experience was placed in stark contrast to the light-hearted way his friends were able to engage with the issue. In such ways, the intellectual appears to be deeply entangled with the social, even when the intellectual is at the fore in subjective accounts.

Working with US apostates, Phil Zuckerman has observed that for many people, 'their loss of faith was frightening, emotionally and psychologically, and yet they had to admit and accept their loss of faith, despite the consequences' (2011: 173–4). Like other people in this research, Alfie was finding ways to cope and, to some extent, seemed to simply be 'acclimatizing' to a new, much more secular and much more non-religious socio-cultural context. The role of the social appeared to be deeply ambivalent, implicated both in the trauma experienced and in processes of healing. Consistent with recognizing the non-religious as substantial, these data draw attention to the dynamic processes of socialization that may be involved not only in the formation of religious subjectivities but in the formation of non-religious ones, too (see also Lanman 2012; Merino 2012; Zuckerman 2012).

TAKEN-FOR-GRANTED SOLIDARITIES

This study found a clear contrast between how embedded people are in non-religious, religious, and spiritual social networks and their awareness of these connections. It appeared that conflations of the secular with the insubstantial and of the non-religious with the intellectual conspire against the individual in their ability to recognize social aspects of non-religious life. Comedian Marcus Brigstocke's 'anti-fennelism' analogy can be understood in this context:

> I'm [...] an atheist but by default really. Because, you know, atheism is an *absence* of a thing: it's saying, 'I'm not one of *them*'. I mean, I don't like fennel [but] I don't *hang out* with other 'anti-fennelists' at the weekends. So I don't think you should be defined by something you *don't* believe in. (*Something for the Weekend*, 2010)

Despite not 'hanging out' with other non-theists, Brigstocke presented his non-theism and atheist identity to audiences at his comedy tour, 'The God Collar', which visited London over the course of my fieldwork and which I attended as part of this research. In relation to this, Brigstocke also developed promotional work associated with that tour (including the television appearance cited here) and published a book on the topic (Brigstocke 2011). Despite his idea that the absence of something could not bring people together, in all of these appearances Brigstocke forged social relationships with his audience through what Thompson (1995) calls mediated quasi-interaction and based, in large part, around his own non-religiosity.

At the show I attended, Brigstocke announced to the audience of people who, if not identifying as non-theistic themselves, found Brigstocke's non-theism (or agnosticism, as he sometimes termed it) sufficiently appealing to attend a comedy event which was expressly non-religious in character. The audience laughed in recognition of the absurdity of socializing with other 'atheists' and 'anti-fennelists'—and yet this was a large group of people coming together on the basis of a shared interest in this topic, bound together by their common sense that this experience would and could never happen. As well as the informal modes of socializing discussed above, it is striking that, even in more structured social occasions, the idea of secularity as anti- or asocial is such a powerful one that it can, in fact, bind people together.

The intellectualization of non-religiosity appears to be a major contributor to the taken-for-grantedness of non-religious solidarities. Many people focus on beliefs in their non-religious autobiographical accounts while being much less conscious of the diverse social engagements and the religious and non-religious norms that inform this thought. Alfie's focus on his formal philosophical education is one example of this, in which his own ideas rather than the ideas and cultures shared with others in his classroom come to the fore. Similarly, Matthew focused on ideas from the schoolroom in his account of becoming a Unitarian as a young man growing up in the US in the 1950s. Yet he also explained that, in this socio-cultural context, a religious identification was an expectation and necessity and that he consequently found himself shopping around from the available Protestant and Protestant-influenced denominations. The appeal of Unitarian ideas is at least partly explained by this context and the need to manoeuvre around and negotiate local norms and cultural possibilities. The role of the social was clearer still when Matthew talked about moving away from Unitarian practice, social identity, and self-understanding as a result of participating in new religious and non-religious socio-cultural contexts: when he moved to Germany and then to the UK, it was different expectations about religious identity that gave rise to his shelving his Unitarian practice and adopting a new non-religious identity and self-understanding.

In fact, changing social contexts often precede changing beliefs and identities so that becoming non-religious seems to follow familial and peer-group cultures (see also Merino 2012; Zuckerman 2012; Lanman 2012). So, for example, Gemma, a 26-year-old researcher, identifying herself as a nominal Christian and atheist, had been brought up in a Christian family and educated in a Christian school. Although she and her friends did not, she said, take Christianity very seriously, it was only in the first years of university, in which religious culture ceased to play such a central role in her environment, that she had developed her non-theistic views and sense of self. Thus, the change in her cultural environment anticipated the intellectual shift by some months. In contrast, for people whose non-religious views were more or less shared by their parents, the moments at which they became conscious of themselves as non-religious often occurred at a much younger age. One man who had, as a child, travelled frequently between Wales and Ireland by boat spoke about 'testing' his non-theism by ceasing to pray for his safety on these trips, as had been his habit. As he was quite aware, however, it was likely that the real change in belief had occurred sometime before undertaking what would otherwise have been a highly risky test. His story illustrates, though, how non-religious positions may crystallize in certain ideational and aesthetic moments and forms, which then act as markers in the non-religious autobiography while also obscuring longer-term and more complicated processes of social change from view.

NON-RELIGION AND SOCIETY

If non-religion is a deeply social phenomenon, then, it also takes up all of the ambivalence associated with that. This section examines the positive and negative social effects of non-religion and the ways in which it both facilitates and inhibits relationships.

Pro-Social Non-Religion

The first of these effects is the role of shared non-religiosity in creating and sustaining social relationships. Many of the examples given above are of this sort and many people saw shared non-religion as an important characteristic of their relationships. One man who identified himself as an atheist and also as indifferent to religion said that atheism was something he discussed with his friends a lot, explaining:

> Definitely, I think anyone who is a close friend of mine is highly likely to be atheist or at least agnostic too—the vast majority—and they would have heard me going on about this at great length.

Here, shared non-religion is a valued, even necessary characteristic of friendship. Other examples were more negative. As we saw in Claire's discussion in Chapter 4, a sense of shared irreligious views can also facilitate relationships—especially via the open expression of anti-religious views. Although these cases 'other' religious people and are overtly anti-religious, they also contribute to the construction of in-group identities and are constructively social to that degree—something that critics of anti-religiosity are not usually sensitive too. These data also show how secularist notions about the social settings and situations in which religious, spiritual, and non-religious concerns are (and are not) central also shape social life. This can involve the exclusion of such topics from particular types of relationship and not others. For people like James, it might be reasonable to know and understand one's partner and family's religiosity, but not that of friends. By contrast, Natalie talked about lengthy discussions that she had with friends and family about religious and spiritual theories (as she described them) and she presented these discussions in a positive light. On the other hand, when asked to describe the religious or non-religious positions of some of her friends, she said she didn't know because it was just 'not something you talk about'. In this way, Natalie drew a distinction between the role of abstract religious questions and personal religious beliefs in her social interactions: the former was considered to be a public matter, the latter a highly personal one. Natalie's experience contrasts with Emily's, a student from London, training as an actress. Emily also said that she enjoyed talking about religion and non-religion in both personal and abstract terms with family and friends, saying that this was a major source of fulfilment in her life and that, because of these 'discussions or intellectual debates', she did not experience her non-religiosity as an absence: because of these conversations, she said, 'I don't feel like I have a void which religion would fill'. Taken together, these cases complicate simple notions of the 'not religious' as agents of religious privatization. Not only may privatization incorporate the non-religious and spiritual as well as the religious, but it is heterogeneous, varying according to different aspects of these phenomena and to different types of relation.

As well as affirmative relations between people as non-religious, these data also highlight positive social relations across religious, spiritual, and non-religious difference. Again, detailed accounts are necessary because such relations are more and less positive according to how people are disposed to the religious, spiritual, and non-religious cultures at hand. Emily, for example, said that she enjoyed visiting religious buildings and participating in ceremonies, all except those related to the religion that she had once been a member of, the

Church of England. Emily said that she might identify herself as 'Church of England' because she had been christened, and she would sing Christmas carols 'because they're nice songs'. By contrast, she felt she could not go to church at Christmas because in that context she would feel like a 'hypocrite' or a 'dissenter in their midst'. Or, talking about a friend's church wedding, she said:

> I don't think I could get married in a church—I think that would be awful [. . .] I hate the fact that when [a friend of mine got married], she got married in a church: she never bloody goes to church! I find something icky about it.

At other points, her experience of Christian ceremonies and rites of passage was more antagonistic: she felt angry, frustrated, and rebellious. But, she said, her relationship with Christianity was different from other religions:

> My cousin [. . .] went to a Sikh wedding in India and he said it was *amazing*, a four- [. . .] or five-day celebration [. . .] and he said it was completely *amazing*, it was the most incredible experience. But I could go and do that because it would be *fascinating*, but I wouldn't feel like [. . .] my beliefs were being, I don't know—I wouldn't feel like I *had* to conform to their beliefs. I could watch as an outsider, whereas within the Christian thing, I felt *very* uncomfortable sitting at the front of the church at [my friend's] wedding, to be honest. [. . .] I kind of felt like, I'm a witness to this, and I kind of feel I shouldn't be.

Other non-religious people retained a fondness for the religion of their upbringing, feeling able to participate in a voluntary capacity and enjoying doing so. While some people made new, non-religious rituals out of participating in religious ceremonies (participating in Christmas services, for example, while not only maintaining a sense of non-religious difference from proceedings, but enjoying a sense of their shared otherness with companions), others rejected this approach entirely. In general, the data suggest nuanced variety and a need to understand the emotional responses non-religious people have to the religions they encounter in more detail. Again, these are distinctions which do not come out in prevalent, post-secularist critiques of how, 'religious people—Christian, Jewish, and Muslim—are being asked to keep their religious beliefs, identities and norms "private"' (Casanova 2006: 67; in Berger et al. 2008: 61–2).

Even overtly anti-religious cultures may play a role in the development of positive relationships with people from familiar as well as less familiar religious traditions. One man—my neighbour for the day at a non-religious activist event—told me about the enormous sense of recognition and relief he had felt when he had read Dawkins' work on non-theism. Now in his 50s or 60s, this man had spent most of his life without an articulated position in relation to religion and Dawkins' work had been an important resource for him. Significantly, for all of Dawkins' strong critique of theism and religion, for this man having an articulated sense of his own non-religiosity had facilitated friendly debate with a cleric friend in the village where he lived. This shows the importance of reception studies in relation to New Atheist and other non-religious cultural outputs, the effects of which may be complicated and even counter-intuitive. Here, an apparently unforgiving stance towards religion is transformed into constructive religious–non-religious relations. Rather than assuming that these relations are universally antagonistic and defined by struggle, then, such cases demonstrate the need to untangle different dimensions of religion and non-religion and examine carefully the ways in which these create as well as inhibit points of connection.

Anti-Social Non-Religion

None of this is to say that exclusionary practices are not a feature—and a significant one—of the social side of non-religion. Moreover, the particular anti-religious antagonism that post-secularist critics of 'secularity' have highlighted, involving scientistic and rationalist rejections of religious claims, is clearly visible in this research. It was expressed in the view, for example, that religious belief is associated with some kind of brain malfunction: religious people as 'stupid', 'insane', 'mad', 'abnormal'. It was also expressed in more sympathetic terms, as in an attempt to explain (away) religious belief by reference to people's struggles and their need for comfort: this focus on comfort is at once a kindly and condescending way of expressing the view that religion involves dampened critical faculties. Yet, these data do not support the view that the rationalist anti-religious mode is as ubiquitous or indeed as wholly negative as most critics imply. On the one hand, rationalist approaches can, as we have seen, facilitate positive and warm engagements with religious people, providing a shared basis for debate and discussion. On the other hand, not all anti-religious views are rationalist. Instead, there are several fault lines along which the non-religious reject religious others. Some non-religious people are even hostile to religiosity for reasons that run at odds with rationalist perspectives. For example, some participants in this research criticized particular or all religious actors on the grounds that they were hypocritical, a charge premised on a belief in the religious person's ability to understand their own actions and ethical positions and ability therefore to assess whether the former is consistent with the latter.

Another complexity is the role of anti-spiritual views as well as anti-religious ones. In these the subjective modes of reasoning associated with spiritual cultures (Heelas and Woodhead 2005) were also associated with stupidity or with moral weakness. The former critique could be couched in exactly the same scientific, rationalist terms invoked in some anti-religious positions and noticed by critics of certain Enlightenment cultures, but, whereas anti-religious cases take issue with people deferring to religious authority, doctrine, and dogma, anti-spirituality focuses on the inflation of the self as an arbiter of knowledge. Anti-religious and anti-spiritual lines of critique could be consistent with one another or mutually exclusive. A critic might, for example, treat the spiritual person as admirable, if not necessarily legitimate, for being 'true to themselves', whereas the religious person was criticized for following dogma unquestioningly; or they might reject individualistic modes and respect and forgive the religious person who, though faulty in their beliefs, was commendable in wishing to honour and maintain cultural traditions and communal life.

The following examples, both of anti-religious stances, illustrate such differences of logic, while demonstrating the ways in which different negative conceptions of religion can also be used by people to negotiate religious others in constructive ways—how, that is, the anti- and pro-social can be seen as two sides of a coin. The examples come from young women with very similar religious, cultural, educational, and professional backgrounds, similarities that make their different outlooks all the more striking. In these sections of discussion, both women are describing how they view the religiosity of close friends. The first account gives something close to the non-religious rationalist view of religion that post-secularists anticipate. For this woman (Emily, 25, non-nominational), encountering religiosity in her personal interactions is unacceptable if the religious person attempts to make a rational explanation for that position—an explanation that, for her, is bound to fail. Talking about her ability to enjoy a friendship with a strongly religious friend, she says:

> I think the difference is that I don't know, for example, any Born-Again Christians: I'd find that alarming. Whereas someone who's been born into that, it's like the way your mum used to a cook a Sunday roast, it's kind of who you are,... therefore you'd be doing something fairly major to say, 'I don't believe in it'. Especially because [my friend's father] was a 'man of the cloth'. That's very different to not having [a religion in your background] and then choosing it. Because, if you *choose* it, you really have to have a real reason to choose all these mad things.

In this account, religion is inexplicable as a rational choice, and religiosity is therefore more problematic and confusing when it is presented as such. Emily regards religion as irrational, but considers that the individual might be socialized into religious cultures. She is ambivalent about this: she clearly struggles to understand religiosity, but, on the other hand, she respects the way that common cultures bind families together and become part of 'who you are'. For Emily, when religion is part of a person's cultural heritage, it is therefore intelligible and easier to negotiate.

Describing a similar situation, another woman, Hermione (36, 'atheist') uses a reverse logic to come to terms with a culture she feels distant from. I asked her how her relationships had been affected by her friends' religiosity—was it a source of interest, perhaps? Or a source of tension? She said:

> Of interest much more than tension. I think... all of my friends who have any kind of religious bent I think do so from a really sort of open-minded, intellectual, spiritual, searching kind of a standpoint. So they're thinking about God and the world from within the context of, say, the Catholic Church, but... they're not sitting there and accepting, repeating dogma or doctrine. So, as a result, I can sort of respect that, to an extent.

Hermione's attempt to understand the religious 'other' is, like Emily's, qualified, but it is significant that an entirely different rationale is being used to think about and negotiate the religiosity she encounters in her social life. In this case, it is precisely the unquestioning upholding of a cultural heritage that is problematic, whereas a considered religious position is something she can relate to and respect ('to an extent').

Thus, while both women see religiosity as problematic in some way, the nature of the problem and the methods for negotiating it are quite different: where the one finds cultural practice salient and intellectual commitment problematic, the other finds unthinking cultural reproduction problematic and intellectual engagement salient. Not only do differences such as these complicate existing accounts of anti-religiosity, but they also paint an ambivalent picture in which logics of anti-religiosity are combined with pro-religious logics in order to negotiate religious others. It is not, by this light, sufficient to criticize people in such situations for directing their frustration towards religious others, nor is it convincing to say that the non-religious do not take on 'cognitive burdens' involved in negotiating different religious, non-religious, and secular practice as Habermas suggests (2006; Berger et al. 2008). Such accounts fail to recognize the compromises that non-religious people make and the restrictions they may experience in negotiating religious, spiritual, and non-religious others. Instead of simplified accounts of anti-religious positions and experiences, these findings point to the need to understand different secularist regimes as complicated embodied realities to which people have cultural and social ties as well as theoretical ones.

THE SHAPE OF THE NON-RELIGIOUS SOCIAL

Most of the examples encountered in this project and discussed here exhibit a general affinity to Spencer and Pahl's (2006; Pahl and Spencer 2004) notion of hidden solidarities and to decentred network morphologies of social interaction. The term 'network' is used to distinguish a loose associational structure founded on fewer and/or weaker ties, contrasted with tighter, more bounded associational structures involving many overlapping and/or stronger ties. While they strive to distance themselves from bleaker images of network sociality—Bauman's 'liquid society', in particular (2000; in Spencer and Pahl, 2006: 191)— the informal nature of the relationships they describe do make them less rigidly and deeply embedded than would be the case with more communitarian models. Spencer and Pahl (2006) argue that the decline of place-based and organizational solidarities has misled many scholars into thinking that solidarities in general are disappearing. Their qualitative research uncovers a range of informal relationships that can be established and stable as well as narrow in focus and transient. For them, the issue is less to do with differences between strong and weak, stable and transient, or dedicated and generalized in the formation of social relationships, as it is to do with subtle and qualitative shifts in how people 'fraternize' and in how 'fraternities' are represented in symbolic form.

This network morphology describes how many of the non-religious positions I observed in southeast England are integrated into social life. Non-religion mediated between people, feeding into their relatively stable and long-term relationships; at the same time, engagements forged around non-religiosity represented only one thread in much more complicated social and cultural ties and played different roles in different relationships and contexts. At largely anonymous non-religious cultural events, people came in small groups of friends; at meeting and activist groups, people met for an hour every month, participating in other types of social network in the interim; within families and friendship groups, people exhibited tacit knowledge of religious, spiritual, and non-religious positions; outside these groups, encounters with religious, spiritual, and non-religious cultures briefly brought people together and drove them apart. In these ways, the non-religious was embedded in relationships, but not tightly or extensively prescriptive over them.

Despite the salience of Spencer and Pahl's model of 'hidden solidarity', given the exploratory nature of this project it is important to consider other possibilities, too. This networked mode of solidarity was useful for understanding many of the social aspects of non-religion that I encountered in this research, the methodology of which—working in urban settings and focusing on personal social networks rather than more formal ones such as occupational networks—may be particularly attuned to this form. But this project also contained indications that, on the one hand, non-religion could be expressed in more tightly bounded communitarian forms of association and that, on the other, being non-religious could be an isolating experience. In fact, all of the forms of association outlined above were observed at one time or another in relation to the non-religious. At large, commercial comedy gigs, for example, 'tribes' of strangers gathered to consume non-religious cultural products, disbanding at the end of the evening. Others participated in more centralized and bounded meet-up and activist groups, motivated by particular interest in non-religious and secularist themes, by the desire for the company of old friends who were long-standing members of a group or, for university students and other migrants to unfamiliar towns and countries, for the company of new friends, or by the need for support after traumatic experiences in relation to religion. Other participants recalled feeling isolated at times in their non-religiosity, especially while going through the processes of leaving a religious community, but at other times too—when negotiating difficult life events with a sense that religious traditions might have provided support, if only they did not feel so unable to connect with those traditions.

The finding is not, therefore, that there is a natural fit between non-religion and distributed, networked modes of solidarity. Indeed, exactly the same networked patterns of association have been seen in relation to contemporary religious cultures. 'Centralized, state-like, religious bureaucracies and hierarchies of leadership have', says Linda Woodhead (2012a: 27), 'lost influence relative to much looser forms of association including small groups, occasional gatherings and festivals, and real and virtual networks'. The following sections explore in a little more detail, therefore, how non-religiosity may be manifest in other types of solidarity or in its absence.

Atomism and Insufficient Solidarity

These data include some evidence of insufficient social resources for non-religious people, particularly associated with the non-institutionalization of non-religious cultures. As well as limited space for discussion, this fieldwork suggests that the non-religious sometimes lack channels for sharing other kinds of symbolic resources. For example, while several participants had taken part in non-religious and civil lifecycle ceremonies, some participants discussed not knowing where to turn when this kind of ritualization was needed. Bob, a man in his mid-thirties who described himself as an 'atheist', spoke about the experience of arranging a non-religious funeral for a non-theistic university friend who had died at a young age. He and other friends had wanted to honour their friend's beliefs, but had no guidance on how to go about this. The result was a group of young people, gathered together but unsure of the best thing to do or the best thing to say. While others described finding support from humanist and other organizations in similar circumstances, Bob had felt the lack of structure and guidance—all the more acute as it was partially felt as a failure, that he and his friends had, in some way, let their friend down. Bob's experience is, in one way, an example of a pro-social non-religious experience, with he and his friends having collectively worked to prepare this non-religious commemoration. Nevertheless, the example also shows the importance of attending to the shortcomings in the communication of secular and non-religious cultures. It demonstrates how practical or tacit forms of social life may not always provide sufficient socio-cultural resources for unreligious people and that, for some people at least, there may be a lack of or impoverishment in more intimate discursive spaces as well as more public ones.

Another area in which a lack of symbolic resource is visible in these data is in relation to attempts to articulate moral or ethical codes. The positive correlation between religion and morality is a corollary of the association between religion and 'dogma'-based morality, thus the relationship between ethics and religion/non-religion is a contested and controversial one (Campbell 2013: 97–102). The methodology of this research does not test this relationship, nor does it investigate the nature of morality in non-religious populations. Its exploration of non-religious cultural forms does, however, reveal the sometimes poverty of explicit moral discursive strategies, which in turn, seems related to a lack of cultural resources to draw on in articulating moral positions.

So, for example, an interview question concerning whether participants could judge the difference between right or wrong and how this judgement might be made, proved particularly difficult for several interviewees to answer. People almost always expressed confidence in their ability to know and assess right and wrong, but they struggled to describe the foundations of their assessments—to say not what but why something was right or wrong. I sometimes prompted the discussion by referring to murder as a concrete example and participants were able to break down the problem into specific cases, in which taking human life might be considered more or less problematic for different reasons and to different degrees. What was lacking was not an ability to make moral decisions, therefore, but to connect these decisions to a wider moral code and to defend moral views in more abstract terms. People varied in whether they viewed their inability to articulate moral perspectives as a problem. Nevertheless, studying the non-religious does raise questions about the sufficiency of non-institutionalized non-religious cultures in facilitating ethical knowledge—questions that are relevant to non-institutionalized religious cultures, too.

People more closely involved with popular non-religious cultures and organizations, such as New Atheist discourses or the British Humanist Association, were sometimes more confident in their views—though it is not clear whether their interest in codified ethical and existential cultures drew them to these resources or whether, having come by this material for other reasons, it had helped them articulate those views. Notions of morality were frequently associated with something 'inherent' to humanity as a species, 'hard-wired' into our psyches, or with the 'Golden Rule'. The Golden Rule, normally presented as the duty to treat others as you would like to be treated yourself, was seen as the common denominator of religious moralities—a commonplace view in British Humanist Association and other non-religious literatures. The centrality of the Golden Rule in some non-religious culture may require further scholarly attention in coming years, relevant, for example, to new social scientific work investigating the typically uncodified ethics that govern everyday social relations. The frequent use of the Golden Rule does illustrate, though, an appetite for some codification and circulation of non-religious cultural resources.

Other cases showed how a lack of social support might manifest in festering anxieties about non-religious selves and religious others. In one acute example, Clarissa, a researcher in her mid-fifties, told me about a strong fear she had of being treated by a theist doctor. Her concern was that, because they believed in the afterlife or that his or her own agency was in some sense subservient to the will of a higher being, a theist surgeon might battle less hard to save her life if the situation came to a crisis: the doctor's belief in the afterlife, she considered, might make keeping the patient alive a less urgent concern, and he or she might also be less inclined to fight for the patient's life if they thought that the patient's ailing was God's will. Clarissa communicated an acute feeling of vulnerability and disempowerment in the face of such fears, and she also talked about desiring to have a forum in which to discuss her concerns.

In interrogating the notion of secularism, scholars have begun to attend to the significant ways in which religious voices are delegitimized in or excluded from the 'public sphere'. The issues facing non-religious people are different: the issue is a lack of visibility within the public sphere rather than one of legitimacy. But both are issues of recognition, and these data show that we need to attend more closely to the ways in which non-religious voices also struggle to be heard within 'secular' and other public spaces.

Consolidating Hidden Solidarities

According to Durkheim (2001), religion partly concerns the needs of a community to objectify or 'worship' itself. The idea here is that the self-representation of the community helps consolidate and sustain that community. Following this, Spencer and Pahl's (2006) notion of hidden solidarity may be a contradiction in terms—or at least a social model with intrinsic problems when it comes to its reproduction over time. Indeed, while for some people, hidden solidarities were satisfactory, for other people these informal and diffuse solidarities were unsatisfying and they wanted to replace hidden solidarities with more explicit ones.

This was commonly expressed as a desire to socialize more with like-minded non-religious people. Some illustrative examples of this are found in responses to the questionnaire given to some audience members at the 'Nine Lessons and Carols for Godless People' annual event, held in central London since 2008 and drawing together comedians and other performers in a non-theist celebration of Christmas. In the year that I attended one of these events, several informants had been drawn to it as an opportunity to engage with non-religious cultures in a more social and celebratory way. For example, Amy, a 21-year-old who identified as a 'strong agnostic', explaining that she considered 'hard atheism to be as much a mistake as hard theism', described the appeal of the event as follows:

> Richard Dawkins' website mentioned it, and I thought it would be wonderful to attend something so unique. I celebrate Christmas secularly, but have never come across an event which sought to bring together people with the same views as me. I know a lot of atheists, and being a philosophy student, I'm not lacking in opportunities to discuss religion, but this is always within an academic context, and the celebratory nature of Nine Lessons made it very appealing.

Amy is clear that her social life is shaped by non-religion and religion in a number of ways, but the focus is on the intellectual and she feels that she specifically lacks opportunities to celebrate those views communally. Her non-religion finds expression in epistemic communities

(Haas 1992), in which people are brought together around an intellectual interest; what she seeks, however, is to experience a more general kind of non-religious solidarity.

It is not only a shared non-religious view but an intensity of feeling that some people wish to share with others. Amy had attended the event with a friend who she identified as non-religious—'A university friend, whom is atheist'—and indicated that they not only shared the same views but the same interest in non-religion:

QUESTION: If you share non-religious views, did you know that this was the case before deciding to attend this event?
AMY: Yes, I was [aware of this]. We talk about it a lot, and I knew it would appeal to him for similar reasons as it appealed to me.

In contrast, David, a 36-year-old who describes himself as 'devoutly atheist', had also attended the event with a non-religious friend but expressed a desire to build social relationships with people who felt more strongly on the topic.

QUESTION: Have you given the show any further thought since? Have you discussed it with anyone since?
DAVID: It's made me realize that I should stop ranting to friends about these issues and find some sort of rationalist or humanist organization to become involved with.

Amy and David both have existing non-religious networks, then, but they also have a desire for more dedicated and reciprocal non-religious relationships.

Other people observed that their existing non-religious relationships were going through a period of consolidation, in which they became more self-aware and articulate about their non-religiosities and non-religious solidarities became less 'hidden'. Answering the same question, Shiv, a 23-year-old 'atheist', said:

> Yes. I think it's intriguing how secularism is 'coming out'. It's been generally seen to be ok to be atheist but people have tended not to crow about it. With this event, and the atheist bus campaign, I think we're seeing a demand for communal secularism—a celebration of what we believe about life and the universe. It's not just intellectuals like Dawkins leading the way anymore.

For this participant, 'communal secularism' is not about forging new social experiences, but about extending the range of practice associated with existing ones. Shiv also highlights the need for a celebratory mode of non-religiosity culture, which he sees as lacking.

While these informants demonstrated a desire for more communal forms of non-religion and, to some extent, a sense that these forms are developing around them, they also provided confirmatory data about the way in which non-religion frequently manifests in informal social networks. Everyone had come to the event with friends and, regardless of whether they thought this was significant or not, they knew the religious, spiritual, or non-religious perspective of their companions prior to attending. Some people had attended for social reasons: a friend had bought them a ticket; another had been given a ticket as a Christmas present from another friend; one person said that they had seen the advert and thought immediately of a particular friend. But this companionable non-religion was combined with a sense of non-religion as appealing for intellectual reasons or as socially underdeveloped. On the one hand, these hidden solidarities are established and taken for granted; on the other hand, they may not be solidary enough.

Nevertheless, this research suggests that more centralized forms of non-religious community build on existing social networks mediated by non-religion and religion, too. They do not much conform to Turner's (2010) model of tribal interactions or Bauman's idea of 'peg communities' (2000 cited in Spencer and Pahl 2006: 190), which involve 'a momentary gathering around a nail on which many solitary individuals hang their solitary individual fears', a pause in an otherwise erratic shifting 'from one target to another and drifting in a forever inconclusive search for a secure haven; communities of shared worries, shared anxieties, shared hatreds'. Rather, new non-religious gatherings build on longer-term, informal—sometimes overly informal—social networks.

Communal Forms?

In this research, I did not encounter any highly centralized communal forms of non-religious culture. Commercial non-religious forms are decentralized; meet-up groups are held only every few weeks; informal social networks are diffuse and, in culturally diverse southeast England, inclusive, with people engaging with non-religious, religious, and spiritual people of various types every day. However, non-religious communities were also emerging and centralizing over the course of this research and since. Similar to 'materialist religions' such as Auguste Comte's nineteenth-century 'religion of humanity', recent years have seen the emergence of new non-religious collectives. Alain de Botton's (2013) 'Religion for Atheists' and the School for Life or Sanderson Jones and Pippa Evans' Sunday Assembly have both emerged in central north London since this research began and attempt to replicate at least some aspects of religious communal life. Yet none of these has rivalled religious traditions in terms of their scope. Their focus is on existential philosophical questions, day-to-day well-being, and community for community's sake; but they do not give detailed direction in terms of, say, how to dress, what to eat, how to wash the body, and so on. This may indicate a limitation in terms of the areas of life that non-religious cultures address and how comprehensive and how bounded a community they are capable of generating or supporting. If there is, then, a possible affinity between non-religious cultures and looser network-style associations, in contrast to the more centralized and centralizing nature of theistic thought, as Durkheim suggests, this is a complicated question requiring a much wider survey of the non-religious field and a much deeper understanding of the different socio-cultural formations found within it.

CONCLUSION

These data suggest that non-religion is part of social life, both structuring networks of relations and being structured by them. Though these social structures are often informal rather than explicit, in a way that is salient in decentralized, liberal societies, they can still be meaningful for people. On the other hand, the hiddenness of these relationships has its problems. Some people want these social structures to be more overt and more central in their lives, while others express the desire or need for improved social channels through which non-religious social and cultural resources can circulate. Hidden solidarities may also be insufficiently open to critical enquiries about how these patterns of association shape social spaces in ways that are necessarily exclusive as well as inclusive.

It is not possible on the basis of this qualitative study to say anything general about the relationship between non-religion and different forms of association. This chapter has presented an analysis of some social morphologies associated with non-religion and these present possible ways of approaching non-religious solidarity in future research. These data do clearly demonstrate, however, the variety of ways in which so-called secular populations are involved in explicitly non-religious social relations, as well as the possibility that they are often oblivious of this. Whether this is, ultimately, evidence of robust 'hidden solidarities' or of insufficient solidarity, these findings echo the sense of non-religion as banal, mundane, tacit, and taken-for-granted discussed in the previous chapters. As in those discussions, the fact that a real and embedded aspect of our social lives is identifiable—and identified as unrecognized—provides further support for the suggestion that the condition we may have taken to be 'indifference to religion' or 'post-religion' is really an invested form of non-religion, and that we require the substantial rather than the insubstantial—or subtractive—understanding of 'secularity' to understand it.

6

Disaffiliation and Misaffiliation

Identifying Non-Religion in Public Life

Academic ideas and discourses do not develop in isolation from popular ones. Rather, they are mutually influential and even mutually constituting, and they emerge out of shared cultural contexts which they help to recreate in turn. This chapter considers the ways in which notions of the insubstantial secular seen in academic work are also expressed in non-religious cultures more widely. It demonstrates how negative concepts—'atheism', 'not religious', 'non-religious', 'indifference to religion'—are taken up in reflection of this idea of the insubstantial secular, but are also reformed into positive and often intricate non-religious identities, used to express specific cultural positions that the terms themselves may not hint at.

This chapter focuses on self-classification according to typical social survey formats—an exploration of which opened most of the formal interview discussions in this research. Identifications instigated by researchers and taking place in research settings are, of course, set apart from the business of everyday life and are artificial in that sense. At the same time, though, survey categories reflect emic ones to some extent (necessary, after all, if people are to make sense of the concepts that are put in front of them in survey research), and they also produce classificatory possibilities that are woven into daily life in numerous ways. Survey classes are reported in academic and media treatments of religion and religious identification, for example, and they are used to develop and defend local and national policy decisions. The impact of social researchers' systems of identification on wider discourses is visible in the emergence of the phrase 'the Nones' to label and understand non-affiliates (Pasquale 2007: np):

this phrase that has no meaning except in relation to multiple-choice grammars. Thus, in accommodating and attending to non-affiliation, academics are implicated in the creation not only of a population but of a social group. 'Hospital clipboard' identities, as one interviewee described them, are therefore instructive about 'real-world' trends as well as about academic ones.

At the same time, generic non-religious identifications are not merely imposed on people by social researchers but can be made and performed by them in their everyday lives. This may not be true of 'the Nones', but that is a specific case. More generally, as discussions presented in this and the previous chapters show, identifying oneself in contradistinction to religion is something that takes place quite frequently outside research settings. It can occur, for example, in the course of making decisions about, explaining, and performing life-cycle ceremonies that are experienced as alternative to religious ones; it can occur in conversations between parents as they make decisions about their children's religious education. People position themselves as non-religious formally, in taking legal affirmations instead of religious oaths (though this choice can reflect other values too, including religious ones), and they may also do so privately or in informal groups, in negotiating media representations of religion, spirituality, and non-religion, or in interaction with the religious, spiritual, and non-religious people encountered in familial, occupational, and other social settings. In fact, as this chapter discusses, a dearth of positive concepts for the self-representation of religious-like, non-religious commitments means that people often *rely* on distinctions with religion as a sole method of self-identification, even when the experiences they are identifying are far more complicated and richer than a strict etymology of terms such as 'atheism' would suggest.

The chapter outlines three central forms of 'disaffiliation' that people in fact use to affiliate with certain positions in socio-cultural space: 'atheism'; 'non-religion' in reflection of an alternative non-religious culture; and 'non-religion' or 'indifference to religion' as the representation of the self as detached from such matters. With regards to the latter, because people identifying as detached often display multiple engagements with religious, spiritual, and non-religious cultures, this brings us back to the idea of the insubstantial secular as a cultural form which is itself substantial and impacts on social life. The ideological force of the idea of the secular as insubstantial is something that post-colonial scholars have drawn attention to and critiqued. The discussion here builds on this but also emphasizes the ambivalent nature of misaffilating as 'indifferent', which is bound up with struggles for power and resources that do not always work in the 'secular' person's favour.

In all these ways, apparently negative identities emerge as reflections of concrete and sometimes complicated self-understandings, used to indicate a sense of the secular as insubstantial but combined with attempts to reflect richer, culturally and socially contingent meanings. Though these identities take up the notion of the insubstantial secular, then, they simultaneously make it the wrong analytical category by which to describe them. This chapter concludes by reflecting on the implications of this for survey research, reporting of quantitative data and other methods of describing 'religious' landscapes generally and comprehensively. The non-religious currents that often anchor non-affiliations also call into question the idea that these data can be used, on their own, as a meaningful measure of secularity and secularization, as they are often assumed. Instead, they are more convincingly used as a measure of substantive non-religious identification—and of the 'non-religionization' of society (Lee 2014). Non-affiliation can, that is, be used to gauge not how secular a society is but how non-religious it is. Following this approach, it may be reasonable to describe the UK as a non-religious society as much as a secular one.

'BRITISH ATHEISM'

Alongside 'non-religion' or 'not religious', 'atheism' was one of two central terms used to identify non-religious cultures over the course of this research. As the discussion of academic discourses has already indicated in Chapter 1 of this volume, 'atheism' is a familiar term and one that is apparently easy to understand. In interviews, those people who classified themselves as 'atheist' were often able to provide concise definitions of what this identification implied—normally making a short statement of unbelief in the existence of God. In practice, however, 'atheism' is used to indicate much more than its core definition implies. In this cultural context, it emerges as proxies for a general non-religious outlook, an intellectualist conception of why and how people are non-religious, and a clearly articulated, confident, or over-confident expression of non-religion in society. 'Atheism' has also become a deeply ambivalent classificatory category. It has a wide currency and is useful for identifying non-religiosity therefore, but it also has particular connotations that, for some people, limit its usefulness or desirability.

First, then, and in line with the sense used by academics, 'atheism' is frequently used in popular discourses to indicate non-religiosity in general. The pairing of 'religion' with 'atheism' takes place outside of academic discourses as well as inside of them. For example, the *Guardian*'s religion blog (the 'Belief' section of the 'Comment is Free' site) for a long time used a photograph of New Atheist Richard Dawkins as a header to its non-religious section, and this section took then and still takes 'atheism' as its title, rather than, say, 'non-religion' or 'secularity'. The website does not include a section on 'theism' but rather locates 'atheism' alongside cultural denominations: the list reads, Anglicanism, Atheism, Catholicism, Evangelicalism, Islam, and Judaism, as well as a final Philosophy tab. Alongside these other 'isms', then, 'atheism' is constructed as a or *the* non-religious cultural position. The centrality of New Atheism has consolidated the role of 'atheism' in British and other Western discourses, bolstered by its quasi-institutionalization in Internet forums (e.g. <www.richarddawkins.net>), organizations such as the Richard Dawkins Foundation for Reason and Science (a registered charity that 'promotes rationalism, humanism, and science in a quest to overcome religious fundamentalism, superstition, intolerance, and suffering'[1] and even in A. C. Grayling's new university, housed within the auspices of the University of London and which, through the participation of Dawkins as well as Grayling, can lay some claim to being Britain's first 'atheological college'. This collapsing of non-religion into 'atheism' is bound up with the same intellectualist assumptions about what it means to be religious and non-religious that I have outlined in discussion of theoretical approaches in Chapter 2 within this volume and in fieldwork it was also particularly associated with people taking rationalist, scientific, and humanist approaches to non-religiosity.

Atheist identifications are also used as a proxy for a number of more specific forms of non-religion, three in particular. First, 'atheism' is used to identify a non-religious outlook that is markedly clear

---

[1] <www.richarddawkinsfoundation.org>, accessed 11 July 2014.

or strident. One woman, Claire, explained that she preferred to identify as 'non-religious' rather than 'atheist' because, she said:

> If I was to say I was 'atheist', it sort of suggests I actively pursue that in a kind of formal way. Whereas I don't really give it a huge amount of thought very often.

On the other hand, later in the interview, Claire called on this notion of 'atheism' in discussion of issues on which she did in fact wish to take a 'formal' stance. She said, 'I'm not probably keen on marriage, but were I to want to get married, there's no way I would have a church wedding—and if someone was to [ask why], I would say, "because I'm an atheist", I suppose'.

In this way, participants like Claire noticed and reflected on contradictions that emerged in different parts of our discussion. Claire observed that, contrary to her earlier statement, 'atheism' was an identity that she *would* call on, and came to the conclusion that the way she identified herself would actually vary according to how firmly she wanted her non-religiosity to be understood. 'I suppose it depends who you're talking to', she explained, 'cause, if I was talking to someone who was really religious, it might somehow seem a bit, um, *aggressive* to say I was an "atheist", or something, so I'd probably say I'm "not religious"'. Claire's consistent sense is of 'atheism' as a considered and confident non-religious stance, while 'non-religiosity' emerges as a gentler and more moderate one. Moreover, the difference is, she feels, recognized by others such that she can take up different strategies of identification according to different social settings and requirements.

Another woman who, this time, primarily identified as an 'atheist', raised similar concerns. Hermione told me:

> Yeah, I am [happy to call myself an 'atheist']. The only—my only concern with it is it often comes across as being quite aggressive. Calling yourself an 'atheist' in *company*, can occasionally seem like holding up a big sign saying, 'if any of you are anything other than atheists, I think you're all fucking morons'. Um, which is disrespectful, in the extreme. Obviously.

Thus, 'atheism' was seen as a provocative or aggressive form of identification, and not only by those who would avoid identifying themselves with the term. In another case, Jane explained why she called on 'atheism' as one of the several religious and non-religious identities she said that she used. One reason she used the term was to irritate her (religious) mother; the other was to identify herself to a general audience. Jane's approach summarizes this dual aspect that 'atheism' has in British culture—as, on the one hand, a widely understood generic term for non-religiosity and, on the other, as a particularly committed and confident brand of non-religiosity. In a sense, then, the survey category of 'convinced atheist' that Steve Bruce sensibly critiques as incomparable to the unqualified denominational categories offered alongside it (2002: 193) actually reflects an established understanding of what 'atheism' means, at least in this cultural context.

As well as indicating an explicit non-religious stance, 'atheism' has also come to be associated with what Tariq Modood (2010) calls 'radical secularism'. James, a 24-year-old journalist from Cambridge said he would describe himself on a survey as having 'no religion'. He told me that he was beginning to question his 'atheism', not because he was reconsidering the existence of God (as this statement might literally imply), but because he was becoming increasingly critical of the absolutist secularist views that he had previously held and of the anti-religious ideas underpinning them. His mind was changing as to the value and dangers of religion for individuals and societies. James was not the only person to raise these kinds of objections to a thick set of values associated with the term 'atheism': over the course of research, I met many people who said, 'I'm an atheist but...'—'I'm an atheist but I don't like Richard Dawkins', for example. Their objections reveal an understanding of 'atheism' that extends far beyond godlessness itself. Instead, 'atheism' is translated into more detailed cultural forms, one of which implies antagonism towards religion, certain political and ethical demands, modes of engagement and styles of address, as well as non-theism itself. Consequently, James and others felt uncomfortable with the 'atheism' label, though they were uncertain what to call themselves in its stead. Running through this research was a sense that more non-religious classifications are needed to help people understand themselves in relation to religious, spiritual, non-religious, and also areligious others—the rarity of which is partially a consequence of the pervasive understanding of the secular as insubstantial.

The 'aggressive' connotation of 'atheism' is partly informed by negative stances towards New Atheism. While New Atheist work has provided many people with important socio-cultural resources for negotiating 'religious' contexts that they do not have an obvious or articulated place in relation to, other people were critical or concerned by popular perceptions of it. One woman told me that when she first encountered Dawkins' work, she had identified with it and started to think of herself as an 'atheist'. More recently, though, she had come into contact with media critiques of New Atheism as comparable to—or 'as bad as'—religious cultures. For someone who saw her outlook as meaningfully different from a religious one, she was left casting off her 'atheist' identity but, like James, not sure then what to call herself. Such cases draw attention to the way that non-religious identifications can be more changeable than the outlooks and feelings they are used to describe, and they also highlight the way that British media contexts have been involved both in the construction of 'atheism' as a form of self-classification and in its partial demolition. As Hermione speculated:

> I think there's this idea that if you're an atheist then you wander around saying that everything is permitted and, you know, it's regarded as being analogous with 'out for yourself and yourself alone' [. . .] so people kind of edge away from that term and use other ones—like 'humanist', or 'secularist' or 'atheist plus' or 'superstitious atheist' or so on, and they're really just [. . .] reactions to other people's hate figures rather than anything fundamentally wrong with the term 'atheist'.

Hermione, then, was attempting to reclaim the 'atheism' that she identified with in the face of popular discourses that had turned on the notion and come to associate it with a particular way of doing—or practising—non-religion.

Thirdly, 'atheism' is sometimes associated with elite positions and socio-economic privilege. In many parts of the world, various demographic correlates with non-theism and non-religion have this in common: people who state that they do not believe in God or who identify themselves as 'not religious' are disproportionately likely to be white, male, middle-aged, and educated (Hayes 2000; Voas and McAndrew 2012; Keysar and Navarro-Rivera 2013). The explanation for these correlations is likely to be complicated and multifaceted, but a compelling general interpretation is that, in previously religious societies, being non-religious is to go against the grain and it is people in positions of relative power who are first able to take up views and practices that deviate from existing norms (Campbell 2013, cited in Voas 2009b). Consistent with the pervasive, intellectualist view of non-religion, though, the people I talked with did not tend to identify non-religiosity as a socio-cultural phenomenon or with any of these demographic factors, education levels apart. As well as educational disadvantage, people did identify theism with economic vulnerability, excusing belief in God as a product of marginalization in the face of which religion might provide comfort. This interpretation had sympathetic as well as condescending aspects and also reflects an intellectualist approach to non-religion. On the one hand, this view does not appreciate the comforts that a non-religious world-view might also provide in times of hardship and crisis and, on the other, it implies that religious belief is intellectually untenable though there may be obstacles to or even good reasons for putting intellectual matters to one side. In this way, a classed understanding of 'atheism' —as the intellectualist expression of non-religion—becomes a significant prospect for scholars to contend with.

An understanding of 'atheism' as an intersectional identity that combines a number of different powerful positions is expressed in the following piece, extracted from an article in the high-brow literary magazine, the *London Review of Books*. The author is thinking about the London Riots, which took place in 2011 towards the end of this research, and the social and economic divisions in north-east London that he sees as underlying them. He writes:

> On the face of it my area's mixed, ethnically and socially. They've just built a new Hindu temple on Rhondda Grove. The students at the girls' school across the road are almost entirely Muslim. The church along the way which would, I assume, be derelict otherwise, has been taken over by a black congregation. *Middle-class white atheists like me sail around on our bikes to buy our coffee beans in Broadway Market or Victoria Park Village*; there are Georgian houses round the corner that a million pounds wouldn't buy you, and there's the eastern stretch of Roman Road, with pound stores and pawn shops and elderly geezers who never made it out to Essex, and a market that makes Albert Square look posh. But this isn't mixing. It's the ingredients for something—nobody knows what—laid out side by side and not being mixed, not touching. (Meek, 2011: np; emphasis added)

The people of Hackney and Tower Hamlets are, here, differentiated from one another by wealth, race, and religion, and by patterns of consumption and practices of movement. While not everyone is identified according to all of these dimensions—Muslims and Hindus are not described in terms of class or ethnicity; the people using the church have an ethnicity but no class identity—the description of himself and people like him as white, middle class, and atheist gives a completed intersectional identity that encourages the reader to position these other groups in relation to it. By implication, it is the 'atheists' who occupy 'million-pound houses', whose security and even complacency is expressed by their 'sailing' happily around unimpeded, about and above others like the immobile people that 'never made it out to Essex'. It is a powerful and concerning statement of an embodied, classed, and substantively non-religious identity, and not only in the ways that the author intends. The piece forcefully expresses the elite position that some Atheist cultures are associated with, as well as the construction of 'atheism' as at once a cultural equivalent to religions and as the absence of cultural ties—presented in the lower-case in contrast to named religious cultures.

Consistent with this, we may observe that non-theist popular cultures in the UK are mainly associated with elites and are not representative of non-theist approaches in general. The leading figures in the New Atheist and other non-theist cultural movements such as Alain de Botton's 'Religion for Atheists' are typically establishment figures. The classes offered by de Botton's 'School of Life' in Bloomsbury are expensive. The spread of the free Sunday Assembly (named 'the atheist church' in media discussions) from its initial homes in Islington, Hackney, and Camden in London to other cities with large, cosmopolitan elites raises questions about how 'radically inclusive' the movement really is, as it intends. Stephen Bullivant (2010: 119) draws attention to a contrast between British non-religious cultures—associated with establishment figures, trained and working in elite institutions and, moreover, typically male, white, and affluent—and American ones, which have been associated historically with women and (other) 'outsiders'. Scholars focusing on non-religion in the US also point to the way that 'atheism' (that they sometimes identify as a cultural category, sometimes not) is seen as a deviant position that is excluded from public settings, disliked, and discriminated against.[2] As well as throwing the British connotations of 'atheism' into relief, this comparison also reminds us that 'atheism' is a contingent, cultural construction, and that its meaning will vary across contexts.

---

[2] For example, Smith (2011) discusses the use of 'atheist' identities to combat experiences of marginality; on discrimination of atheists in the US, see also Edgell et al. (2006), Cimino and Smith (2007; 2010), Cragun and Hammer (2011), and Cragun et al. (2012).

I interviewed a woman from Poland who had heard about my project and was eager to be involved. Her notion of 'atheism' was, in several respects, different from others and was, she explained, bound up with the role of religious and non-religious institutions in Poland's political history. These cross-cultural differences demonstrate the need for a cultural approach to 'atheism'—or Atheism—that attends to variations in meaning. As a first step to identifying this heterogeneity, we might begin by contrasting 'British atheism' with 'American', 'Polish', and other nation-specific non-religious cultures as I do here.

The concerns that people raised about 'atheism' as an aggressive identity can be understood in light of these socio-cultural factors: it may be that identifying as 'atheist' appears to be gratuitous, pointed, or even bullying in contexts where the power and normative status of non-religion is assumed. It may be that identifying as 'atheist' is seen as throwing one's weight around unnecessarily, in much the same way as, in the British context, identifying with dominant groups—as white, for example, or as English—is problematic in ways that identifying with minority and minoritized ethnicities and nations are not. For people occupying elite positions, that is, making use of the extra resources that identifying with bounded cultural groups provides is problematic, given that they already have a disproportionate share of power.

This is, though, only one socio-economic mooring of 'atheism' amongst others in the UK—though it is perhaps particularly significant in affluent areas of Camden and Islington that were central to this fieldwork. On the other hand, some atheist identities were situated in relation to working-class autobiographies, for example, and others drew on 'atheism' *qua* a considered and forceful non-religiosity precisely because they felt marginalized in society or at risk, using this notion of atheism as a resource in the face of these challenges. It is also important to consider how the resources that religions undoubtedly provide for vulnerable groups are not always available to those who understand themselves as non-religious, especially when their vulnerability is the direct product of traumatic experiences of religion. In such cases, overt non-religious cultures can be an invaluable resource, just as religious cultures can be to others. That the former is often much more difficult to come by than the latter may, by this light, be a matter of concern.

Disaffiliation and Misaffiliation 141

Nevertheless, the issues that the association between 'atheism' and elites raises—exacerbated by the parallel association between 'atheism' and intellectual capability—has potentially serious implications for societies and for social scientists seeking to understand and critique them. Given the well-documented relationship between religion and social respectability it is perhaps not surprising that we might need to view non-religion in similar sociological terms, but this has not always been recognized. Identifying non-religiosity as a cultural absence or as a merely intellectual phenomenon is a major obstacle here. Regardless of whether it is used to express a confident form of non-religiosity or is drawn on to gather strength in the face of felt and real vulnerabilities, these examples show that identifying as 'atheist' is as much related to structural relationships as it is to philosophical beliefs and secularist politics.

SUBSTANTIVE 'NON-RELIGIOUS' CULTURES

Generic non-religious identities—'not religious', 'non-religious'—can be used to express moderate modes of non-religiosity that emphasize contingency and the importance of practice and community and are often explicitly placed in contrast to local notions of 'atheism'. Some of the examples given above demonstrate this. On the other hand, some people never turn to 'atheist' or other categories and this is because 'non-religious' classifications serve their purposes very well. As with 'atheism', the idea of 'non-religion' has several related meanings, though these can be distinguished into two main types. One involves the construction of the self as detached from religion (but not religious)—an expression of the 'indifferentism' that I discuss below. The other is an attempt to reflect less narrow forms of non-religion than 'atheism' is seen to describe.

In the first place, though it is etymologically similar to 'atheism' in its negative formulation, in the ethnographic context of this study 'non-religion' and 'not religious' were typically considered to be useful to describe more open modes of non-religiosity. They were used by people who rejected the few non-religious concepts available to them—'atheism', 'humanism', and so on—and found themselves in a cultural predicament, not sure how to describe themselves but still with a sense of themselves as not religious. The perceived openness of 'non-religious' or 'not religious' categories also makes them appealing to those who only have a vague sense of themselves in relation to religion—though it is significant that this classification is general while nevertheless still situating people, quite firmly, as other than religious. This underlying fixity suggests that there might be more to these ostensible undeveloped identities than first appears. As Bagg and Voas (2010: 108) comment in their study of British 'indifference to religion', it may be that poorly articulated beliefs and identities only exist because they have rarely been challenged and therefore rarely articulated.

On the other hand, some people in this study described themselves as 'not religious' or 'non-religious' because openness was a particular value they held dear. People adopting this approach rejected the practice of categorizing in general. Sharing similarities with some alternatively spiritual cultures, people of this view questioned whether single categories were sufficient to describe complicated realities; we might perhaps think of them, therefore, as the 'non-religious but not atheist' equivalent to the 'spiritual but not religious' group. To this end, generic non-religious labels were taken up as the most minimal form of self-classification. However, it is again important to note that 'not religious' does still position the person in relation to, and specifically outside of, religious cultures. 'Merely' describing oneself as 'not religious' is not the same thing as disavowing labels altogether. In later interviews, I started to ask people whether they would mind being (mis-)identified as religious and many said they would. This, then, brought to light commitments underlying apparently generic non-religious identifications. What is more, such attachments to generic non-religious labels may be bound up with a fuller 'world-view', emphasizing relativity and fluidity (discussed at greater length in Chapter 7).

Finally, in addition to acting as a placeholder for as-yet unidentified non-religious positions or as a way of expressing a particular relativistic one, another reason that people prefer to identify with 'non' categories is that these terms have become increasingly visible in British public life and media discourses over recent years and have, therefore, become significant and mainstream ways of talking about and identifying non-religion. One reason for this is the high profile in recent years of surveys dealing with religious identification, particularly in relation to the introduction of a 'religion question' to the census in 2001 (see Day and Lee 2014; Field 2014). As well as reports of findings from this and the 2011 survey, census figures have been widely discussed and debated in the media and have given rise to various social and political campaigns (see Singler 2014 on 'Jedi Knights' and Crowley 2014 on census campaigning by pagan groups). The media presence of 'the nones' (2001) and the 'not religious' (2011) has made generic non-religious categories increasingly visible in British public life. What is more, one census campaign actively worked to consolidate non-religious identities. This was the British Humanist Association's 'Census Campaign', conducted in the run-up to the 2011 Census for England and Wales and addressing concerns about the number of people identifying as not religious in the 2001 Census (many fewer than had said they had no religion in other survey research (Voas and Day 2007)). The campaign used the striking graphic design made familiar in the 2009 'Bus Campaign', discussed in Chapter 3 in relation to material non-religious cultures. This time, however, the adverts lobbied people who were not practising any religion, encouraging them to opt for the 'not religious' category. The BHA attempted to 'school' people towards the category of 'not religious', changed from the 'none' option provided in 2001 precisely in recognition of the affirmative statement that selecting this option involves (Day 2013; Lee 2014). Although individuals involved with the BHA have raised concerns about the term 'non-religion' used as a noun (Andrew Copson, Chief Executive of the BHA CE, *personal communication*), this campaign increased the public profile of the 'non-religious' as an affiliation and as a group and highlighted the virtues of using it as a way of identifying with a collective: 'If You're Not Religious, For God's Sake Say So', the campaign ran, while the campaign website warned that, 'The Census cuts non-religious people in half!'. In addition, the campaign encouraged people who were largely secular and uninterested in these debates and who might have maintained a 'superficial' cultural affiliation with a religion to reflect on this practice and to re-identify as 'not religious' if that was appropriate. Secular people are probably more likely to identify with a religious culture than a non-religious one in settings where the former is or has been predominant: to do so is to follow the path of least resistance (Lee 2014). Discourses surrounding religious identification statistics are therefore involved in the formation of substantive non-religious identities, while at the same time calling attention to the limited degree to which these identities can, in practice, truly be secular: identifying as religious, as the BHA point out, is not neutral but rather feeds feeds into discussions and claims about religious cultures.

Somewhat perversely, the design of the census survey led to the Census Campaign also seeking to discourage non-religious people from taking the opportunity provided to volunteer what, in this cultural context, are considered to be more developed and determined identifications: in 2001, some people had described their 'religion' in the box provided as 'atheist', 'agnostic', 'secularist', and, of course, 'humanist'. These numbers were quite small—tens of thousands only—and the argument was that they were misleading because the format of the survey discouraged people from identifying in this way by requiring respondents to actively volunteer these identities and by describing them as other *religious* affiliations rather than non-religious ones. In addition, is the problem—for the BHA at least—that many non-theists actually prefer to identify themselves as 'non-religious'.

What is more, despite the prevalence of 'atheism' in popular discourses, the BHA's literature uses both this term and 'non-religiosity', and the latter is, if anything, more prominent. This can be seen in the introduction to the BHA provided on their website (BHA 2011c; emphasis added):

Who we are
The British Humanist Association...
... is the national charity working on behalf of *non-religious people* who seek to live ethical and fulfilling lives on the basis of reason and humanity. We promote Humanism, *support and represent the non-religious*, and promote a secular state and equal treatment in law and policy of everyone, regardless of religion or belief.
Humanists...
... are *atheists and agnostics* who make sense of the world using reason, experience and shared human values. [...]

In such ways, 'non-religiosity' is actually widely visible in the public domain, while at the same time attracting much less attention than 'atheism'. It is the more banal of the two categories but, as proposed throughout this book, not necessarily the less influential for that.

INDIFFERENCE AND INDIFFERENTISM

A second use of 'non-religion' for identification relates to an understanding of the self as neutral towards religious, spiritual, and even non-religious people and cultures and/or as having no interest in questions of religious belief. Matthew, an American in his seventies who had lived for a long time in the UK, affiliated with 'the nones' before taking up the term 'areligion' when this was raised as a suggestion in order to describe himself as not 'irreligious' so much as 'just uninvolved'. That is, Matthew uses these terms to describe himself as 'secular', in contradistinction from engaged religious *and* non-religious stances. Similarly, Claire—who rejected the 'atheist' label on the grounds that it might suggest that her non-religion was 'actively [pursued] in a kind of formal way'—preferred to describe herself as 'non-religious' because, in her view, it more accurately reflected her limited engagement. As we have seen, she and others classify themselves as 'atheist' when they wish to make more forceful, affirmative statements, whereas the 'non-religious' label is useful in order to make more general statements. In a similar way, the idea of the self as indifferent was sometimes presented in conjunction with concrete self-understandings: as non-partisan, uninterested, disinterested, non-pious, tolerant, and open to other people's views.

What is more, people identifying as more or less indifferent to religion often displayed a range of engagements with and commitments to religious, spiritual, and non-religious cultures. As we have seen, Claire also said she was committed to her non-theist outlook and that there was 'no way' she would have a church wedding. She was also able to identify the largely non-religious orientations of many of her close acquaintances, including a detailed description of her partner's religious biography and his current views on the topic, and the ways in which his perspective was similar and different to her own. She raised strong ethical objections to and was personally upset by the use of religious funerals for non-religious people. Thus, Claire communicated a number of considered and strongly felt engagements with religious, spiritual, and non-religious cultures—less visible to her, maybe, because they emerged in brief moments and particular contexts, rather than in institutional or 'formal' settings.

Likewise, Matthew also identified himself as largely indifferent to religion. He did not feel that his non-religious identity was something that came up in social scenarios—'It doesn't happen'; 'I've never been asked'; 'I've never volunteered the information'—and continuously used his own lack of interest as a yardstick to measure others' religiosity. Describing one friend's religious identity, he says, 'he's not interested in religion; it's not part of his life as it is not part of mine', while of his daughter he says that religion is 'more important to her than it is to us'—'us' being he and his wife. Having previously practised as a Unitarian, Matthew was blasé about becoming inactive, equating it with falling out of the habit of participating in certain sports that he had once enjoyed. Like Claire, Matthew said explicitly that religion was not something he thought about, and even questioned whether he really was suitable as a participant in my research.

But, like Claire, he also revealed numerous ways in which non-religiosity and religiosity were significant in his life. He gave ready and sometimes detailed answers to interview questions concerning 'religious' beliefs—God or higher powers, the afterlife, morality, and so on. Matthew also gave a clear indication of a committed non-religious rationalist world-view: when I asked him if the concept of 'the sacred' had any meaning for him, he said:

> Well, science is what is important to me. I believe in science as a frame of reference, I think [...] the sense of finding one's place in the universe is that... yeah, and the method and the whole... perspective of a scientific age is one that I find very comforting. I don't need supernatural explanations because I have the... nature in itself is impressive enough.

And, prompted to say how strongly he would agree or disagree with a statement positing the existence of God or a higher power, the discussion unfolded in the following way:

MATTHEW: Er, probably on the 'strongly disagree' [end of the spectrum] but of course, it's all contingent on definitions, isn't it. So, it's a semantic question.
LOIS: So, please tell me your thoughts about [these] definitions so I—
MATTHEW: Oh, we can go on for most of the afternoon!

Matthew's ability to 'go on all afternoon' on this topic is at odds, then, with his idea of himself as 'uninvolved'. Indeed, this discussion immediately followed Matthew's statement that religious topics were not something he thought about; but he did not notice the contrast.

As well as these intellectual and cultural commitments, Matthew also identified a stronger social engagement with religion, spirituality, and non-religion than he reported. I began each interview with a demographic questionnaire, including a question about the participant's parents' religious positions. When I asked Matthew about this religious background, he answered by providing a concise, but three-centuries-long religious family history, which began:

So, my family, my father's family, was Presbyterian. They had been Presbyterian for three hundred years, three hundred and *fifty* years actually and they had—they were forced out before the [English] Civil War because they were radical Puritans of what later became Presbyterianism...

Similarly, Matthew had a detailed sense of many of his friends and family members' involvement with religious, spiritual, and non-religious cultures, as well as their conceptions of the religious, spiritual, and non-religious lives of others. He described his son, for example, as 'very tolerant of religious people' and his daughter as less so. Indeed, in discussing his daughter's views he set out one reason why even a person of secular inclinations may have to develop a religious, spiritual, or non-religious sense of self in relation to the interests of those around them. I asked him what sort of indications he had concerning his daughter's outlook, commenting that he seemed quite confident in his knowledge of this. Matthew thought about this and said:

> Mmmm, well, we have discussed it because it's more important to her than it is to us. So she raises the issue from time to time, and she says, 'Atheism is very well, but what if they're wrong!'

Though Matthew marginalizes his interest relative to his daughter's, this statement also gives away the relevance of these issues to different social relationships—an outlook shared with his wife and discussed with his daughter. In discussing his wife's views, Matthew described a shared 'wavelength' and implied that this was something he valued. And in discussion of other friends and family members, he presented himself as indifferent in contrast to the more anti-religious and religious amongst his personal network, demonstrating how 'indifference' is an identity that is visible and performed in social settings. He also communicated sympathy with anti-religious views that he said he did not share: he was, he said, entertained by a passionately anti-religious friend and said also that he understood why his friend holds the views that he does.

In fact, people who conceived of themselves as indifferent while at the same time revealing various ways in which they were anything but was a common thread running through this research, encountered in both face-to-face and media contexts. 'Indifferent' identifications were even visible at large, organized non-religious events. The idea presented by comedian Marcus Brigstocke, that it is as absurd to think that people would socialize on the basis of their non-theism as it is that they would associate on the basis of their 'anti-fennelism', contrasted with the various ways in which this statement mediated between people: between he and his theatre, television, and radio audiences; between the groups that participated in these audiences as small collectives (families around television sets; couples and friends talking about and around the show in the theatre interval); and between theatre audiences as a group, whose laughter and applause is shaped, as Durkheim highlights, by co-presence and the experience of collectivity. Taking the same view as Brigstocke, one respondent to my questionnaire concerning the Nine Lessons and Carols for Godless People event in London said, of herself, 'I don't really have a position—I'm not religious and I don't tend to think about it much'. But she also reported that she had attended the event with a friend, who had known enough of her interests to have bought her the ticket as a Christmas present, and of whose views she also had a clear sense: they shared the same opinions, she said, 'though his are more defined than mine'; 'I like to give things and people the benefit of the doubt, and have some very close religious friends; he is vehemently anti-religion'. Again, it is clear that in fact her own and her friend's religious views are something that she has thought about, and, despite her sense that her friend's views are the 'more defined', uses the contrast between them to present a clear picture of her own.

Finally, self-understanding as 'indifferent' emerged as a mode of engagement with religion, spirituality, and non-religion when people drew on this outlook in order to explain their interest in these cultures. This comes out in Steph Berns's (2014) research, conducted concurrently with my own and also based in London. She discusses how visitors to British Museum exhibitions with religious subject matter explain that their own 'indifference' makes religious cultures seem fascinatingly 'other'. She recounts how one woman, in her thirties, was captivated by the more 'bizarre' and 'other worldly' exhibits 'as they constituted elements of ritual networks that were alien and exotic' (Berns 2014: 256). This woman had described herself as an 'atheist', 'having been brought up with complete indifference'. Berns's work shows how uncomfortably the notion of 'indifference' sits with social and culture realities full of relations and encounters between religious and non-religious people and objects.

The point here is not that everyone is highly engaged with religious, spiritual, and non-religious cultures at all times. As others have also found in the study of religion and non-religion, these cultures are situated and become more and less relevant at different moments in time. What is more, detachment from religion (steering away, here, from the tricky concept of 'indifference') is observable on particular occasions where attachment might be expected and as a general disposition. In seeking to identify the religious, spiritual, and especially the non-religious currents that run beneath apparently 'secular' life, this volume forgoes the interesting problem of how immersed people are in each of these cultures, that is, their degree of areligiosity. This is an important question. The point here, however, is that people are not always aware of the extent of their own engagement. At least sometimes the construction of the self as indifferent can be seen, therefore, as a social and cultural practice with concrete effects and can be recognized as *indifferentism* rather than actual indifference (Lee 2014).

Explaining Indifferentism

To some extent, indifferentism is like other negative identities such as 'atheism' or 'non-religion' that indicate distance from religious cultures rather than explicitly describing alternative ones. But there are a number of other factors to take into account as well. For one, the notion of indifference is typically presented as a general and encompassing stance, but it often reflects detachment from particular phenomena that people think are 'really religious' (Woodhead 2010), as well as from phenomena that they see as 'really spiritual' or 'really non-religious'. So a flip side of the notion that authentic non-religion is fundamentally intellectual, for example, is that people may discount other forms of non-religiosity and lines of othering. Some of the examples given earlier illustrate this. In these, people think of themselves as indifferent because religious issues are not something they *think* about: 'If I was to say I was "atheist", it sort of suggests I actively pursue that in a kind of formal way. *Whereas, I don't really give it a huge amount of thought very often*'; and 'I don't really have a position—I'm not religious and *I don't tend to think about it much*'. And it is not only thought-work that is important, but particular types of thought-work; as we have seen, all of these people have actually given over some notable time to thinking about religious, spiritual, and non-religious issues and cultures, but they do not view all of these thoughts as meaningful or significant. There is a related issue here about the fact that many non-religious positions and cultures are developed outside of centralized organizations or institutions, and are instead associated with forms of solidarity that tend to be hidden (Spencer and Pahl 2006).

As well as being obscured, engagements can also be taken for granted because they operate as norms. At the end of one of the longer interviews, involving a wide-ranging discussion of humanist values, non-theist rituals, and religious 'others', one man reflected, 'I tend to think that I don't really care—you know, like I said before: I'm *such an* atheist that I don't care. But obviously I do'.

Finally, participants understand themselves as indifferent for the ideological reasons that post-colonial scholars observe in the notion of a rational, secular neutrality towards religions. As they point out, positioning as detached—or disinterested, to use a term that rulers have relied on since time immemorial to justify their claims to power—allows people to differentiate themselves from the partisanship, irrationality, unthinkingness, or other undesirable characteristics that are seen to constrain the religious mind and sometimes the non-religious one too. The idea of the self as insubstantially secular also has great costs, though: it restricts opportunities for self-knowledge and for making the kinds of cultural claims that people involved with recognized traditions have access to. Consequently, it is helpful to remain ambivalent about the causes and effects of indifferentism—at least until more extensive empirical research has been undertaken. Such work should be careful to attend to the ways that people who falsely understand themselves as indifferent not only impact on the lives of others but on their own ability to thrive.

FOR WANT OF A BETTER WORD

This chapter has focused on 'atheism' and 'non-religion', partly because of their prominence in the ethnographic field and partly because of their theoretical significance. These are not, of course, the only terms that British people use to identify themselves as non-religious. 'Humanism' came up a lot, as did 'agnosticism', and 'secularism'. All of these have a strong presence in British discourse, though perhaps not so pronounced as 'atheism' and the generic 'not religious'; the focus on 'atheism' in the *Guardian*'s 'Belief' blog is a case

Disaffiliation and Misaffiliation 151

in point. A few people like labels such as 'rationalist', 'sceptic', and 'freethinker', terms that have a lineage in organized non-religious cultural movements and remain particularly associated with those traditions.

But although the availability of these terms would seem to be a resource for capturing different non-religious experiences, in fact they appear to converge on the same, narrow set of meanings. 'Secularism', for example, clearly enacts the contradictory notions of the secular that this book draws attention to, used on the one hand to locate oneself and others away from 'theist–atheist' debates and, on the other, to describe an active interest in constraining religion—and only religion—in politics. (Given that British religious and non-religious history is marked by the demarcation of religion as a highly personal matter, the fact that both these senses prioritize public life may explain why this category was not frequently used as a primary self-description in interview discussions.) 'Humanism' was sometimes associated with official Humanist organizations, local and national. It was also used by people seeking to frame a materialist stance in positive terms, though these stances might actually be quite similar to those identified as 'atheist' or 'non-religious'. In fact, 'humanism' was associated with two streams that replicate the distinction described above: some associated it with rationalist non-theist cultures, while others saw it as a more open and sympathetic but also non-theist identification. Put in the negative by some participants, 'humanism' was sometimes seen as adding little to a core 'atheist' identity (as in Hermione's view, earlier), while others saw 'humanism' as a more 'wishy-washy' or 'hippy' non-religious orientation, involving leanings towards the alternatively spiritual. The overlapping meanings of apparently different categories was also illustrated by people who rejected or accepted them all when prompted with a long list of possibilities. In fact, despite seeing himself as not very interested in such matters, Matthew responded to a long list by saying, 'Yeah, I'd put "all of the above"!'

This finding draws attention to the lack of diversity that these concepts present and the extent to which they are tied to a tradition of rationalist and materialist non-theism, with several of them explicitly prioritizing the intellectual: 'rationalist', 'freethinker', 'sceptic', or the Anglo-American 'Bright' identity, which alludes to a sunny disposition and a superior intellect. As I discuss in the next chapter, the anthropocentric philosophy that the concept of 'humanism' connotes also prioritizes human intelligence and, in that way, the term can be understood as part of this rationalist framework. It is because of this that 'not religious' identities are sometimes taken up: for want of a better word. One woman said she liked either 'not religious' or 'agnostic' as labels, explaining:

> Well both of them in a way feel a bit lazy—like, well, I can't be bothered to really have a determined argument for myself as to *why* I'm an atheist... but I *know* I feel no kind of gut affiliation to any religion, or I have ethical and moral issues with all of the religions, you know, in the detail of them. Therefore, what's the alternative, you know?

It is sometimes argued that the relatively small numbers of people identifying explicitly as 'atheist' or 'humanist' in large-scale surveys indicates that committed 'secularity' is not widespread. Meanwhile, generic non-religious identifications are dismissed as second order categories, an assumption captured in the idea of 'disaffiliation'. In contrast, this work draws attention to the potential weightiness of apparently generic non-religious identifications and suggests that these affiliations, as they are, may be examples of hidden or banal commitments. To continue a theme, they may be another ostensibly hollow symbolic form that masks more complicated and concrete realities.

Non-religious identifications are also hidden because they do not exist, as people think, in overt experiences of deliberating about and making propositions about beliefs. Rather, non-religious identities emerge in relation to everyday interactions. Identifications are necessarily socially contingent, so it is perhaps not surprising that they particularly emerge in thinking about the views of others and interaction with those others. The many identities that Jane mentioned in our interview illustrate how the means and purposes of identifying in relation to religion are situational. Jane, a 33-year-old, working for an agency of the British government, had given her religious/non-religious identity some thought: when I asked her by email whether she would generally identify as 'religious' or 'non-religious' (the eligibility question for interview recruitment), she problematized both notions and said the question was opening up a 'can of worms'. In our interview, though, she proposed different identifications to different social ends. Over the course of our meeting, Jane told me that she would classify herself as a member of the Church of England on a census survey as she (incorrectly) believed that funds are allocated to the Church on that basis and, feeling fondly towards it, wanted the

Church to benefit in this way. She would classify herself as an 'atheist' on any other survey, as a widely recognizable way of identifying her world-view; as a 'natural pantheist' to open deeper conversations with close relatives and friends; as an 'atheist' (again) in order to irritate her mother, who is a practising Methodist; and as practising a religion in encounters with proselytizing religious people. She felt that saying she was 'atheist' would suggest too much room for negotiation in such encounters, so she preferred to indicate an active religious life by saying that she was 'just off to temple' or similar in order to cut short any longer discussions. The problems that such multiple identities pose for quantitative research are known, but the issue is particularly acute for the study of non-religious identities, where common categories have been given less attention and in relation to which the possibility of multiple, hybrid, and 'syncretic' identities has only recently begun to gather attention.

NONES AND NOTHINGNESS

All of the cases discussed here—atheist, the 'open-minded' non-religious, and the indifferent—are affirmative identifications that relate to locations within and movements around socio-cultural contexts. This means that it is wrong to assume that 'nones' are always 'nothings', and raises issues about using non-affiliation data to measure secularity.

Further support for this conclusion comes from three sources. The most important of these is the inclusion of real 'opt-out' options in addition to non-religious categories in some quantitative instruments, demonstrating that 'not religious' options are not being used to step outside religiously defined frameworks. The Census for England and Wales is one example of this because its 'religion question' was, unlike every other question on the Census, voluntary and respondents were made aware that they did not need to answer it. As a result, the censuses of 2001 and 2011 not only record the number of people who said they had 'none' or 'no religion' respectively, but also made a separate record of the number of people who declined to answer the question entirely. In both years, the 'not stated' category was, in fact, the third most popular one in the population, after the 'Christian' and 'none'/'no religion' categories, and it was double the size of the next largest category, the 'Muslim' group: in 2011,

4,038,032 did not state a religion, a decline from 4,433,520 in 2001. Representing a slight decline in percentage terms, the nearly 400,000 more people who decided to state a 'religion' in 2011 as compared to 2001 is a significant figure in its own right, larger than any of the minority religious affiliations, Muslim apart—more than the 263,346 people who said that they were Jewish on the 2011 census, for example. And, although the 'voluntary' status of this question is particular to obligatory surveys like the census, other surveys allow people to record a 'not sure' or 'not stated' option. The scale and significance of these 'opt-out' groups is interesting and deserves further research. For the purposes of this discussion, the important point is that these real opt-out options highlight the extent to which generic non-religious categories are *opt-in* ones. Accurate reporting would therefore describe the 'not stated' group as having made neither a religious *nor a non-religious* identification.

Secondly, there is statistical evidence that people are really committed to non-religious identities. In their reporting of British Social Attitudes findings concerning British religion and non-religion, Voas and Ling (2010) include data concerning how religious or *non-religious* British and American respondents consider themselves to be and find that a large number of non-religious people feel determined in their non-religiosity. In fact, more people identify as strongly non-religious (26 per cent) than identify as strongly religious (7 per cent). In total, 37 per cent of the UK population appear to say that non-religiosity is something that matters, exactly the same number who identified as non-theist or agnostic in relation to the existence of God in that year and only slightly less than the number who said they had no religion. Though it may not have been designed for this purpose, this item is notable as a possible measure of engaged non-religiosity and as a rare case in which indifference (if that is what the alternative, 'neither religious nor non-religious' option implies) was measured relative to both 'religion' *and* 'non-religion'.

Finally, there is the logical point, already made, that people who are basically detached from religious, spiritual, and non-religious cultures are more likely to go along with traditional identities—religious, in this case—as they are to adopt less established 'not religious' ones. So, for example, Karen, a student at Cambridge told me that she (probably) did not believe in God, thought that her whole being would end with her material body (when I asked her what she thought would happen after death, she said simply, 'You rot'); but also said that she

Disaffiliation and Misaffiliation 155

would identify herself as a Christian on a survey, 'because I've been christened'. Alternatively put, in contexts of religious decline, people are more likely to be 'nominally religious', to use Abby Day's (2011) category, than they are to be 'nominally non-religious'.

People describe themselves as 'not religious' for reasons not discussed here, for example in order to identify an alternatively spiritual orientation not provided for. 'Atheist' and 'non-religious' identities may not map perfectly onto those captured in survey data as the meaning of both is intrinsically relational and alters with their context. Those identifying as 'non-religious' on a survey may do so, for example, to express a 'spiritual but not religious' or alternatively spiritual self-understanding, especially if the survey options only include a restricted list of confessional identities and a 'not religious' option. But there are some indications that a sizeable portion of the non-affiliate population is generally non-religious. Some studies show that non-affiliate identities cluster with other dimensions of non-religious culture (e.g. Voas and Crockett 2005) and Siegers (2010) analysis of data from the turn of the millennium suggests that alternatively spiritual populations account for approximately 10 per cent of the British population as compared to the 27 per cent who are actively non-religious. If this is correct, alternatively spiritual people form a sizeable share of the British religious landscape but only account, at a maximum, for about a quarter of those identifying as 'not religious' as recorded in the British Social Attitudes survey in the same year. It is also reasonable to assume that alternatively spiritual people have prior ways of identifying themselves than in contradistinction to religion which they use when they have the option. Because, as this chapter proposes, non-religious identities are culturally contingent and are therefore embedded in national as well as transnational cultural networks, this means that what is true for the UK may not be true elsewhere. By triangulating data in this way, though, it is possible to say something about the extent of non-religious identification in different places. In Britain, some types of non-religious positioning are, it would seem, widespread.

Recognizing the cultural moorings of non-religious identifications makes it possible to take up innovative analytical approaches developed in the study of religion and to apply these to non-religious populations. For example, Day (2006; 2011) and Voas and Day (2007) have highlighted the ethnicization of the 'Christian' category in Britain, so that 'Christian' is perceived to be an expression of especially white Britishness; Voas and Day use this to understand the unusually high numbers of people who identified as Christian in the 2001 Census for England and Wales as the religion question came immediately after one asking people to describe their ethnicity. If 'not religious' categories are also historicized, it is possible to build on this analysis to consider how cultural connotations of this category also might have impacted on the number of people selecting it. The use of a generic non-religious category to position oneself as non-partisan and disinterested might have been less salient when given alongside the ethnicity question, for the reasons that Day and Voas observe, while non-religious categories that are perceived to be substantive—'atheism' and 'humanism'—might have fared relatively well.

On the other hand, recognizing the value that 'not religious' categories can have for survey respondents suggests that they should remain a central part of research designs in future. Attempts to give more considered options for 'secular' populations have led to these categories being replaced with ones such as 'atheist', 'agnostic', and 'humanist', yet, as we have seen, these options may still leave non-religious people unsatisfied. It may be, in fact, that to remove a general non-religious category is to remove one of the most popular identifications out there. Similarly, in individualizing cultural contexts, it may also be the case that general-sounding identities are increasingly salient and popular, not only for non-religious people but for religious and spiritual ones, too. Rather, survey designers may want to consider including general options such as 'religious' and 'spiritual' alongside the more obviously substantial, local 'denominational' cultural categories—'Christian', 'Muslim', 'Pagan', 'Humanist', to take some examples that are relevant to the British case. These should be included alongside an opt-out category, too, in order to capture those who incline towards secularity proper. In such ways, recognizing that 'secular' categories circulate through society as substantive culture forms allows us to attend to these and other methodological possibilities and deepen our knowledge of contemporary religious landscapes.

CONCLUSION

While several scholars have criticized survey methodologies for having too few and/or poorly theorized 'secular' categories (Bruce

2002: 193) and for treating the unreligious as a largely undifferentiated mass (e.g. Campbell 2013; Pasquale 2007; O'Brian Baker and Smith 2009), there has been little research into how people actually understand the common categories—'not religious', 'non-religious', 'atheist', 'agnostic', 'humanist', 'secular', 'rationalist', 'freethinker', 'secularist'—of which they make use. The discursive study of non-religion, similar to the discursive study of religion that James A. Beckford (2003; 2012) and others have encouraged, is therefore helpful, as are other qualitative methodologies for interpreting these 'hospital-clipboard' categories. As a result of this work, commonplace representations such as 'atheism', 'not religious', 'non-religious', and 'indifferent to religion' emerge as much more than negative and purely reactive classifications. Instead, in the British context, these identifications are shaped by and reflect an understanding of the secular as insubstantial and, at the same time, are augmented by people to indicate much richer and autonomous non-religious commitments. As a result, terms that appear to 'disaffiliate' people from cultural forms take on concrete characteristics so that they compete with more explicitly positive identities such as 'humanist', while the insubstantial secular becomes more relevant, in these cases, as an emic rather than an etic form.

This work corroborates other indications that people understand non-religious classifications in different ways and that self-classifications are unreliable as predictors of other aspects of non-religious subjectivities (Bullivant 2008a; Gibson and Barnes 2011a; 2011b). Indeed, the large discrepancy between the number of people who say that they do not believe in God and who identify themselves as 'atheist', which Bullivant (2010: 114) gives as a ratio of 28 to 5, is also illustrative of complexities surrounding apparently self-evident non-religious identifications. But this work also draws attention to the way that the insubstantial secular has impacted on non-religious identifications in general. When people say they are not religious and not theistic, then, they tend to mean that they are not religious and not theistic in *particular ways*. Even when they say they are extensively uninterested in such matters, they again typically have particular religious forms in mind that they are either not interested in or reject outright. Understanding this not only provides the opportunity to typologize meanings associated with different categories, but highlights the problematic effects of relying on positively inscribed negative identifications. The negativity of these categories appears—especially in the context of this volume—to be bound up with the banality and hiddenness of non-religious cultural forms, meaning that these forms are neither subjected to as much critical attention as they deserve, nor made visible in a way that would help people develop articulated self-understandings and know where to turn for social and symbolic resources when they need them. As we have seen, some non-religious people are equipped with these understandings, but some are not: in contrast to more extreme accounts, the nature of non-religiosity in the UK seems to reflect a more mixed experience, so that the non-religious do identify themselves and others in constructive ways, but are also sometimes lacking codified forms that are sufficiently detailed and sufficiently visible to mediate between people in all the ways that might be required of them.

Building on the discussion of social life in the last chapter, then, this work shows the wider significance of understanding the non-religious in socio-cultural terms. In the UK at least, non-religion is a useful example of the decentralized cultures and communities that are such a central concern to sociologists and others thinking about the particular challenges that modernity poses in terms of the age-old struggle for equilibrium between individual autonomy and a fulfilling communal life.

7

Beyond Unbelief

Non-Religion and Existential Culture

The idea that 'secular moderns' find substitutes for religious practice and belief is commonplace in both academic and popular discourses. The 'Football is my Religion' slogan discussed earlier in the book is one manifestation of this view. The idea of football as an analogy to religion is found in everyday discourses and owes something to the Durkheimian functionalist tradition in the social sciences, which explores the ends that religious thought and culture have served and the extent to which these ends may be fulfilled by other means. But a wide array of substitutes for religion has been suggested. Indeed, literary critic Terry Eagleton (2014: 44) has recently argued that the widespread 'displacement of divinity' is one characteristic of the modern period. For Eagleton, 'the history of the modern age is among other things the search for a viceroy for God', and 'Reason, Nature, *Geist*, culture, art, the sublime, the nation, the state, science, humanity, Being, Society, the Other, desire, the life force and personal relations: all of these have acted from time to time as forms of displaced divinity'.

This chapter corroborates the view that alternatives to at least some aspects of religious culture can be found outside religious traditions. However, instead of looking to secular domains as the above examples do—that is, to phenomena that can be identified independently of religion (football as a sporting activity, for example, or nationalism as a political ideology)—this chapter draws attention to a set of phenomena that has been much more closely tied to the concept of religion. These phenomena are described in this chapter as *existential cultures*. Existential cultures incarnate ideas about the origins of life and human consciousness and about how both are transformed or expire after death—what have been called 'ultimate questions' in the literature before now. These existential beliefs are bound up with distinctive notions of meaning and purpose in life, as well as with epistemological theories about how it is that humans are able to take a stance on existential matters. Finally, these existential positions are manifest in particular ethical practices—not the unspecified ethics imagined when people speak of 'religion and ethics', but ethics that can be identified concretely as anchored in existential principles and cultures and distinct from other ethical forms.

This is a return to belief, then, but not to the religionized and Christianized orthodox beliefs (and orthodox unbeliefs) that frequently take centre stage in Western social scientific research. Moreover, while belief and philosophy are used to identify distinct existential cultures, this return to belief seeks to highlight the ways in which thought is manifest in and is a manifestation *of* cultural traditions and social relations. Unreligious existential commitments are not always significantly intellectual in practice—just as religious ones are not always driven by theology. People come to existential cultures, religious or otherwise, for non-intellectual reasons: they might participate in existential rituals because those rituals are favoured by friends and family, or because they are the only ones locally available; they might belong to existential communities out of habit or out of need. In fact, people become involved in cultures of all sorts for diverse reasons—economic, social, emotional, political, and so on—and they often do so incidentally to intellectual goals and interests. Yet the existential helps understand and demarcate these engagements, just as territorial claims and constructions give form to the notion of nationalism even when they do account for people's participation in specific nationalist cultures and movements.

Despite blurred boundaries and complicated, multidimensional realities, the concept of existential culture is also presented as one possible way of identifying a distinct set of practices and 'a particular type of social behaviour' (Weber 1993:1) that is inclusive of so-called secular populations alongside religious ones and may operate alongside existing categories—occupational cultures and familial ones, territorial cultures and economic ones, ethnic cultures and existential ones. Existential ideas and their manifestation in cultural forms and social relations also play a central role in religion and alternative spirituality, but this chapter is situated against the prevailing assumption that they are *solely* manifest in these traditions. This chapter seeks to show that existential issues are still relevant and still ritualized outside religious settings. In so doing, however, it draws attention to important similarities between religious, spiritual, and non-religious experiences, while keeping the important differences between them in view. It also examines the relationship between unreligious existential cultures and non-religious discourses. People have numerous reasons for describing themselves non-religiously, that is, in contradistinction to religion—to express political positions, cultural divisions, ideas of legitimate religiosity and non-religiosity that emerge in relation to secularism, and so on. Without, then, conflating unreligious existential cultures with non-religiosity, this chapter draws attention to the significant ways in which non-religious distinctions are animated by existential commitments.

The chapter proceeds by providing a general outline of the five types of existential culture identified in this analysis—the humanist, agnostic, theist, subjectivist, and anti-existential—before providing examples from fieldwork to illustrate different ways in which existential cultures can manifest. Because this typology is empirically grounded, emerging from a sense of *lived* existential cultures, it is developed with a strong sense of the messy and ambivalent nature of existential cultures in practice. The distinct existential cultural types described here are frequently combined in everyday life, and different orientations may be more or less salient in different moments and contexts. It is impossible to describe most people according to a single type, though one or other orientation may come to the fore at times. It is certainly difficult to understand the effects of different existential cultures in the straightforward terms presented in more theoretical accounts, such as the idea that all humanists are lost souls, for example; or that all of those with a romantic, non-theistic disposition revel in pain and death (Taylor 2007). Instead, existential cultures are recognized here as having diverse effects, including the capacity to support human and social well-being alongside the capacity to damage both.

EXISTENTIAL CULTURES TYPOLOGY

The types of existential culture identified in this research have something in common with work that differentiates theocentric and anthropocentric orientations, and theist, humanist, and romantic orientations but identifies five types in total. These types are as follows.

Humanism

The first existential culture is perhaps the one most commonly associated with 'secular' philosophies. The notion of humanism arising from this empirical work involves an idea of existence as purely material and an emphasis on humanity as a whole, as special and as a repository of existential, including moral knowledge. So, for example, people of this disposition used terms such as 'inbuilt', 'innate', and 'genetic' to justify moral judgements and believe that individuals can find this knowledge within themselves only because it is universal to the human species as a whole. Humanism is, then, about respect for other people *qua* humans and it is this centrality of the human species that makes sense of the concept 'humanism'.

The valorization of humanity is expressed in other ways, too. This orientation places, for example, particular emphasis on science and the scientific method as a peculiarly human art: the scientific concept of 'objective truth' is arrived at, after all, by testing claims made by individuals to determine if these would be true according to the perception of humans in general. The humanist epistemology rejects subjective knowledge claims as well as theist ones (described later), and celebrates the knowledge that humans have accumulated over time. The veneration of humanity and its ability to generate knowledge and control its environment plays a central role in the aesthetics of this culture, too, as do images of that environment and of the human being itself. Humanism emphasizes also the knowability of the world, and the possibility of reducing complexity—not necessarily denying the existence of complexity and the unknown, but motivated by and finding meaning in what humanity can do to master it. Ethically, humanism implies a prioritization of genetic resources and rational deliberation between humans to make moral decisions, involving some reliance on individual intuitions because these are not perceived to be subjective so much as a way of accessing the inherent ability of humanity to act well.

Grand narratives about meaning, purpose, and the afterlife relate to contributing to humanity's collective knowledge, sometimes called 'science', sometimes 'progress', sometimes described more vaguely in terms of making the world a better place. Contributing to the accumulated body of human knowledge, broadly conceived, informs a sense of legacy and, through contributing to this transcendent body of knowledge, gives the individual an afterlife of a sort. Humanism is, as philosophers have observed, teleological and Hegelian in the sense that perfect knowledge is conceived of as an end point, albeit an end point that people see as unreachable. But it has resonances, too, with widespread ideas of improvement, perfectibility, and, indeed, salvation. The distinguishing feature is not, therefore, a modernist narrative of progress—and in fact it is important to emphasize that all of these existential cultures can take optimistic and pessimistic forms—but rather the association of progress with human knowledge. In other words, humanism is not so much characterized by an interest in human flourishing, as Taylor (2007) puts it, as it is by a particular conception of what human flourishing entails.

This notion of humanism builds on existing philosophical conceptions and captures something of what terms such as 'scientism' and 'rationalism' are getting at when they are applied to examples of this existential culture. The epistemological conviction that scientific methods are the most significant or even sole source of legitimate knowledge can be a feature of this orientation, as can the engagement with scientific cultures as sources of meaning and enjoyment. Rationalism, which has come to be associated with non-religious cultures in popular discourses, describes an approach that can also be manifest in religious cultures (Martin 1990: 488–9). But humanism does frequently exhibit rationalism in its focus on and faith in humans to know the world through systematic thought, as well as through their innate faculties. Hence, the concept of humanism gets to the heart of the matter, but keys into other, I would argue, subsidiary aspects of this existential orientation.

Agnosticism

The second existential culture that I encountered in the field I have called agnosticism. Like humanism, agnosticism is a materialist perspective that conceives of scientific methods as the most legitimate means by which humans can know the world. In contrast to humanists, however, agnostics consider that this knowledge of the world is profoundly limited. Thus, although humanism and agnosticism share similar outlooks in some respects, there are important differences. Where humanism emphasizes what humanity knows, agnostics emphasize what humanity does not and actually cannot know. Instead of experiences of discovery and tangibility, the emphasis is on the connectedness of people and things, complexity and contingency. Concomitantly, focus is shifted from humanity to a wider network of people, animals, and things. Coined by T. H. Huxley (1825–1895) in 1869, the concept of 'agnosticism', which has specifically emerged in the non-religious cultural field, is helpful here for capturing the view that humans are without (*a-*) knowledge of forces that transcend humanity (*gnosis*). Yet, paradoxically, this philosophy provides its own transcendent understanding of life and experience.

Given the emphasis on complexity and irreducibility it may not be surprising that this existential culture has less obvious expressions in symbolic form, and agnostics often struggle to or actively resist identifying themselves or objectifying their outlook in other ways. Whereas people with humanist inclinations often described themselves in more explicit terms, as 'atheist' or 'humanist', people involved in agnostic cultures were amongst those who identified themselves as 'not religious' in what they conceived of as general terms. Complexity, connectivity, and unknowability could also be objectified, in similarly general terms, as 'love', 'energy', and 'mystery'—as 'some arbitrary nurturing goodness', in one woman's words—or in the stated pleasures of the ineffable. Agnostic cultures celebrate the limits of knowledge and narrativize the importance of the experiential over the investigative—the sensual aspects of being and moving through the world rather than the intellectual pursuit of knowing and understanding it. This form of romanticism was, however, distinct from others which narrativize experience of the unknown and sensual in reference of an external, knowledgable agent (theism) and from those that elevate individual experience to a form of legitimate knowledge (subjectivism).

In terms of ethics, this agnostic attitude was associated with relativism. Agnostics problematized categories of 'right' and 'wrong', for example, and viewed morality as a constructed phenomenon. Crudely put, where humanists emphasized 'nature', agnostics emphasized 'nurture'. This relativism was, however, positioned in opposition to subjectivist forms of relativism because agnostics have a more radical sense of the illegitimacy of knowledge claims. Though agnosticism identifies the fundamental contingency of knowledge claims and calls for these claims to be understood in context, the idea of limited knowledge itself is a central and absolute fixture in this existential culture. The agnostic is permanently sceptical of those claiming extensive knowledge, whether the claim is that knowledge has been objectively, subjectively, or authoritatively acquired.

This distinction between humanist and agnostic models of existential culture has received some initial support from statistical work conducted in Germany. Schnell and Keenan's (2011) work with 'atheists' differentiates between three types: 'low-commitment atheists', typified by meaninglessness and crises of meaning (discussed in relation to that 'anti-existential' type discussed later); 'broad-commitment atheists', who emphasize well-being, community, love, self-knowledge, freedom, and individualism, and set less store by knowledge and reason; and 'self-actualization atheists', who have a knowledge-based world-view shaped by individualism and an interest in self-knowledge, but particularly focused on the satisfactions of reason. These latter two types have strong similarities to the agnostic and humanist types respectively, and point to tensions between them: between non-rationalist and rationalist atheist cultures, and between gender divisions that see women more likely to be of the broad commitment or agnostic type and men more likely to be of the self-actualization or humanist type (Schnell and Keenan 2011: 74). The differences between these two groups cut across, as Schnell and Keenan say, simple connections between rationalism, science, and secularity, as well as other correlations—between men and non-religiosity, for example, or any other correlation based on a binary religious/unreligious distinction.

Theism and Subjectivism

As well as three existential cultures that particularly come into view as a result of working with so-called secular populations—humanism, agnosticism, and the anti-existential (discussed later)—some participants expressed positions that did not fit into these frameworks and had more in common with religious and alternatively spiritual cultures. In addition, several other participants articulated their existential orientations in contradistinction to these other modes. Drawing on these data as well as helpful approaches in the literatures dealing with religion and alternative spirituality, I developed an account of the theist and subjectivist existential cultures which, alongside the humanist, agnostic, and anti-existential, complete the picture when it comes to the existential cultures encountered in the field.

Theism understands the origins and outcome of life in terms of a centralized, autonomous being. While humanists see humanity as the repository of existential knowledge, theists associate existential knowledge with this external being. The distinctive existential feature of alternative spirituality is its subjectivism. As in agnosticism, alternative spirituality tends to see the physical world as a complex and connected network. However, where agnostics translate connectivity into scepticism, alternative spirituality translates it into the idea of individual experience as a central way of knowing.

In interviews, some participants discussed theist and subjectivist modes in positive terms, while others distanced themselves from religious and spiritual cultures according to the idea of a pre-given, that is, theist approach to the existential or to subjectivist claims. For example, Leila, a 19-year-old woman just finishing her studies and describing herself as an 'atheist', talked about her frustration with a close friend who would justify her views according to her own experience. Leila, whose orientation largely conformed to the humanist mode, found this prioritizing of individual experience and of subjective epistemology difficult to cope with and it was a source of tension in an otherwise close relationship.

Notwithstanding a possible subjectivist turn in how we think about *religion* (Luckmann 1967, in Woodhead 2011), the theist and subjectivist existential cultures described here are informed by some existing notions of 'religion' and 'spirituality' in the literature. In particular, I have drawn on Heelas and Woodhead's (2005: 3) distinction between religion as 'life-as' and spirituality as 'subjective-life', in which the former is described as life lived according to externally prescribed roles, as 'dutiful wife, father, husband, strong leader, self-made man, etc.' and the latter as 'life lived in deep connection with the unique experiences of myself-in-relation'. Their idea of religion as an experience of an 'objective' or external other as the point of authority for truth claims (Heelas and Woodhead 2005: 5–6) can be understood in terms of the idea of theism outlined here. Bringing unreligious populations into the frame draws out interesting similarities between theism and humanism in terms of a centralized and external notion of existential authority, for example, both of which can be seen as distinct from the decentralized vision incorporated into both subjectivist and agnostic existential modes.

As well as work that understands religion and spirituality in ways that are very close to the notion of existential cultures suggested here, some scholars, especially philosophers, have proposed models in which religious and non-religious cultures are treated as ontologically similar. Charles Taylor's (2007) pluralist vision of secularity does this, for example, identifying three philosophical orientations, one religious, two non-religious, that make up the 'secular age'. Taylor's types derive from Western philosophical traditions, as critics highlight and Taylor concedes, and include a humanist type ('exclusive humanism'), a materialist Romantic type ('immanent counter-Enlightenment'), and a Christianized theist type.

Taylor's two non-religious modes have a lot in common with the humanist and agnostic modes I outline, but Taylor provides much thicker descriptions of both that are not always flexible enough to describe the orientations and experiences I encountered. For example, Taylor's humanists are unable to cope with mortality, whereas his 'post-Schopenhaureian' Romantics revel in concepts of death and suffering. In this study, however, several humanists expressed equanimity and contentment in relation to their understanding of mortality and its implications in terms of meaning and purpose in life. On the other hand, there was not much evidence of anyone—agnostic Romantics, or otherwise—taking pleasure in oblivion and pain. Instead, this account of *lived* existential cultures is much more emphatic of the ambivalent—of the possibility of positive and negative effects.

It is interesting that, though Taylor is critical of the idea of the insubstantial secular, he still conceives of materialist existential cultures in terms of loss: these cultures are defined by 'the sense of an absence' which, in his view, is concomitant with a 'sense that all order, all meaning comes from us'; and exclusive humanism encourages a killing off of transcendent sensibilities and is therefore 'a victory for darkness' (Taylor 2007: 376). Yet, working with materialist existential cultures via empirical methods calls attention to the way in which a sense that 'all meaning comes from us' involves a cultural transformation, rather than exhibiting the sad residue that is left over when the transcendent has been cast off. More than that, this work actually suggests that existential cultures, theist or otherwise, have, in a certain sense, a conception of the transcendent. Each culture involves superempirical, metaphysical, or 'supersocial' (Woodhead 2011) abstractions about the world, which necessarily transcend the empirical, physical, and the social. These are objectified into universalized forms—natural laws, mathematical formulae, notions of connectivity, and so on, with which people then commune. Several respondents talked about experiences of awe in response to physical complexity or magnitude—in considering the human brain, for example, or observing an expansive landscape from a mountain top. Such moments provide people with opportunities to commune with what the individual experiences as a transcendent truth but this truth is expressed according to different existential frames. For example, one interviewee said that, when confronted with such phenomena, she experienced a profound sense of a creator of super-human capacity as the only way of making sense of these awe-inspiring, incomprehensible realities. By contrast, those of a more agnostic orientation described revelling in this same incomprehensibility. The humanist response was different still: one interviewee recounted a point made by Dawkins that understanding the processes that give rise to extraordinary material phenomena such as a rainbow deepens their amazingness. In direct experiences of the awe-inspiring, what took her breath away was that such apparently incomprehensible forms had been made sense of. The 'sublime' provided a gateway to the natural laws that humans, fantastically, have come to understand.

In these ways, being confronted with similar material phenomena was refracted through different existential cultures and provided comparable but distinct opportunities for communion with transcendent 'truths'. Thus, the social scientific study of existential cultures encourages and deepens philosophically informed approaches such as Taylor's and complicates binary approaches to the religious and secular. This binary is actually expressed through several overlapping binaries, with the aesthetic, experiential, intuitive, non-empirical, metaphysical, and transcendent on the one hand and the explanatory, scientific, empirical, physical, and immanent on the other—distinctions bound up with the idea of the cultural religious and the insubstantial secular. The existential cultures described here do not fall neatly into one or other side of this divide, but exhibit shared and distinctive characteristics that cut across it.

The Anti-Existential

As well as humanistic, agnostic, theist, and subjectivist frames, an additional and more ambiguous orientation emerged in this research. This attitude primarily involved the rejection of existential philosophies and cultures in general. This was expressed in a number of ways. Some people struggled to understand why anyone would care about theological questions enough to uphold them or dispute them; others resisted thinking about life in terms of implications and meaning. Instead of paying attention to abstractions that transcend the material world and are metaphysical in that sense, these responses emphasized the immediate—everyday needs, responsibilities, and pleasures.

Throughout this research, I struggled with how to understand these practical, social, and intellectual refutations of the existential, and remain uncertain. On the face of it, the rejection of any and all existential cultural frameworks—as a basis for understanding or narrativizing birth and death, or for thinking about how humans relate to one another in their shared environments—appears to differ quantitatively rather than qualitatively from the humanist, agnostic, theist, and subjectivist existential cultures: these people do not care about or participate in an alternative existential culture but rather care about and participate in existential cultures less. To that extent, the anti-existential—or unexistential as it might be more correctly termed if this interpretation is the right one—may be a manifestation of secularity as it is understood here, as a subordination of religious and 'religious-like' concerns. This notion of the unexistential mirrors what Tatjana Schnell (2010) has termed 'existential indifference' and observed in her Germany-based research.

But it is also possible to argue that an anti-existential stance actually rests on existential claims. It may be that the ostensible rejection of existential cultures involves a deep affirmation of the material as opposed to the ideal, such that the immediate and the immanent are all that matters, and the existential is void of meaning and an indulgent distraction. It is also the case that the anti-existential has concrete effects and is a substantive form in that sense. So, for example, this stance implies that ethical issues are attended to intuitively and pragmatically, according to immediate rather than abstract concerns. Anti-existential stances might also be expressed in social conventions, such as the restriction of existential cultural practice in specified places or relationships, or the denigration of existential others as, for example, unproductive, misguided, or superficial. The rejection of existential life is meaning-giving, too, with a sense of purpose derived from the fulfilment of the individual's immediate needs and the needs of others around them—a sense of purpose that has its own ethical and aesthetic dimensions. In addition, following the relational logic presented throughout this book, we can highlight the way that people of anti-existential perspectives are confronted with the existential cultures described here, yet are able to maintain their anti-existential attitude. This suggests some kind of commitment to the anti-existential orientation. Billig (1995) says that everyone is a nationalist because everyone lives in a world of nations; in the same way, we may conceive of everyone as existential because everyone lives in a world of existential cultures.

There is, however, one clear difference between the anti-existential attitude and the other existential orientations described here. The contrast is between existential cultures that propose some kind of abstract force that transcends human life—natural laws, the ineffable, centralized 'higher powers', or the elevation of subjectivity as a higher truth—and the absence of these abstractions in the anti-existential orientation. This distinction raises interesting and, to my mind, open and complicated questions about where the boundary between transcendent and immanent truly lies, as well as new possibilities for understanding what underlies non-religious positionings in order to reimagine the secular.

These issues are socially and politically significant, as well as theoretical. They impact, for example, on how people and practices are included and protected in the law. Egalitarian approaches to religion (Laborde 2014a) have drawn attention to broader, generic characteristics—such as having a conception of the good life, participating in 'meaning-giving' cultures (MacLure and Taylor 2011) or believing, widely conceived—as ways to extend to others the protections that have been offered to the religious. These suggestions have been surrounded by debates about how to evaluate claims to 'meaning-giving' cultures or beliefs, imperfectly resolved by the use of sincerity to decide on the legitimacy of such claims (Laborde 2014b). Not only is there a problem here to do with whether habitual practices can be protected as well as 'sincerely held' beliefs (Laborde 2014b), but there is also an issue of inclusion that arises for people like 'anti-existentials' who may profess to have no sincere belief at all.

There is a more general egalitarian concern at stake here, too. There is, as we have seen, a long history of understanding religion and secularity in some kind of hierarchical relationship, and sensitivity to this should make us wary of understanding certain experiences as unequal rather than different—as 'unexistential' rather than 'anti-existential'. Recognizing 'non-religious' existential cultures alongside 'religious' ones unsettles a rationalist explanation of secularization in which people turn to religious cultures when they need comfort or because they are, to use Norris and Inglehart's (2004) phrase, 'existentially insecure', because these other existential cultures appear to be equally capable of providing this comfort. Identifying some outlooks as less existential may open up new lines of critical analysis concerning the unequal distribution of meaning-making resources, associated in new research with differential health outcomes (Schnell 2010), but it may also reopen condescending and often classed ways of thinking about existential cultures. One established line of prejudice precisely concerns those who neither engage with religious nor non-religious cultures, who are 'given up to low sensual indulgence' (*Congregational Year Book*, in Kitson Clark 1965: 164). In less pejorative tones, scholars continue to associate interest in the existential with higher levels of education and intellectualism. Phil Zuckerman (2008: 68–9), for example, has questioned whether Weberian, rational choice, and other approaches to religion are right to prioritize issues of meaning, arguing that such concerns may be of interest only to a very small number of people with a high degree of education:

> I started to think that perhaps for maybe a very small, select proportion of humanity existential questions of the ultimate meaning of life are of constant, visceral concern and that these types of people perhaps do ponder the matter deeply and for long periods of time. And they probably go on to get degrees in philosophy or religious studies. And they are probably not like most people. (Zuckerman 2008: 73)

This is an important proposition to consider, and it brings issues of power and class to the fore. Related arguments include Langmead Casserley's (in Campbell 2013: 71) view that irreligion is a class ideology for the middle classes, involving an intellectualized form of retreat as well as an intellectualized mode of distinction from the indifferent working classes. On the other hand, the existential is a part of daily life, not in the abstract, but in our direct and indirect experiences of birth, death, and ill-health, and in the ethical decisions we make about the value of human life in our responses to an array of personal and political issues such as abortion, euthanasia, murder, and war. Thinking of meaning-making, not as a narrow, philosophical practice but as something enacted in multiple ways, small and large, in everyday life calls into question the idea that large groups of people can be easily located outside the existential cultural field. If it is the case that such a group exists, there is an acute need for careful sociological, anthropological, and critical accounts of it.

EXISTENTIAL CULTURES IN PRACTICE

This notion of existential cultures emerged through a process of inductive analysis as I attempted to understand the different experiences and accounts that I was encountering. These existential commitments were rarely expressed in developed, abstract propositions. Rather, existential cultures tend to emerge through fragments of articulated belief and also in accounts of real-world encounters of various sorts. The following examples illustrate how existential cultures are formed in and through practice and how different cultural frames are combined in creative and self-contradictory ways—how existential cultures are *lived*.

Everyday Abstractions

Victoria, an editor in her late twenties, described herself as 'non-religious' and as an 'atheist' and she associated herself with agnostic as well as humanist and anti-existential positions. After preliminary discussions of this project, I arranged to interview Victoria in her London flat. I had given her some examples of the questions I might ask her before the interview, and when I asked her whether the concept of the 'sacred' had any meaning for her, Victoria said I had mentioned this before and that she had been giving it some thought. She had been wondering, she said, 'was there anything?' 'And', she said, 'this sounds really cheesy, but when you said that, the first thing I thought of was *love*.' Victoria said the word 'love' self-consciously, and laughed. Continuing, she said, 'But then I thought, [...] how is that sacred? And I don't exactly know what I mean by that. But it's something about, like...' and at this point, Victoria broke off in emotion, and we discussed whether or not to continue the interview. She brushed this off, and resumed, more calmly:

> It's something about the bond or something, between people. [Some friends were talking about] whether love was material, or something, and it just seemed really, like, *sacrilegious* to me, to say that love was material, or something. Because I suppose I imagine that—like, to me it seems really sort of ineffable or something, the way I imagine a sort of religious person would sort of feel about, I don't know, God or faith or something. Yeah, I suppose that's what it's like: it's kind of like a sort of faith because [...] it's really important or something, and you don't quite—sometimes you have to [...] kind of go with it, even if you're feeling unsure.

Victoria's speech was typical of many others who made faltering attempts to articulate commitments that appeared, nevertheless, to carry meaning and emotional weight. And it is from speeches like this that a sense of existential frames emerge. In this case, the thread of the agnostic is visible in the value Victoria gives to the intangible. For Victoria, describing something that she thinks of as fundamentally 'ineffable' as having concrete, material form profanes it. While celebrating the 'ineffable', she does, on the other hand, offer an objectification of this same form: it concerns connectedness; 'love'; 'the bond between people'—giving her philosophy a humanistic inflection at this point in her focus on people to the exclusion of non-human animals and objects. Though she lends it no supernatural agency, Victoria's concept of 'love' is something that transcends the material and is extra-empirical. It is a way of understanding and experiencing the world that is beyond question, not a matter for investigation but of 'faith'.

In another example, Victoria's discussion of morality drew on agnosticism, again with a humanistic inflection. In considering the question of how she might assess whether an action is right or wrong, she says:

> Well, I suppose [that judgement would be] by instinct in this case. I mean, it's been ingrained in you from, like, such a young age, through, you know, nature and nurture, whatever—well, I suppose mostly nurture; I don't know if it's anything to do with nature.

The humanistic inclination to 'instinct' and 'nature' shifts to a more agnostic, relativistic focus on nurture and socialization. And, in giving closer attention to whether murder might be conceived of as right or wrong, Victoria's morality becomes more expressly agnostic, in which murder is wrong because nobody has the knowledge and authority to empower themselves over others:

> I feel strongly that [murder is] wrong. Like, well, I think there's obviously gradations, like, if it's like a woman who's been raped by her husband for years on end, then she murders him, that's like less wrong—probably still wrong, but, like, just totally justifiable. Um, but, I just feel—yeah—that it's wrong for one person, or a group of people, whatever, to take someone else's life. [. . .] I suppose because I sort of feel like it's not, it shouldn't be *up to you*, the individual; but then again, that suggests that it *is* up to some higher power, which I don't think either.

Thus, Victoria's agnosticism largely emerges through distinctions, in rejections of subjectivist and theistic decision-making, as well as humanistic logics.

This articulation of existential culture through distinction is notable in itself. It is partly typical of the agnostic orientation, which is sceptical of labels and therefore describes positions in relative, apparently negative terms. But Victoria's faltering attempt to express existential positions is typical of many interview discussions, agnostic and otherwise. These convictions and cultures were frequently expressed, not through lofty philosophical propositions, but through everyday language and in consideration of concrete problems or situations. Several participants found articulating their views in abstract ways unfamiliar—maybe because they lack cultural resources for developing codified and reflexive moral and philosophical positions; maybe because these resources are superfluous in their day-to day-lives. At the same time, such speeches indicate firm and committed existential commitments. These are matters of 'faith' and can be understood in relation to the sacred, while challenges to these positions provoke strong emotional responses and social divisions.

Discussion with Walt, a 36-year-old from London, demonstrates a similar notion of existential culture as faith, this time in relation to humanistic commitments. In discussing how he would identify himself in relation to religion, and responding to my long list of possibly classifications, Walt had said, 'if I could choose more than one, I'd choose "atheist", "humanist", "rationalist"; I think these are most important to me'—an answer that illustrates the convergence of meanings behind apparently alternative terms discussed elsewhere

Beyond Unbelief

in this book. We talked about what appealed to him in these concepts and what the terms meant. In relation to 'humanism', Walt said:

> That is a good question. I think it is arbitrary choice on my part. I like humans. I think humans are great. [Laughs] For the most part, I think humans are intelligent and I happen personally to value intelligence. The thing with that, and why I say 'arbitrarily' [is that] in a sort of wider rational sense, I don't really believe [in] absolute values—like intelligence is good or killing people is good. I kind of believe that it's within a human-centric viewpoint, that being intelligent is good. [. . .] Intelligence is not a value that matters particularly [. . .] and, say, matters less to a dog. I suppose [what] I mean is I'm a humanist [because] I'm human-centric; I have a human viewpoint and in a sense, for me, being religious detracts from the kind of dignity of being human because you set up this boss character who's supposedly made or set down all these rules that we're supposed to follow unquestionably and that to me is rather undignified.

As with Victoria, it helps Walt to understand his humanism non-religiously, in contradistinction to the theistic notion of an external authority. There is also an agnostic inflection to Walt's humanism: in theory, he rejects absolute values and the fundamental validity of his humanism. On the other hand, he embraces and enjoys his humanism: he takes pleasure in capacities that he experiences as unique to the human species. In a strikingly self-reflexive account, Walt identifies a desire to participate in a humanist existential culture and to live in the world as a humanist. Human intelligence is at once a nonsense to Walt and a matter of deep meaningfulness.

Existential Cultures in Public Life

As this notion of existential culture developed from interview discussions, I also started to attend to expressions of it in public discourses and consider how these ostensibly non-institutional cultures might have voice in public life. New Atheist culture, for example, is a firmly humanist one and had particular currency in the years of this fieldwork. It was interesting, too, to notice expressions of agnosticism and the anti-existential in these spaces, as well as alternative humanist approaches. One example that I have used in presentation of this research comes from a feature article, published in 2010 in the *Guardian*'s glossy Saturday magazine. The piece paired 'Gods of

Science'—scientists and science communicators: Stephen Hawking, Brian Cox, Richard Dawkins, and David Attenborough. One pairing was between Sir David Attenborough, naturalist and broadcaster, and Richard Dawkins, who were both asked by the *Guardian*, 'What is the one bit of science from your field that you think everyone should know?' Attenborough says, briefly, 'the unity of life'—with a possibly agnostic emphasis on interconnectedness. Dawkins then takes up Attenborough's answer, developing it as an explicitly humanistic response. The 'bit of science' that everyone should know is, in Dawkins' view:

> The unity of life that comes about through evolution, since we're all descended from a single common ancestor. It's almost too good to be true, that on one planet this extraordinary complexity of life should have been brought about by what is pretty much an intelligible process. And we're the only species capable of understanding it.

Here, Dawkins takes up Attenborough's more open-ended comment to revel in the way humans are, in his view, able to reduce complexity. His lexicon is geared towards this task in a number of ways: the big amorphous population—'we all'—is descended from a 'single' common ancestor; the 'extraordinary complexity of life' is presented only to show how amazing it is—'almost too good to be true'—that this can be reduced to a single process; the repeated use of concepts constructing simplicity and singularity: *single* and *common* ancestry, *one* planet, the *only* species, a single process. There is also the scientifically gratuitous celebration of human knowledge—'And we're the only species capable of understanding it'—and the glorying in evolution is not just for its own sake, but is as something vastly complicated rendered 'intelligible'. Dawkins' humanism is of the archetypal—and stereotypical—non-theistic Enlightenment modernist model, with a Cartesian valorization of human knowledge as 'the only thing that makes us men and distinguishes us from the beasts' (Descartes 1988, in Badmington 2003: 16).

Attenborough and Dawkins were then asked about the most exciting moment of their careers. Again, Attenborough answered first: 'One would be', he says, 'when I first dived on a coral reef and I was able to move among a world of unrevealed complexity'. This answer is explicitly agnostic in its orientation. In marked contrast to Dawkins' joy in single, masterfully simple explanations, Attenborough observes complexity and communicates excitement in the unknown—in a complexity that is 'unrevealed'. He also stresses the sensual and experiential sides of connection, emphasizing the 'dive' and the ability to 'move among' this unknown world. In contrast, Dawkins' answer puts the human's ability to know the world at the fore: the most exciting moment of his career is, he says: 'Something to do with a puzzle being solved—things fall into place and you see a different way of looking at things which suddenly makes sense'. For both men, enjoyment is shaped by a philosophical sensibility that is not solely philosophical: these different existential cultures are experienced and excite emotion. But they do so according to different logics.

An instructive example of the anti-existential in the public sphere comes from a poem written by artist and poet Heather Phillipson. She is writing about life in the London borough of Islington and performed this poem at readings in central and north London at the time of this research. The poem explores and objectifies the limits of abstract theories of meaning in favour of lived experience. It is reproduced here in full.

'German Phenomenology Makes Me Want to Strip and
   Run through North London'

Page seven – I've had enough of *Being and Time*
and of clothing. Many streakers seek quieter locations
and Marlborough Road's unreasonably quiet tonight.
If it were winter I'd be intellectual, but it's Tuesday
and I'd rather lap the tarmac escarpment of Archway Roundabout
wearing only a rucksack. It might come in useful.
I can't take any more of Heidegger's *Dasein*-diction,
I say as I jettison my slippers.

When I speak of my ambition
it is not to be a Doctor of Letters
or to marry Friedrich Nietzsche, it turns out,
or to think better.
It is to give up this fashion for dressing.
It is to drop my robe on the communal stairs
and open the front door to the commuter hour,
my neighbour, his Labrador, and say nothing
of what I know or do not know, except what my body announces.

The poem prioritizes the immediate and the sensual, but it is not because the speaker is embracing the limits of knowledge: at least for a time, they want to 'say nothing of what [they] know or do not know', and to participate in the world another way.

These media representations of existential culture extend, then, beyond the work of New Atheist contributors. The *Guardian* discussion includes a New Atheist figurehead, but also the views of a figure feted as a 'national treasure' in the British media, warmly regarded—a mainstream and far less controversial figure than Dawkins. Phillipson's poem demonstrates how unreligious existential cultures may be visible in local cultural life and also, in its intellectualism, provides a useful corrective to an assumed association between the anti-existential and lower levels of education or intelligence—with 'low forms of sensual indulgence'. When they are not attached to any centralized and institutionalized culture, representations of existential culture may be diffuse. As such, they present a challenge for research designers. But they are an important bridge between scholars of substantive non-religious cultures, which have focused on New Atheist examples almost exclusively, and more open, theoretical discussions of a 'secular imaginary'.

'Public' and 'Private'

These latter representations of existential culture are part of the media contexts in relation to which people live their lives. Although public and elite figures such as David Attenborough and others may seem remote from the daily lives of ordinary people living in the southeast, they expressed feelings and perspectives shared by others in my interview and ethnographic research in London. So, for example, David Attenborough's joy in an 'unrevealed complexity' echoes Victoria's veneration of the ineffable. Jude, a PhD student in her thirties, drew a similar connection between the unknown and the exciting when I interviewed her in the initial Cambridge study:

> I think that at times there's a sense of knowing within myself that it's something that doesn't require scientific or rational explanation, and it works on its own regardless. [. . .] I think over-analysing that space kills it; I think belonging to religion kills it; because I prefer the idea that it's unexplained—because that makes life more exciting. [. . .] What I'm trying to say is that it's why I wouldn't be religious then, because it's the same thing as what science offers me: it offers me an end explanation. I'm not sure whether it's necessary to require an end explanation.

For Jude, as for Attenborough, the unknown is moving and meaningful, and has a vitality of its own.

In the same way, connections can be made between Walt's outlook and Dawkins'. For all the differences of their speeches, both express pleasure in human mental capacities. Elsewhere in our interview, Walt exalted in what he saw as the joyful absurdity of evolution, as well as in humanity's extraordinary abilities of creation:

> [When] I read about the brain and its effects at all, I have a sense of awe and wonder about it [and] *that* I find very pleasurable and satisfying. When I think that all this—you know, biros and paper and socialism and jazz—has come out of some chemicals [...] that happened to get hot enough to mix together and form something called life, I think that is an object of awe and wonder, in the same way that I imagine that Kevin [a religious friend] felt when he contemplated God [...]. It might happen that there might be something that sparks it off, like listening to beautiful music or reading a great book or having a smashing time with good people: I think it's wonderful that this has happened. Sometimes I really have it from, I don't know, suddenly realizing that there's a factory that makes the little porcelain dividers [...] and I think that's *so* amazing that they've come up with this funny little thing, so un-functional and that arose out of, yeah, chemicals in a pond.

Walt explained that these experiences were not constant but were 'little moments' of what William Connolly (2011: 651) calls 'gratitude in existence'. He compared these moments to something that might be experienced by Christian, Sufic, or Buddhist mystics—his emphasis on mysticism suggesting an agnostic sense of 'moving among' rather than explanation. But his pleasure follows a distinctive logic—according to models of evolution and some sense of invention, drawing on both agnostic and humanistic existential cultures. Against the idea of always anti-religious secular moderns, people like Walt drew out similarities between their own and religious experience, while also differentiating their experiences in important ways. These accounts seem distant from the 'secularist assumptions' of the 'many (if not all) social and political commentators' (Berger et al. 2008: 61–3), and, while the relationship between everyday and media accounts is certainly variable, it is probably also the case that media representations of non-religion and unreligious existential cultures extend beyond the polarizing and controversial examples that often absorb our interest.

Existential Cultures, Religion, and Non-Religion

Some of these examples illustrate how people can understand existential cultures in relation to contemporary notions of religion and non-religion. The fact that these cultures became visible in the course of interview discussions concerning religion and non-religion likewise demonstrates a perceived tie between them. Judging from these data, it seems likely that positioning the self in social space as non-religious, spiritual, or religious is, in fact, often an attempt to express underlying existential cultures. But this is not the same as saying that some existential cultures are non-religious, or that others are religious. Instead, existential cultures and religious, spiritual, and non-religious ones operate on different dimensions—sometimes in relation to each other, to be sure, but not always and not according to fixed patterns. There are, for example, types of non-religious otherness that are not expressly to do with existential culture, but instead respond to the actions of or stereotypes about religious institutions and groups. More clearly still, particular religious, spiritual, and non-religious organizations might, like the individuals discussed here, combine existential cultures in complicated ways. For example, mystical religious traditions combine elements of theist and agnostic orientations, drawing together faith in an external and autonomous power with a sense of the absolute limits of humanity to know this power. Such traditions might have more in common with materialist forms of agnosticism than they do with some other theistic ones. Likewise, people involved with the Humanist movement and its non-religious positioning, discourse, and action may participate in the humanist existential cultures described here but may also have agnostic attitudes or even anti-existential ones. These different strains of Humanism might be one reason for tensions within that movement, as in other non-religious ones. Despite some commonplace connections between particular religious and existential cultures, therefore, they are not mapped on to one another in one single way.

Because existential cultures deal with matters of the life course—related to how we come into the world, how we have children, how we live with death, and how we die—one of their key expressions is in life-cycle rituals. These often take place in religious and non-religious institutional settings, while civil ceremonies conducted outside these settings are shaped by religious and non-religious cultures as well, in content and format and in the way they are set apart from more overtly religious, spiritual, and non-religious cultural forms. Because these ceremonies do, however, reflect existential cultural positions, many people—religious and otherwise—make thoughtful decisions about what kinds of rituals to use, weighing up these issues with family, and in relation to national and other traditions. Existential cultural difference also emerged as a cause of tension surrounding these religious, spiritual, and non-religious rituals. Couples deciding if and how to perform and celebrate a marriage might take different views on the value of tradition, for example, or they might disagree on the type of narrative being told about the meaning and purpose of their marriage. People expressed particularly strong views about participating in funerals that did not reflect their own or the deceased person's existential views and cultures. Emily, for example, spoke strongly about her experiences of a cousin's funeral:

> When my cousin died last year, we went to the funeral—I *just* wanted to leave. I found the service absolutely revolting. I couldn't stand all the, 'he's now a child of god,' and 'he's now being looked after by Jesus,' and all this stuff. I just—it made me feel sick, because I didn't believe in it, at all, *and* because I was *pretty* sure [my cousin] didn't believe in it [...] I didn't believe that that was what had happened; I just believed he'd died, on his own [...]—and I didn't *believe* that there were any warm comforting arms that were looking after him. So that, for me, was sad.

While unfamiliar ideas, narratives, and rituals surrounding death can be welcome, inspiring, and soothing, they can also be intensely upsetting, especially as they occur when people are particularly vulnerable. The issue can be even more acute when the existential culture is refracted through a religious one from which people feel particularly estranged. Elsewhere in her interview, for example, Emily expressed openness and interest in learning about religious traditions in general, but said that she found it difficult to take this kind of interest or otherwise participate in the Christian religious tradition that was part of her background and against which she had differentiated her own existential and non-religious identity.

Recognizing the life-cycle rituals that take place outside traditionally religious settings is at odds with the idea that societies have experienced the loss of culture implied in ideas such as secularization and disenchantment. Social scientists have recently started to take these rituals more seriously in their work, presenting a shift away from the idea of the insubstantial secular. The idea that non-religious rituals may express different existential cultures and that the change that societies have experienced is one of cultural transformation rather than cultural decline goes even further in support of this positive approach to 'secular' life. Earlier in this volume I discuss Anthony Giddens's (1991: 204) comments on what is diminished with the decline of religious practice in the modern age. Something profound, he says, 'is lost together with traditional forms of ritual' because these rituals put people 'in touch with wider cosmic forces relating individual life to more encompassing existential issues'. Yet, societies such as the UK continue to conduct these rites in civil and non-religious contexts—that is important in itself—and it is my suggestion that these rites also continue to place participants in touch with the existential. This is not necessarily their central feature, but it is their characteristic one.

This is not even to think of the informal or 'hidden' rituals that may go on. Even in deciding *against* naming ceremonies, weddings, and funerals, the positionings, negotiations, and agreements that go into making these decisions may be important in themselves, as well as the quiet, private celebrations and commemorations that can occur as part of the process of coming to shared understandings. In these ways, it seems rash to describe 'modernization' in terms of cultural impoverishment rather than cultural change, or to say that existential and metaphysical issues and cultures are 'bracketed' from public life and political discourse as theorists such as Habermas and Rawls have suggested.

Likewise, it seems that these opportunities to participate in shared as well as personal existential cultures undercut the idea that people might turn to religion at certain crucial moments or later on in the life course. It is true that certain experiences can make the existential more pressing but, because there are, as we have seen, multiple ways of fulfilling these needs, it cannot be assumed that people will turn to religious cultures or theist existential ones in particular. Experiences of bereavement were at the fore in several of my research interviews and the acute moments of these experiences also emerged as highly creative ones, in which people developed new relationships with people and cultures, deepened existing ones, and cast off others. There was certainly no sense of unidirectional movement towards the religious. For Gavin, a retired care-worker in his sixties, the illness and death of his wife had brought him into closer contact with a local Humanist organization and precipitated the transformation of his identity from the long-held 'atheist' one he had shared with his parents and others in his family to his new 'humanist' one. He also drew on ideas from religious traditions to understand and describe his experiences—so that he might be perceived by others to be, he said, a 'mixed-up humanist'. Gavin's experience shows the diverse cultural resources available to understand existential questions and to support people through existential struggle and pain, as well as the way in which different, apparently contradictory options, refracted through religious and non-religious cultures, can be held together.

CONCLUSION

In some ways, highlighting the significance of the existential in relation to religious and non-religious life is conventional, harking back to intellectualist philosophies of religion in which religious cultures provide answers to 'ultimate questions'. And certainly these approaches have much in common. The focus on the concept of 'existential cultures' rather than 'ultimate questions' builds on the latter approach in two particular ways, however. First, focusing on the 'existential' rather than the 'ultimate' is an attempt to move away from the hierarchical approaches to religion and the secular that several scholars have identified by providing a more roundly qualitative description (the existential) rather than a comparative one (the ultimate). The idea that religious cultures deal with something that is intrinsically more important than other issues is also expressed in terms such as 'foundational', 'comprehensive', or 'transcendent', all of which have been used to describe the kinds of commitments at hand. It is not clear, however, how appropriate this is for understanding the role of existential and religious cultures in human life because, in addressing them sociologically and anthropologically, they often seem to be quite similar to our other cultural commitments: they may be expressed in philosophically 'superficial' ways—in habit, convention, aesthetic preferences, and social relations (Laborde 2014b). On the other hand, it is not clear in what sense political questions about capital punishment or arrangements for the distribution of wealth that lead to unequal health outcomes and life expectancies are less 'ultimate' or 'fundamental' than existential questions. It is also possible that people may be more deeply committed to other groups and cultures than they are to those built around existential cultures, such that being severed from the former is as profound an experience that may strike us at our core. It does not necessarily make sense, therefore, to distinguish existential cultures according to their significance or profundity.

Secondly, the concept of existential cultures attempts to make it clear that what is at stake is more than philosophical responses to philosophical questions. Rather the philosophical is incarnated in diverse and discrete symbolic forms, social formations, and everyday ethics. Existential cultures, then, can be expressed in rituals and practices, and involved not only in consolidating moral codes but expressed in embodied ethics. Often mediated through religious, spiritual, and non-religious references, these cultures are encountered in social life—something people can be born or marry into, move closer to through their friendships, or develop intersubjectively in late-night conversations at formative moments. Moreover, to the extent that these existential cultures are refracted through religion, spirituality, and non-religion, they take on all of the material, embodied, social, and public aspects that have been discussed throughout this book. Existential cultures may be meaning-giving then, to use Maclure and Taylor's (2011) phrase, but they are also lived. Thus the idea of existential cultures draws on different strands in the philosophy of religion in an approach that makes space for the intellectual but understands it in relation to its socio-cultural moorings.

The study of existential cultures may, then, provide an opportunity to broaden those aspects of religious studies that are related to it, and to integrate it with the study of 'secular' modern life from which it has stood apart. As Schnell and Keenan (2011: 75) say, 'it may be the case that what were widely thought to be 'separate' incommensurable worlds of meaning and belief—the dualistic, bifurcated worlds of religiosity and secularity (Berger, 2010; Gellner, 2003)—do, in fact, share, in the contexts of lived experience, a degree of common ground in terms of meaning and commitments'. Though it challenges the claims to power that both religious and non-religious actors have made (Fitzgerald 2000) and may encounter resistance as a result, finding this common ground presents one of the most exciting prospects that there is for the study of religion and 'secular modernity' for years to come.

Conclusion

Reimagining the Secular

So, after all, *is* modernity secular?

This volume argues that this question can only be tackled by breaking it down—by unpacking or disaggregating 'the secular' into the separate and ontologically incommensurable concepts that have been collapsed into it. Most importantly, it distinguishes between insubstantial and substantial conceptions of the secular. It points to engagements with substantial 'secularity'—as irreligion, anti-religious modes of secularism, active and activist non-theistic perspectives and cultures, and pluralist configurations of religious and non-religious cultures—and demonstrates how scholars can build on this to create a more rounded and theoretically coherent notion of the non-religious as that which exists, is expressed, or is identified in contradistinction from the religious.

This first stage of recognizing the non-religious is conceptual and methodological, consolidating the idea as a way to access and interrogate substantive features of contemporary social life that have largely been neglected by researchers and by social commentators of all sorts. In a sense, however, this work temporarily takes us further away from questions about secularity because recognizing the non-religious involves recognizing—sometimes more clearly, sometimes for the first time—a number of prior questions about the nature, variety, and pervasiveness of non-religion, all of which are necessary if we are to distinguish this phenomenon from secularity and compare their scale and significance. This work poses questions about 'indifference to religion' as a category, and the ambiguity surrounding whether 'indifference' implies a degree of remoteness from religious, spiritual, and non-religious concerns or a form of rejection that is embedded, embodied, and taken for granted. Certainly, this research suggests that representations of indifference cannot be taken at face value and require much closer scrutiny. In order to compare the significance of non-religiosity and non-religionization processes to secularity and secularization processes, then, we need deeper, empirically grounded accounts of what non-religious cultures actually involve—a question that requires methodological creativity, as several researchers have noted, and which also requires the accumulation of initial knowledge so that new methods can be developed incrementally.

Central to this work are questions about how non-religious cultures impact on religious ones, and vice versa, which need attention before we can assess rival theories of the secular that ascribe different roles not only to the religious but to the non-religious and alternatively spiritual too. New accounts of 'religious' plurality and pluralism such as Charles Taylor's (2007) show how non-religious cultures can be brought into and taken seriously within models for understanding contemporary societies and psyches, while renewed interest in non-religious secularist movements revives a question that Colin Campbell (2013) raised so many decades ago about the role of these activists in bringing about secularization through social and political struggle with certain religious actors—and, we might suggest, with certain alternatively spiritual and non-religious actors, too. All of these investigations of the non-religious will give rise to new, next, and subsidiary questions that will also require some attention. The idea proposed here, for example, that religious, spiritual, and non-religious cultures can be understood as forms of existential culture, all providing viable responses—salient ideas, satisfying socio-cultural experiences—to what have been termed 'ultimate questions' is a hypothesis that requires further testing. Were it established, this would generate subsequent questions about the relationship between *these* cultures and secularity and secularism.

Such qualitative studies that we have—be they of unbelief and materialism, organized non-religious groups, or existential cultures—indicate, in their very richness and detail, the vast potential of the study of non-religious beliefs and practices, and how limited our current empirical knowledge is. Recognizing the non-religious is in large part about recognizing how open this field of enquiry is. This volume has sought to facilitate this enquiry by considering and identifying some of the ways in which human life *can* be non-religious, giving particular attention to manifestations beyond the primarily philosophical and political that have been focused on elsewhere. This volume seeks to build on such contributions in two ways: by locating cases of organized non-religious culture in relation to more diffuse, less codified forms; and by taking up the multidimensional approach that is encouraged by anthropologists of religion.

First, this volume challenges ideas about the location of active non-religion in society by steering away from intellectual and anti-religious expressions as well as highly visible cases such as secularist lobby organizations and local social and activist meet-up groups. Instead, it emphasizes everyday engagements with religious, spiritual, and non-religious 'others' and the quiet performances of the self as non-religious that take place in interaction with but also independently from those others. Unremarkable displays of non-religion in material environments, bodies, and social relations may be, I argue, as important as the more exotic expressions of non-religion that occur in small moments and bright colours, to adapt Billig's (1995: 6) phrase, such as the crystallizing and memorable moments that punctuate much more protracted processes of becoming non-religious, or the high-profile 'god wars' that have taken centre stage in media coverage. It is often through banal forms and hidden solidarities that cultures are at their most influential in human life, woven into the social as taken-for-granted norms. In addition to the study of more widely recognized non-religious cultural movements, therefore, this volume suggests that equal consideration be given to the more subtle forms of non-religious culture that may also underlie and even undergird so-called secular society.

Building on the work of Quack (2011) and others, this volume draws attention to the way that non-religious activism is a cultural as well as intellectual movement and therefore has, like other non-religious culture, local inflections that effect its passage through societies. As Colin Campbell (2013) says, non-religious cultures emerge in relation to religious ones and they therefore take on characteristics and logics of the very cultures to which they are set in contrast. Grace Davie (2012: 260) has used France and Norway as an instructive comparison of the ways in which these nations' 'communities of unbelief' are formed as 'mirror images' of their respective state churches—and makes the intriguing proposal that non-religious cultures may have been stymied in the US precisely because there is no state church for them to replicate. Anna Strhan (2014) and Matthew Engelke (2013) have explored the way that British non-religious organizations emerge in relation to and often in explicit dialogue with religious ones, as a result of which these non-religious cultures are expressed in languages and with foci that facilitate their relationships with certain actors while simultaneously making them unintelligible or unsympathetic to others. Engagements between public intellectuals—establishment figures in the main—that form the large part of the contemporary 'god wars' between New Atheists and 'Old Theists' are an example of this: even though these engagements can be antagonistic, they are based on shared assumptions about what religion is and on common lines of interest and modes of address. By the same token, this 'war' may be less intelligible and appealing to people who do not share those same assumptions and tastes. Indeed, the significance of shared culture to understanding the diffusion of non-religious ideas has been observed in geographic clustering effects (Voas and McAndrew 2012). This volume lends weight to the view that social scientific approaches to understanding provocative and fascinating non-religious cultures such as New Atheism are therefore necessary alongside intellectual interlocutions.

Related to this, this work builds on contributions especially from anthropology in highlighting the ways in which diverse and sometimes diffuse non-religious cultures are expressed not only as sets of ideas, but are manifest also in material environments, bodies, patterns of associations, aesthetic pleasures, and symbolic forms. Ideas influence our lives, directly and indirectly, but the material, embodied, symbolic, and social have structuring effects of their own—effects that may not be all that closely related to intellectual ones. The impact of the same non-theist sentiment is quite different when it is presented on the side of a soap bottle rather than the side of a city bus. What is more, the ways in which non-religion is expressed are much more diverse than most accounts of the 'secular' have imagined. Indeed, a cultural approach to non-religion can be challenging because it unsettles established ways of thinking about secularity as insubstantial and, at the same time and paradoxically, as intellectual—conceptions of the secular that are themselves lived and embodied. Objecting to my suggestion that people might not only share their non-religious cultures with those around them but also therefore be non-religious at least partially as a result of these shared experiences, one woman accepted the logic but exclaimed, 'But it *feels* rational!'—a succint expression of the embodiment of ideas. Nevertheless, as sociologists of knowledge, science, and politics have demonstrated, recognizing ideas as inseparable from social and cultural life deepens our understanding of them and opens up new lines of critical engagement with the complicated material, social, and intellectual dynamics that produce them.

The suggestion of this work is, then, that, almost regardless of whether they are secular or not, so-called modern societies such as the UK may be significantly non-religious. This means that some of the experiences and appetites of a more religious age remain, but that they now revolve around new cultures that have emerged as alternatives to religious ones and are frequently expressed in contrast to them. It is misleading to describe those 'secular moderns' as 'areligious', as experiencing life quite without religion, but it is equally problematic to describe them as 'religious'; to do so is to obscure differences between these and religious lives that are analytically and ethnographically meaningful. Recognizing the non-religious is, then, a way of identifying a mode of experience that is of the same order as religion and spirituality while also taking seriously the specificities of these modes. Precisely *how* non-religious contemporary societies are, and how the relationship between non-religious cultures and modernities are configured are outside of the scope of this work—though they are important questions with wide-ranging implications for theory development, and they are precisely the questions that this work has attempted to draw out and make more concrete. Questions about how modernization undermines religious cultural forms can be turned into more positive projects, by asking, for example, how modernization processes give rise to or encourage non-religious cultures.

REVISITING THE SECULAR

If non-religiosity is quite distinct from the secular, though, this provokes new questions about the extent to which the latter is dependent on the former, if at all—questions that must be approached today in relation to reinvigorated debates about how religion relates to secularity too. Our ability to recognize the non-religious opens up a broader project of reimagining the secular, therefore. It also makes an initial contribution to that process by distinguishing the substantial non-religious from the insubstantial—or analytical—secular and thereby refining our notions of the latter. Specifically, placing the non-religious to one side allows us to hone in on the single central meaning that the concept of 'secularity' has always had, that is, the subordination of religious authorities and concerns to other ones. This is the one meaning that cannot be expressed by other existing terms; it is what is left after those senses of secularity that really conflate it with other phenomena—the absence of religion (areligion), antipathy towards religion (anti-religion), religious pluralism, and so on—have been set apart. As scholars have rightly shown, subordination of the religious is itself a vastly complicated and ambivalent phenomenon, and it is one that enables certain ways of being religious even while it constrains others. Subordinating religion in particular contexts can be a cornerstone of religious practice or it can be an imposition that stifles it. Recognizing that secularity also involves subjugating alternatively spiritual and non-religious concerns and authorities to exactly the same forces only deepens the complexity. At the same time, it provides new ways of articulating it.

This kind of conceptual precision contributes to other debates too. It allows us, for example, to say quite simply what the problematic concept of 'post-secularity' is often trying to capture—that some forms of secularism are anti-religious, whereas others are not. Likewise, because religion and secularism are no longer set in opposition to one another, it is possible to avoid complicated descriptions of, for example, those who are involved in religious existential cultures but are politically secularist—simply a 'religious secularist' in this conceptual scheme. By contrast, previous distinctions between 'personal' and 'political' secularism have obscured, for example, the personal dimensions of political secularism and the political effects of 'private' religion; and they could not help but imply that being 'personally secularist' or 'personally secular' have a closer affinity with political secularism than the 'personally religious' person has. Using the same root term to describe these two quite different phenomena puts them into a relationship with each other that, as I hope I have shown, has not been examined. If we instead differentiate between non-religious secularists and religious and spiritual ones, these qualifications and hierarchies are undermined while multidimensional approaches to all of these phenomena—religion, non-religion, and secularism—become more visible, manageable, and amenable to the very research that is required.

Making this and related distinctions between non-religion and secularity therefore makes it easier to see and imagine different theories of the secular and different empirical possibilities that future research might address. If, for example, non-religious beliefs, assumptions, symbols, and social boundaries are found to be a vital force within societies such as the UK, this might then mean that these societies are, in a sense, a lot less secular than we have imagined, with secularist arrangements reflecting these cultural commitments as well as religious and spiritual cultures much more than they do some kind of secular restraint. Scholars have highlighted how some secularist ideas accord to religious, namely Protestant, conceptions of legitimate and illegitimate religious practice, so that the secular is located *within* a larger religious framework and is conceived of as one expression of a more comprehensive religious life, rather than as an alternative to it. If non-religious cultures are likewise implicated in the formation of the secular—to use Asad's (2003) helpful phrase—so the religious model of secularity becomes problematic and it may instead be necessary to look for a non-religious cultural framework that informs some secularisms and creates secular domains.

Alternatively, though, the exact same processes of secularization that have been imagined and observed by social scientists for decades extending into centuries may still emerge as the defining feature of 'modern life': in contemporary societies, the non-religious cultures described here are threads interwoven with many other activities and concerns that have nothing to do with religion, spirituality, or non-religion, and it may be that forces such as economic and social differentiation have equally limited the potential for non-religious as well as spiritual and religious cultures to form 'canopies' (Berger 1967) that contain and influence other aspects of life. Indeed, as Taylor (2007) argues, the emergence of the non-religious may itself lead to the retrenchment of religious and non-religious activity alike. The UK is clearly secular to some extent: most people are not fully immersed in existential cultures—theist, subjectivist, humanist, or agnostic—in all aspects of their everyday lives, in everything that they do, though it is open to question whether this is anything new since scholars do not agree as to whether historic societies were always immersed in religious cultures in this way (see Bruce 2002: 45–59).

The relationship between non-religious cultures and secular states is another area to be investigated in light of this work. For example, scholars sometimes classify Soviet state anti-theism or 'forced secularization' as an extreme form of secularism; at other times, they classify it as a weak form—as an 'atheocracy' with a non-religious ideology and culture at its heart and working at odds with a pluralist ideal of secularist governance. In liberal democracies, it is open to question whether the treatment of religion as special, with its particular dispensations and protections, is a concession to religious interests and undermines the state's secularity or whether it reflects an exclusion of religious authority from the legitimate business of the state, or even perhaps the state's service to a humanist existential culture and 'conception of the good', expressed, for example, in human rights discourses. There are alternative views, too, as to whether the revitalized visibility of religion in public life is part of secularization processes or contrary to it. Post-secular authors argue that attending to religious and non-religious cultures is a challenge to existing modes of secularity, which now need to make more space for these concerns. Others, however, argue precisely the opposite, that religious and non-religious clamour will lead to the consolidation and affirmation of secularist ideologies and the secular state. So, for lawyer Ronan McCrae (2013: n.p.), for example, the growth of new immigrant religions and of non-religious populations will lead to a formalization of the tacit secularism that has shaped many European states. 'As the range of religious and non-religious identities in Europe continues to expand', he writes, 'intensified secularization of the public sphere is the likely, and desirable, result'. In fact, Britain presents a particularly interesting case for considering these issues: religious and non-religious populations in the UK are quite evenly balanced and both cultures have elite representatives that work closely with government and other powerful authorities. It may be because the balance of power is so equal and therefore susceptible to small changes that the 'god wars' have been particularly acute in the UK, with the south-east of England emerging as a centre of contemporary global or at least cosmopolitan non-religious cultural movements.

In short, it is because of its contribution to these diverse and significant questions that recognizing the non-religious is also an exciting prospect for the study of secularity.

ON RECOGNITION

Recognizing the non-religious—described in this book and advocated in the work of the increasing number of scholars involved in the academic study of what has been variously termed atheism, secularism, secularity, irreligion, and, of course, non-religion—contributes to a more open-ended process of reimagining the secular, then. It will be fascinating to see what kinds of innovations and arguments emerge in research that addresses head-on the relationship between non-religion and secularity. But I want to conclude this volume by giving attention to what recognition of the non-religious has already achieved.

Research Subjects

First, recognizing the non-religious has opened up research methodologies to the real and diverse empirical phenomena charted here and elsewhere in 'non-religion studies'. Through this, scholars are able to build more detailed accounts of phenomena that had previously attracted little attention. These include: the impact that being 'other than religious' has on everyday lives and social relations; the ways in which different non-religious perspectives conceive of religious, spiritual, and non-religious others; the ways in which the non-religious engage with questions and practices otherwise dealt with by religious and spiritual cultures, including existential ideas and the demarcating of human existence by life-cycle rituals and ceremonies; and so on. And it will give rise to new approaches not yet acknowledged or imagined.

Like the study of alternative spirituality and the individualization of religion, the study of non-religion also draws attention to the significance of non-institutional cultural forms and experiences in contemporary societies. As media technologies—information and communications technology (ICT) and transportation—advance, social and cultural life is, though not necessarily fragmented or dissolved, certainly decentralized and this helps to understand the kind of occasional non-religious culture and hidden solidarities observed in relation to the British case in this volume. The diffuse forms of culture involved in this pose challenges, not only for societies as they adapt to these systems, but for social researchers seeking to identify them. Recognizing in social research empirical phenomena that are, by nature, easy to ignore is, then, an advance and helps make space for this work within the academy.

This is perhaps the most important aspect of recognition that this volume looks to and it is recognition of an extremely contingent form: what is imagined here is not the recognition of people *as* non-religious in any fixed or bounded sense, but of the existence of non-religious positioning in society that occurs for diverse reasons and with diverse effects. The notion of 'non-religion'—like 'alternative spirituality' and 'spiritual but not religious' categories—speaks to the very initial stage that thinking about and theorizing what non-religion is all about has reached. The recognition this volume has in mind aims to open up these phenomena to more research, not to force these studies along any fixed channels or to recognize non-religion in a way that closes down these enquiries altogether. It recognizes something, certainly, but it is something amorphous—unnoticed, hidden, observed only in relief—that might have to do with existential cultures but not only that. Recognizing the non-religious sufficiently that it can be translated into subjects for research—human and otherwise—will lead to other, better conceptions and the abandonment of 'non-religion' as a concept, at least to describe some things. This is not paradoxical: it is productive.

Non-religion may be a limited category, and it is, like all categories, essentially arbitrary—that is to say, it is historical and contingent. For all that it is used as a positive category to describe real and concrete things that exist in the world, non-religion is etymologically vacuous and this is something that will be addressed in future research. The flourishing study of alternative spirituality—an equally hollow term that relies on a notion of the traditional religion that it is 'alternative' to for its meaning—shows, however, that relative concepts are well able to support the development of analytical and, indeed, social fields. Even if it seems likely that such terms as 'alternative spirituality' and 'non-religion' are placeholders for more developed, qualitative categories, it is probably also the case that it will only be possible to arrive at those categories by making use of placeholders to facilitate empirical and theoretical work. And, of course, relative though they are, it is not true to say that these terms do not already indicate substantial features of the cultures at hand: qualifiers such as 'alternative', 'non-' and 'anti-' have literal meanings and cultural connotations (consider 'alternative cinema', 'non-violence', 'anti-hero') that give them distinctive senses and make them useful as part of the relational vocabulary outlined here (see Chapter 1 within this volume and the Glossary).

Inclusion and Critique

Unlike secularity, the non-religious is always in some sense religious-like. Thus, where a religion–secular binary is intrinsically hierarchical (though which of the two is on top alters with different accounts), non-religion is situated on the same plane as religion and spirituality. Recognizing and turning our attention to it and to the areligious rounds out a field of study and social life that has otherwise been limited and exclusive. It is similar in this respect to recognition of missing pieces in other puzzles, such as the acknowledgement of maleness and masculinity in gender studies, following a prior emphasis on femaleness, femininity, and minority positions. Another example is the recognition in the study of race and ethnicity of whiteness as a social construction and cultural form, following an earlier tradition of only identifying blackness and other minoritized racial and ethnic categories in these terms. In many Western contexts and in the social sciences especially, non-religion shares with these cases a similarly dominant, normative position. When cultures are dominant they become naturalized and the way in which they are socially constructed in relation to other hierarchies of power and inequality is obscured (Ware and Back 2002: 3). Although it does not occupy an elite position in all contexts, in the Western academy it is likely that the position of power that non-religion occupies contributes to its hiddenness and banalness. Elite positions are not typically expressed overtly or in dedicated institutions, but rather tend to be woven through social life and all of its institutions more generally. So it is for scholars of whiteness that it is necessary to make that category 'visible without reifying and naturalizing it' (Ware and Black 2002: 14) in order to learn which systems and structures it runs through (Ware and Black 2002: 5–6). Because socio-cultural positions are intersectional, they can disadvantage those who are part of dominant groups but do not share all of its privilege. Thus, imbalances of power and issues of exclusion are complicated and cut across the very divides that give rise to them. Recognition is then a method, not of revealing fixed identities and new kinds of identity politics, but of shining a light on social constructions that exert influence and exclude even as they lurk in the shadows. It is a mode of recognition that enables critical engagement.

One obstacle to increased inclusion is locating non-religion within the religious field, so that non-religious, spiritual, and religious cultures are understood as types of religion. The issue here is that, just as comparing 'religious secularists' to 'secularist secularists' cannot help but imply that political secularism has a closer affinity with personal secularism—or non-religion, in my language—than with personal religion, so the idea of non-religion et al. as types of religion cannot help but imply that religious cultures are somehow a more perfect example of the type. Consequently, the hierarchies that have prevented the recognition of some experiences are remodelled, but they are not disrupted. This is a problem plaguing the idea of 'religion for atheists' or 'religions without god' that have emerged in popular and academic discourses (e.g. de Botton 2013; Dworkin 2013). In fact, the study of non-religion should illuminate the problems involved in using the concept of religion as both a super- and subordinate concept—as a term for describing a domain of human and social life *and* one option within that domain. Really, the tradition of treating religion in this singular way marks out the study of religion from the study of other general social categories commonly used in social science. Social scientists do not offer 'class' as a category and then provide 'classed' and 'no class' as possible options. There is no 'opt-out' sub-category in the studies of gender, race, politics, nationality, age, education, ethnicity, or any other major sociological category. How examples of these types are differentiated and described is, of course, contested; some are seen as liminal or transitional, yet other sub-categories describe exclusion from mainstream groupings, such as 'unemployed' or 'stateless'. These 'negative' concepts are different from non-religious ones, though, because they are not used to locate the person outside a domain or field, but rather to describe distinctive positions within it. It is possible to reject sociological categories—to consider the possibility of people being non-gendered, living in a classless society, outside the world of nation-states, or with no concept of formal education, politics, and so on. But these rejections are again not the same as irreligious ones because they overturn the whole category, not particular instances of it. Compare the statement 'I'm not religious' to 'I'm not political': within our current ways of thinking, the former statement is commonplace and intelligible in this form; the latter, however, demands qualification ('I'm have no allegiance to a political party', 'I don't vote in general elections', etc.), and is not intrinsically satisfying.

The concept of 'religion' has, then, been doing too much work—or, in another sense, not enough work at all. That is, religion is an exclusive category that has been allowed to masquerade as an inclusive one; but this is a heavy burden that has, at the same time, excluded from view some parties that should be of interest. By demanding more inclusive approaches, the study of non-religion, and of alternative spirituality, too, contribute to critiques of 'religion' as an appropriate universal concept for these domains of human life. It draws attention to research exploring generic and inclusive categories that might replace 'religion' (e.g. Taves 2009; Taylor and Maclure 2011; Dworkin 2013; see also Laborde 2014a). Similarly, it also enriches the understanding of the non-religious experiences that such work needs to take account of, instead of founding inclusive approaches on air—on, that is, the insubstantial notion of the secular. The result of this has been that new inclusive approaches to religion turn their attention to the claims of vegetarians and conscientious objectors alongside religious ones, despite vegetarianism and conscientious objection being categories of a different order to religion; the fact that vegetarianism and conscientious objection can be manifestations of religiosity illustrates the category error. The question of what generic category or categories might create an inclusive understanding of 'religion' is an open one—but it is one that recognizing and working with those who are excluded from existing categorical approaches is bound to contribute to.

Social, Political, and Legal Representation

The imbalance between a substantial, culturally rich notion of religion and a hollow, insubstantial secular also has political effects. As critical religion scholars argue, the idea that religion is special has served religious interests well, but it has also been inverted to serve what they call secular interests and what I would call non-religious ones. On the one hand, religion can be seen as special and set apart, eligible for certain exemptions and protections; on the other hand, if being secular does not mean anything apart from being normal and having no impediment to the functioning of rational thought, then secular actors have free rein over, and do not need to account for their actions. There are ample opportunities here for people to feel or actually be excluded—from protections, exemptions, having freedom to act, being treated as normal. In this research, I met people who experience their non-religiosity as a dominant position, so that they see identifying themselves as non-religious as aggressive or bullying. But I also met people who felt disempowered and excluded as a result of being non-religious. The unusually small number of people reporting that they did not have a religion on the 2001 census informed one man's belief, for example, that the non-religious were a small and beleaguered minority, and he was incredulous when I talked about non-religious populations being sizeable according to other measures and powerful, even, within some elite institutions. Even if the non-religious do sometimes occupy positions of power, as Casanova (2006) and others suggest, it is important to recognize that non-religious people may not always be aware of this or experience their non-religiosity in this way. In that case, the absence of social and legal recognitions can be seen as problematic and unfair. To take another example, for several people I talked with, reading New Atheist books by Richard Dawkins, Christopher Hitchens, and others had been empowering, providing them with ways of understanding and talking about themselves that they experienced as processes of self-recognition. That people might have strong feelings of relief as a result of this process exposes underlying problems for people whose unreligious outlooks are not recognized or recognizable to them. As critical religion and post-structural scholars suggest, by positioning it as neutral and acultural, actors describing themselves as secular are able to claim legitimacy in many spheres of action and, at the same time, constrain those who speak from a religious cultural position, even in their efforts to protect it. This is an important and demonstrable observation, and critical religion scholars especially are also aware of similar claims to power made by religious authorities. However, this research indicates that non-religious actors can also be constrained by secularist frameworks that construct them as insubstantially secular. This limits their opportunities to develop world-views and to congregate with others (non-religious and otherwise) on the basis of those world-views. Hence, explicitly and implicitly, non-religious people often agitate for or celebrate some kind of recognition.

At the same time, neglecting to recognize the non-religious gives this group some powers over recognized ones. A political dimension to indifferentism—the construction of the self as indifferent, despite a strong sense of otherness—is precisely bound up with an attempt to position oneself as more legitimate than recognized social groups. People I talked with during this research sometimes denied their own cultural investments precisely in order to position themselves as different—and better—than those with more explicit cultural identities and commitments—as more rational, perhaps, or more 'freethinking'. Recognition involves taking proper and respectful account of non-religious subjectivities, collectivities, and actions, alongside religious and spiritual ones, but it also makes non-religious people newly accountable for their self-understandings and the way they represent themselves in public. Recognizing the non-religious means, for example, that the non-religious are no longer neglected by the law but also that they are no longer above it either.

There are, then, social and political reasons to recognize the existence of the non-religious as participants in the 'religious life' of societies—but there are difficulties here, too. To formally recognize the non-religious *qua* non-religious is clearly problematic and may feed into an unhelpful identity politics. There is insufficient space here to go into the detail of issues surrounding the politics of official recognition, but it is important to at least draw attention to the different forms that recognition can take and the fact that recognition is always ambivalent, just as unequal recognition is not a simple case of winners and losers. In fact, the argument for finding more inclusive and egalitarian approaches to 'religion' gathers additional momentum from the normative view that, in unequal arrangements, everyone loses. Recognition may not be straightforwardly desirable, but unequal recognition is worse; it gives all parties involved grounds for grievance and, though this might not be an issue at all times, it is a precarious situation that may easily be inflamed—in relation to other social and economic tensions, for example. The contrast between the many ways in which we recognize religion in contemporary Western societies and the very few ways in which we recognize alternative non-religious positions may contribute significantly to charged discourses and social relations surrounding religion today. While recognition makes people more vulnerable in some regards and less vulnerable in others—and invisibility means freedom to act as well as neglect—inequality of recognition is therefore more problematic and more distorting.

In addition, the ways in which people and groups are recognized require careful deliberation. Introducing or selecting terms for this task is to make an intervention that restructures social life in ways that are partly arbitrary and which necessarily distort reality even as they reveal it. As well as identifying non-religious participants in or in relation to the religious field, to take up Quack's (2014) Bourdieusian metaphor, there are other ways of developing inclusive approaches. Scholars have suggested turning away from the category of religion altogether (Fitzgerald 2000), developing more inclusive or generic categories (Fitzgerald 2000; Taves 2009), or exploring egalitarian analogies for religion (see Laborde 2014a) that cut across divides between the religious and the rest. The supposition of this volume is, however, that these approaches have not yet captured everything that is meant by 'religion' and that this explains the continued vitality of the concept, despite well-reasoned attempts to undermine it. Certainly, broadening our attention to religion's 'others' is a significant method of learning more about the concept of 'religion' and even those sceptical about its efficacy agree that the empirical study of non-religious forms provides one way of interrogating it.

Ultimately, attempts to navigate issues of social, political, and legal representation are as important as they are complicated. People must, in the end, 'speak from somewhere' (Seán McLoughlin 2005: 535; see Lee forthcoming): '"Being heard" requires an act of prioritising, of naming oneself, of coming into representation, if only momentarily.'

The diverse non-religious cultural forms identified here and in other work are, like all cultural forms, involved in making social distinctions (Bourdieu 1986) and are intrinsically ambivalent. They not only inhibit social relations but facilitate them; they construct social difference in a way that can be bridging as well as disabling; they can express antagonistic or respectful perspectives towards religious, spiritual, and non-religious 'others', as well as towards those with whom they have much in common; even when they are hostile on the basis of perceived and actual difference, this can be defensive as well as aggressive. Indeed, even in its most apparently hostile forms, non-religious action can be motivated by a desire for self- and public understanding and recognition as much as it is an attempt to encroach on other actors' claims for these things. Recognizing the non-religious is about recognizing all of these possibilities.

What all of these cases illustrate, though, is that non-religion is a relational phenomenon in the widest possible sense: it emerges in our attempts to relate to one another and to the objects around us, several of which are religious. If it is not clear how secular modern—that is, industrial, hyper-mediated, and differentiated—societies are, it is clear that, in having large 'not religious' populations in contact with religious ones, they are significantly and complicatedly non-religious.

Appendices

APPENDIX I

Glossary

This glossary presents one way of allocating terms to different phenomena that are relational to religion. Significant alternative definitions are also provided. Note that all of these concepts are contingent on understandings of 'religion' or 'theism'; because it is relational, the terminology is flexible around different conceptions and aspects of both. These terms require, therefore, that users are clear on their approach to and understanding of 'religion' and 'theism' in using and presenting them.

anti-religion: Opposition to religion.
anti-theism: Opposition to theism.
areligion: The absence of religion.
atheism: The absence of theism. Alternatively called 'negative atheism'. Can also be capitalized to indicate contemporary non-religious movements, as in 'New Atheism'.
indifference to religion: An ambiguous category, suggesting knowledge of religion combined with minor levels of interest and engagement with it. The category implies at least some degree of rejection of religion, but this rejection can be interpreted as a very strong form of rejection or a very weak form. In practice, the idea of indifference to religion is typically applied to specific aspects of religiosity and not others; and usually implies an equal degree of indifference to non-religious cultures, too.
irreligion: The rejection of religion. Alternatively defined as 'hostility or indifference towards religion' (e.g. Campbell 2013), though both may be seen as forms of rejection.
New Atheism: An anti-theistic cultural movement advocating radical secularism in public life and particularly associated with the works of Richard Dawkins, Sam Harris, Daniel Dennett, Christopher Hitchens, and, latterly, A. C. Grayling.
non-religion: A phenomenon primarily identified in contrast to religion; a stance towards religion identified as other than religious, including but not limited to the rejection of religion. The 'non-' prefix here is used as in 'non-violence' to indicate something meaningfully unlike the phenomena at hand;[1] it contrasts with 'areligion'.

---

[1] With thanks to Stacey Gutkowski for this useful analogy.

non-theism: A phenomenon primarily identified in contrast to theism or a stance towards theism that is other than theist; including but not limited to the rejection of theistic claims. Alternatively called 'positive atheism'.

post-religion: A phenomenon shaped in the past, but no longer actively influenced by religion.

post-secular: A critical stance towards areligious and anti-religious modes of secularity. Sometimes called 'post-secularity' or 'post-secularism'.

religion: This volume uses the 'conventional' Western understanding of religion (Knott 2005: 59) as a theistic cultural tradition.

secular: A condition in which religion is a subordinate cultural or political authority or concern (though it may be an important secondary authority or concern). There are numerous alternative understandings of the term in circulation, though the idea of religion being (at least) a secondary authority is common to all of these.

secularism: A theory or ideology that demarcates parts of a whole as secular, notably but not only as stipulated or enacted by the state. Some scholars have a thicker, historical understanding of 'secularism'.

secularity: The quality or state of being secular. Used by other scholars to distinguish personal philosophies that are alternative to religious ones or the absence of any such philosophy from 'secularism' as a political arrangement.

spirituality: Used in this study in relation to 'alternative spirituality' (see Heelas and Woodhead 2005).

theism: Belief in the existence of god or gods.

APPENDIX II

Interview Question Schedule

Part of the exploration involved in this research was methodological, and while the following question schedule gives a good indication of the topics covered and questions asked in most interviews, the subject matter and phrasing have been refined and additions made throughout the process. This annotated schedule includes comments on its future use.

Question Schedule

1. Introduction
Introduction; ethics form; demographic information (including religion in education, and description of parents' religiosity); list of personal network solicited (<10 'people to whom you are close').

2. Self-classification and Primary Ideational Content

   (i) First, can I ask you, if you were completing a survey like the national census and it asked you to state your religious position, how do you think you would describe yourself?
      PROMPT: If you were given the following list, which would you choose—or be tempted by?
      LIST: Christian (or other religious group), no religion, atheist, agnostic, other?

   (ii) What does [CHOSEN TERM/S] mean to you?

   (iii) Are you happy with [CHOSEN TERM/S] as a way of describing your views?

   (iv) Do any of these other classifications appeal to you?
      LIST: Not religious, no religion, areligious, secular, spiritual but not religious, atheist, agnostic, humanist, rationalist, freethinker?

   (v) What would be the best way to describe this type of position?
      PROMPT: Belief? Ideology? Religion? Non-religion? Religion or non-religion? Philosophy? World-view? Moral code?

   (vi) Would you use [CHOSEN TERM/S] to describe yourself to other people? When might you do that?

   (vii) Would you ever use a different word to describe yourself?

   (viii) What do you think other people think you mean when you describe yourself with the word [CHOSEN TERM/S]?

(ix) When did you start using [CHOSEN TERM/S] to think about yourself? How did you think of yourself before that?

3. Religion in Social Life
(See also social network exercise.)

(i) How interested would you say you are in religion? Is it something that comes up in discussion often?
(ii) Whom would you discuss it with, and when might it come up in conversation?

4. Religion in Social and Public Life

(i) Have you used or attended religious ceremonies such as weddings or funerals?
(ii) How did you find those experiences? Is your [CHOSEN TERM/S] important in that context?
(iii) Have you used or attended any non-religious ceremonies, for weddings, funerals, and so on, such as civil or humanist ceremonies?
(iv) How have you found those experiences? Is your [CHOSEN TERM/S] important in that context?
(v) What kind of ceremony have you used or might you use in your own life—say for your own wedding?
(vi) [VIGNETTE] How do you feel about 'faith schools'?
PROMPT: Would you send your child to a faith school, for example, if it was the best school available in your local area? Do you thing that faith schools should receive government funding?

5. Participation in Organized Non-Religious Activity

(i) Have you ever participated in organized non-religious events, such as atheist meet-up groups or secularist political activities?
If NO: Why not?
If YES: Why did you start attending? Do you find this participation rewarding?

6. Common Measures of Religiosity
Discussion of standard religiosity measures, if they have not been raised already.

[Afterlife]	What do you believe happens after you die?
[Origins]	What are your thoughts about how the universe came into being? (Day 2006).
[God]	Do you believe in God or a higher power?
[PROMPT:	Can you locate yourself on a spectrum from strongly agree to strongly disagree?]

[Supernatural]	Have you ever seen a ghost or something else you felt couldn't be explained by science?
[Fate]	Do you believe in 'fate'? How much influence or control do you feel you have over your own life? (Day 2006)
[Superstition]	Do you have any superstitions?
[Morality]	Do you think you have a sense of what is right and wrong? (Day 2006) How do you know if something is right or wrong? (Day 2006)
PROMPT:	In the case of murder say?
[Comfort]	What frightens you? (Day 2006) What do you do to comfort yourself during those times? (Day 2006)
[Sacred]	Does the word 'sacred' mean anything to you? Is there anything you would describe as sacred?

7. Social Network Exercise

   (i) Going back to the list you've made of people you are close to, what I'd like you to do is go back through the names and tell me how you think these people would describe themselves in relation to religion and non-religion. Please don't be shy to say that you don't know, as that is very interesting also.

   (ii) [DISCUSS CONSISTENCY OF LIST] Does this surprise you?

   (iii) Have you ever had a close relationship with anyone [OF ORIENTATIONS DIFFERENT FROM THOSE LISTED]?

   (iv) Has there ever been a time that someone's religion or non-religion has been a source of tension/curiosity/interest?

8. General Prompts
Is this something you can remember thinking about/putting into words before? Can you remember an occasion in which you put this into words?

9. Conclusion

   (i) Do you think there is anything we should have talked about, in thinking about religion, non-religion, and secular society, that we haven't mentioned?

   (ii) Are the things that we've talked about what you might expect to talk about in relation to these themes?

Comments and Suggestions

The following questions arose in individual discussions towards the end of the fieldwork phase, but were particularly fertile.

For section 1, people's definition of their chosen term of self-classification yielded useful data concerning self-understandings of such terms, but also concerning the role these terms are playing in their cultural context. This research takes the individual as the core unit of analysis, but the methodology could be extended in order to explore local discourses and practices by also asking people to define terms that they may or may not associate with themselves: 'humanism', 'agnosticism', 'atheism', 'spirituality'. Bullivant (2008b) has conducted a pilot study in this vein using a questionnaire methodology. The discussions in this research suggest a qualitative approach might be revealing.

For section 3, on religion in social life, some additional questions are suggested:

- Would you mind if anyone assumed you were religious? Would you mind if anyone assumed you were not religious?
- Does everyone on this list know that you identify as [CHOSEN TERM/S]? Would they think of you in those terms?
- Would you feel happy classifying yourself in the same way, as [CHOSEN TERM/S], with all of these people?

APPENDIX III

Event Participation Questionnaire

The following questionnaire was sent to seven people following the 'Nine Lessons and Carols for Godless People' event attended as part of this research. Audience members were approached at the event and subsequently contacted by email. An attempt was made to recruit people of different ages, sex, and ethnicities.

Questionnaire

Please write as much or as little as you wish in the spaces indicated by the text 'YOUR RESPONSE' [removed in this reproduction of the questionnaire]. This is just a simple word document, so you have as much space as you want to answer: just keep writing! If you prefer to contribute a general comment rather than looking through the questions, please do so here:

1. You
Age:
Sex:
Race and ethnicity:
Occupation:

2. Your Non-Religious Views

   (i) How would you classify your own religious or non-religious position?
   (ii) Can you describe or define what this classification means to you?
   (iii) Do you feel that this classification satisfactorily reflects your views?
   (iv) Do you regard it as an important part of your identity?
   (v) Has your religious or non-religious position changed over your lifetime?

3. Your Views of the Nine Lessons Event

   (i) How did you hear of the Nine Lessons event? What made you interested to attend?
   (ii) With whom did you attend? (I.e. friends, your children/parents/ other family, work colleagues etc.)
   (iii) Why did you attend with those people?
   (iv) If you share non-religious views, did you know that this was the case before deciding to attend this event?

4. Your Views of the Nine Lessons Event
    (i) Was there anything you particularly liked about the show or specific performances (either in terms of their subject matter or more generally)?
    (ii) Was there anything you particularly disliked about the show or specific performances?
    (iii) Did you feel the show's content reflected your own views?
    (iv) Did you discuss it with people on your journey home? Can you remember any of the things you discussed?
    (v) Have you given the show any further thought since? Have you discussed it with anyone since?

APPENDIX IV

Research Sample

This appendix provides a summary of the demographic profile of the interview sample as a whole. In order to protect anonymity, complete demographic profiles for individuals are not provided. 'Not recorded' indicates that that information was not formally collected for a participant, either because it was not requested (e.g. some data only collected in second phase of research) or because participants did not want to give that information.

Interview Participants

Total sample size: 42
Phase 1 (Cambridge): 12
Phase 2 (Greater London): 30
(Not including questionnaire respondents)

Gender
Women: 21
Men: 21

Age
18–20: 1
20–30: 20
30–40: 10
40–50: 2
50–60: 4
60–70: 2
70–80: 2
Not recorded: 1

Income, Per Annum
Unwaged: 3
Under £15K: 7
£15K–£30K: 8
£30K–£50K: 8
£50K +: 3
Unrecorded: 13

Highest Education Qualification Attained
Secondary: 6

Undergraduate: 16
Masters: 14
PhD: 3
Not recorded: 3

Participant in Non-Religious Activity
None: 17
Participant: 13
Not recorded: 12

Ethnicity/Race (Self-Reported)
White: 32
White–Asian (or 'English–Pakistani'): 3
Black–African: 1
Indian: 1
South-Eastern European: 1
Not recorded: 4

Other Sample Variables
The following variables had too numerous or complicated categories to present in simple counts, but the following summary provides an overview of the kind of categories considered and sampled.

Religion in Family Background

'Church of England', 'Catholic', 'atheist' and 'not religious' were the most common description of parents' religion.

The sample also included, however, the following classifications of parents' (non-)religion: 'Christian', 'Muslim', 'Evangelical Christian', 'Scientologist', 'atheist Jew', 'atheist', 'lapsed Church of England', 'None', 'strong atheist', 'Baptist', 'Anglican', 'agnostic', 'humanist', 'nominally Christian', 'non-practising Christian', 'agnostic with pagan tendencies', 'lapsed Methodist', 'lapsed Catholic', 'pagan', 'agnosticism (Jewish)', 'Roman Catholicism', 'non-religious theist', 'agnostic/Church of England', 'Church of Jesus Christ of Latterday Saints (Mormon)', 'Quaker'; and some participants did not know the (non)religious positions of their parents.

Non-Religious Background

First generation (one parent non-religious)
First generation (both parents non-religious)
Second generation
Third generation +

National Background

Non-migrant
First-generation migrant
Second-generation migrant
Third-generation migrant +
Non-British nationalities sampled: Irish, Canadian, American, South African, Polish, Romanian, and Nigerian

Education

Religious school ('faith school')
Secular, privately funded
Secular, publicly funded
Secular—religion culturally significant
Secular—religion culturally marginal
Unknown to participant

Bibliography

Amarasingam, Amarnath (ed.). 2010. *Religion and the New Atheism: A Critical Appraisal*. Leiden and Boston: Brill.
Asad, Talal. 1993. *Genealogies of Religion: Discipline and Reasons of Power in Christianity and Islam*. London: Johns Hopkins University Press.
Asad, Talal. 2003. *Formations of the Secular: Christianity, Islam, Modernity*. Stanford, CA: Stanford University Press.
Asad, Talal. 2011. Thinking about the Secular Body, Pain, and Liberal Politics. *Cultural Anthropology* 26 (4): 657–75.
Aston, Katie. 2012. Making Non-Religion: The Practices, Processes and Narratives of Non-Religious Living. Conference paper, presented at the NSRN Conference 2012, 4–6 July 2012.
Atheist Bus Campaign. 2011. FAQ. Atheist Campaign (online), 2011. Available at <http://www.atheistbus.org.uk/faq/> [accessed 19 December 2011].
Aull Davies, Charlotte. 2008. *Reflexive Ethnography: A Guide to Researching Selves and Others*, 2nd edn. London: Routledge.
Bader, Veit. 2011. Beyond Secularisms of All Sorts. *Immanent Frame* (online). SSSR, 11 October 2011. Available at <http://blogs.ssrc.org/tif/2011/10/11/beyond-secularisms-of-all-sorts/> [accessed 9 December 2011].
Badmington, Neil. 2003. Theorizing Posthumanism. *Cultural Critique* 53: 10–27.
Bagg, Samuel and David Voas. 2010. The Triumph of Indifference: Irreligion in British Society. In P. Zuckerman (ed.). *Atheism and Secularity: Volume 2: Global Expressions*. Santa Barbara: Praeger, 91–111.
Bailey, Edward. 1997. *Implicit Religion in Contemporary Society*. Leuven: Peeters.
Bailey, Edward. 2001. *The Secular Faith Controversy: Religion in Three Dimensions*. London: Continuum.
Baker, Joseph O'Brian and Buster Smith. 2009. None Too Simple: Examining Issues of Religious Nonbelief and Nonbelonging in the United States. *Journal for the Scientific Study of Religion* 48 (4): 719–33.
Barker, Eileen. 2007. Preface. In B. A. Kosmin and A. Keysar (eds). *Secularism and Secularity: Contemporary International Perspectives*. Hartford, CA: ISSSC, iii–iv.
Bauman, Zygmunt. 2000. *Liquid Modernity*. Cambridge: Polity.
BBC News. 2011. Phones 4U Mobile Phone Jesus Advert Banned. BBC News (online), 7 September. Available online at <http://www.bbc.co.uk/news/business-14815616> [accessed 7 September 2011].

Beattie, Tina. 2007. *The New Atheists: The Twilight of Reason and the War on Religion*. London: Darton, Longman, and Todd.
Beck, Ulrich. 2010. *A God of One's Own*. Cambridge: Polity.
Beck, Ulrich and Elisabeth Beck-Gernsheim. 2002. *Individualization: Institutionalized Individualism and Its Social and Political Consequences*. London: SAGE.
Becker, Howard. 1950. *Through Values to Social Interpretations*. Durham, NC: Duke University Press.
Beckford, James A. 2003. *Social Theory and Religion*. Cambridge: Cambridge University Press.
Beckford, James A. 2012. SSSR Presidential Address. Public Religions and the Post-secular: Critical Reflections. *Journal for the Scientific Study of Religion* 51 (1): 1–19.
Beit-Hallahmi, Benjamin. 2007. Atheists: A Psychological Profile. In M. Martin (ed.). *The Cambridge Companion to Atheism*. Cambridge: Cambridge University Press, 300–17.
Bellah, Robert N. 1991. *Beyond Belief: Essays on Religion in a Post-Traditional World*. Berkeley, CA: University of California Press.
Bellah, Robert N. and Steven M. Tipton (eds). 2006. *The Robert Bellah Reader*. Durham, NC: Duke University Press.
Bender, Courtney and Ann Taves. 2012. *What Matters? Ethnographies of Value in a Not So Secular Age*. New York, NY: Columbia University Press.
Berger, Peter, Grace Davie, and Effie Fokas. 2008. *Religious America, Secular Europe? A Theme and Variations*. Aldershot: Ashgate.
Berger, Peter L. 1967. *Sacred Canopy: Elements of a Sociological Theory of Religion*. Garden City, NY: Anchor Books.
Berger, Peter L. (ed.). 1999a. *The Desecularization of the World: Resurgent Religion and World Politics*. Washington, DC: Ethics and Public Policy Center.
Berger, Peter L. 1999b. The Desecularization of the World: Global Overview. In P. L Berger (ed.). *The Desecularization of the World: Resurgent Religion and World Politics*. Washington, DC: Ethics and Public Policy Center, 1–18.
Berger, Peter. L. (ed.) 2010. *Between Relativism and Fundamentalism: Religious Resources for a Middle Position*. Grand Rapids, MI: Eerdmans.
Berman, Morris. 1981. *The Reenchantment of the World*. New York, NY: Cornell University Press.
Berns, Steph. 2014. Sacred Entanglements: Studying Interactions between Visitors, Objects and Religion in the Museum. Unpublished PhD thesis, University of Kent.
BHA. 2011a. The Happy Human—The Symbol of Humanism. British Humanist Association (online), 2011. Available at <https://humanism.org.uk/humanism/the-happy-human-symbol/> [accessed 18 December 2011].

BHA. 2011b. The Census Campaign. British Humanist Association (online), 2011. Available at <http://census-campaign.org.uk/> [accessed 18 December 2011].
BHA. 2011c. About Us. British Humanist Association (online), 2011. Available at <https://humanism.org.uk/about/> [accessed 16 September 2011].
Bhargava, Rajeev. 2009. Political Secularism: Why It Is Needed and What Can Be Learnt From Its Indian Version. In G. Brahm Levey and T. Modood (eds). *Secularism, Religion and Multicultural Citizenship*. Cambridge: Cambridge University Press, 82–109.
Bille, Mikkel, Frida Hastrup, and Tim Flohr Soerensen (eds). 2010. *An Anthropology of Absence: Materializations of Transcendence and Loss*. New York, NY: Springer-Verlag.
Billig, Michael. 1995. *Banal Nationalism*. London: SAGE.
Borer, Michael Ian. 2010. The New Atheism and the Secularization Thesis. In A. Amarasingam (ed.). *Religion and the New Atheism: A Critical Appraisal*. Leiden: Brill, 125–37.
Bourdieu, Pierre. 1986. *Distinction: A Social Critique of the Judgement of Taste*, trans. Richard Nice. New York: Routledge.
Bradley, Arthur and Andrew Tate. 2010. *The New Atheist Novel: Fiction, Philosophy and Polemic After 9/11*. London: Continuum.
Brahm Levey, Geoffrey and Tariq Modood. 2009a. *Secularism, Religion and Multicultural Citizenship*. Cambridge: Cambridge University Press.
Brahm Levey, Geoffrey and Tariq Modood. 2009b. Secularism and Religion in a Multicultural Age. In G. Brahm Levey and T. Modood (eds). *Secularism, Religion and Multicultural Citizenship*. Cambridge: Cambridge University Press, 1–24.
Brahm Levey, Geoffrey and Tariq Modood. 2009c. Liberal Democracy, Multicultural Citizenship and the Danish Cartoon Affair. In G. Brahm Levey and T. Modood (eds). *Secularism, Religion and Multicultural Citizenship*. Cambridge: Cambridge University Press, 216–42.
Brigstocke, Marcus. 2011. *God Collar*. London: Transworld.
Brown, Callum G. 2000. *The Death of Christian Britain: Understanding Secularization, 1800–2000*. London: Routledge.
Bruce, Steve. 1996. *Religion in the Modern World: From Cathedrals to Cults*. Oxford: Oxford University Press.
Bruce, Steve. 2011. *Secularization: In Defence of an Unfashionable Theory*. Oxford: Oxford University Press.
Bruce, Steve. 2002. *God is Dead: Secularization in the West*. Oxford: Blackwell.
Budd, Susan. 1977. *Varieties of Unbelief: Atheists and Agnostics in English Society 1850–1960*. London: Heinemann.
Bullivant, Stephen. 2008a. Research Note: Sociology and the Study of Atheism. *Journal of Contemporary Religion* 23 (3): 16–31.

Bullivant, Stephen. 2008b. Introducing Irreligious Experiences. *Implicit Religion* 11 (1): 7–24.
Bullivant, Stephen. 2010. The New Atheism and Sociology: Why Here? Why Now? What Next? In A. Amarasingam (ed.). *Religion and the New Atheism: A Critical Appraisal*. Leiden: Brill, 109–24.
Bullivant, Stephen. 2013. Defining Atheism. In S. Bullivant and M. Ruse (eds). *The Oxford Handbook of Atheism*. Oxford: Oxford University Press, 11–21.
Bullivant, Stephen and Lois Lee. 2012. Introduction: Interdisciplinary Studies of Non-Religion and Secularity: The State of the Union. *Journal of Contemporary Religion* 27 (1): 19–27.
Bullivant, Stephen and Michael Ruse (eds). 2013. *The Oxford Handbook of Atheism*. Oxford: Oxford University Press.
Calhoun, Craig, Mark Juergensmeyer, and Jonathan Vanantwerpen (eds). 2011. *Rethinking Secularism*. Oxford: Oxford University Press.
Campbell, Colin. 1968. Humanism and the Culture of the Professions: A Study of the Rise of the British Humanist Movement, 1967–1963. Unpublished PhD thesis, University of London.
Campbell, Colin. 2007. *The Easternization of the West*. Boulder and London: Paradigm Publishers.
Campbell, Colin. 2013 [1971]. *Toward a Sociology of Irreligion*. Alcuin Academics.
Cannell, Fenella. 2010. The Anthropology of Secularism. *Annual Review of Anthropology* 39: 85–100.
Casanova, José. 2006. Religion, European Secular Identities, and European Integration. In T. A. Byrnes and P. J. Katzenstein (eds). *Religion in an Expanding Europe*. Cambridge: Cambridge University Press, 65–92.
Casanova, José. 2011. The Secular, Secularizations, Secularisms. In C. Calhoun, M. Juergensmeyer, and J. van Antwerpen (eds). *Rethinking Secularism*. Oxford: Oxford University Press, 54–74.
Castells, Manuel. 2010. *The Rise of the Network Society: The Information Age: Economy, Society and Culture: Vol. I*. Malden, MA: Wiley Blackwell.
Cimino, Richard, and Christopher Smith. 2007. Secular Humanism and Atheism beyond Progressive Secularism. *Sociology of Religion* 68 (4): 407–24.
Cimino, Richard and Christopher Smith. 2010. The New Atheism and the Empowerment of American Thinkers. In A. Amarasingam (ed.). *Religion and the New Atheism: A Critical Appraisal*. Leiden: Brill, 139–56.
Cliteur, Paul. 2009. The Definition of Atheism. *Journal of Religion and Society* 11: 1–23. Available at <https://openaccess.leidenuniv.nl> [accessed 9 February 2011].
Connolly, William E. 2011. Some Thesis on Secularism. *Cultural Anthropology* 26 (4): 648–56. DOI: 10.1111/j.1548-1360.2011.01117.x.

Copeman, Jacob and Johannes Quack. 2015. 'Godless People' and Dead Bodies: Materiality and the Morality of Atheist Materialism. *Social Analysis* 59 (2).

Corporale, Rocco and Antonio Grumelli. 1971. *The Culture of Unbelief: Studies and Proceedings from the First International Symposium on Belief Held at Rome, March 22-27, 1969*. Berkeley, CA: University of California Press.

Cotter, Christopher R. 2011a. Consciousness Raising: The Critique, Agenda, and Inherent Precariousness of Contemporary Anglophone Atheism. *International Journal for the Study of New Religions* 2 (1): 77-103.

Cotter, Christopher R. 2011b. Toward a Typology of Nonreligion: A Qualitative Analysis of Everyday Narratives of Scottish University Students. Unpublished MSc thesis, University of Edinburgh.

Cragun, Ryan, Barry Kosmin, Ariela Keysar, Joseph H. Hammer, and Michael Nielsen. 2012. On the Receiving End: Discrimination toward the Non-Religious. *Journal of Contemporary Religion* 27 (1): 105-127.

Cragun, Ryan T. and Joseph H. Hammer. 2011. 'One Person's Apostate is Another Person's Convert': What Terminology Tells Us About Pro-Religious Hegemony in the Sociology of Religion. *Humanity and Society* 35: 149-75.

Crowley, Vivianne. 2014. Standing up to Be Counted: Understanding Pagan Responses to the 2011 British Censuses. *Religion* 44 (3): 483-501. DOI:10.1080/0048721X.2014.903640.

Dant, Tim. 1999. *Material Culture in the Social World: Values, Activities, Lifestyles*. Buckingham: Oxford University Press.

Davie, Grace. 1994. *Religion in Britain since 1945: Believing Without Belonging*. Oxford: Blackwell.

Davie, Grace. 2007. *The Sociology of Religion*. London: SAGE.

Davie, Grace. 2010. Resacralization. In B. S. Turner (ed.). *The New Blackwell Companion to the Sociology of Religion*. Chichester: Wiley-Blackwell, 160-77.

Davie, Grace. 2012. Spirituality and Religion. *Journal for the Study of Spirituality* 2 (2): 163-69.

Dawkins, Richard. 2006. *The God Delusion*. London: Transworld.

Day, Abby. 2006. Believing in Belonging: A Case Study from Yorkshire. Unpublished PhD Thesis, Lancaster University.

Day, Abby. 2011. *Believing in Belonging: Belief and Social Identity in the Modern World*. Oxford: Oxford University Press.

Day, Abby. 2013. Yes, but Not in the North: Nuances in Religion and Language Cultures. *Studies in Ethnicity and Nationalism* 13 (1): 105-8. DOI: 10.1111/sena.12013.

Day, Abby and Lois Lee. 2014. Making Sense of Surveys and Censuses: Issues in Religious Self-Identification. *Religion* 44 (3): 345-56.

de Botton, Alain. 2013. *Religion for Atheists: A Non-Believer's Guide to the Uses of Religion*. London: Penguin.
Descartes, René. 1988. Meditations on First Philosophy in which are Demonstrated the Existence of God and the Distinction between the Human Soul and the Body. In J. Cottingham, R. Stoothoff, and D. Murdoch (eds and trans.). *Descartes: Selected Philosophical Writings*. Cambridge: Cambridge University Press, 73–122.
Dobbelaere, Karel. 1999. Towards an Integrated Perspective of the Processes Related to the Descriptive Concept Secularization. *Sociology of Religion*, 60 (3): 229–47.
Durkheim, Émile. 1984. *The Division of Labour in Society*. Basingstoke: Palgrave.
Durkheim, Émile. 2001. *The Elementary Forms of Religious Life*. Oxford: Oxford University Press.
Dworkin, Ronald. 2013. *Religion Without God*. Cambridge, MA: Harvard University Press.
Eagleton, Terry. 2014. *Culture and the Death of God*. New Haven, CT: Yale University Press.
Edgell, Penny, Joseph Gerteis, and Douglas Hartmann. 2006. Atheists as Other: Moral Boundaries and Cultural Membership in American Society. *American Sociological Review* 71 (2): 211–34.
Eisenstadt, Shmuel N. 2000. Multiple Modernities. *Daedalus* 129: 1–29.
Eller, Jack David. 2010. What Is Atheism? In P. Zuckerman (ed.). *Atheism and Secularity: Volume 1: Issues, Concepts and Definitions*. Santa Barbara. CA: Praeger, 1–18.
Engelke, Matthew. 2011. The Anthropology of After Religion. Paper presented at the 'Atheism and Anthropology: Researching Atheism and Self-Searching Belief and Experience' workshop, University College London, 21 September 2011.
Engelke, Matthew. 2012a. An Ethnography of the British Humanist Association; ESRC End of Award Report, RES-000-22-4157. Swindon: ESRC.
Engelke, Matthew. 2012b. In Spite of Christianity: Humanism and Its Others in Contemporary Britain. NSRN Annual Lecture, Conway Hall, 28 November 2012.
Engelke, Matthew. 2013. *God's Agents: Biblical Publicity in Contemporary England*. Berkeley, CA: University of California Press.
Field, Clive. 2014. Measuring Religious Affiliation in Great Britain: The 2011 Census in Historical and Methodological Context. *Religion* 44 (3): 357–82. DOI:10.1080/0048721X.2014.903643.
Fitzgerald, Timothy. 2000. *The Ideology of Religious Studies*. Oxford: Oxford University Press.
Fitzgerald, Timothy. 2007. *Discourse on Civility and Barbarity: A Critical History of Religion and Related Categories*. Oxford: Oxford University Press.

Gane, Nicholas. 2002. *Max Weber and Postmodern Theory: Rationalization versus Re-enchantment*. Basingstoke: Palgrave.
Gauchet, Marcel. 1997. *The Disenchantment of the World: A Political History of Religion*, trans. Oscar Burge. Princeton, NJ: Princeton University Press.
Geertz, Armin W. and Guðmundur Ingi Markússon. 2010. Religion is Natural, Atheism is Not: On Why Everybody is Both Right and Wrong. *Religion* 40: 152–65.
Gellner, Ernest. 2003. *Postmodernism, Reason and Religion*. London: Routledge.
Gibson, Nicholas J. S. and Kirsten Barnes. 2011a. Toward a Psychology of Atheism I: Measuring Dimensions of Non-religiosity. Poster presented at the biennial congress of the International Association for the Psychology of Religion, Bari, Italy.
Gibson, Nicholas J. S. and Kirsten Barnes. 2011b. Toward a Psychology of Atheism II: An Empirically Derived Typology of Non-religiosity. Paper presented at the biennial congress of the International Association for the Psychology of Religion, Bari, Italy.
Giddens, Anthony. 1991. *Modernity and Self-Identity: Self and Society in the Late Modern Age*. Cambridge: Polity.
Giddens, Anthony. 1992. *The Transformation of Intimacy: Sexuality, Love, and Eroticism in Modern Societies*. Stanford, CA: Standford University Press.
Gill, Robin, C. Kirk Hadaway, and Penny Long Marler. 1998. Is Religious Belief Declining in Britain? *Journal for the Scientific Study of Religion* 37 (3): 507–16.
Gutkowski, Stacey. 2012. The British Secular habitus and the War on Terror. *Journal of Contemporary Religion* 27 (1): 87–103.
Haas, Peter M. 1992. Introduction: Epistemic Communities and International Policy Coordination. *International Organization* 46 (1): 1–35.
Habermas, Jürgen. 1998. *Postmetaphysical Thinking*. Cambridge: Polity.
Habermas, Jürgen. 2006. Religion in the Public Sphere. *European Journal of Philosophy* 14 (1): 1–25.
Hall, Julian. 2010. Marcus Brigstocke: God Collar, Vaudeville Theatre, London. *The Independent*, 10 February 2010. Available at <http://www.independent.co.uk/arts-entertainment/comedy/reviews/marcus-brigstocke-god-collar-vaudeville-theatre-london-1894259.html> [accessed 21 November 2011].
Halman, Loek and Ruud de Moor. 1994. Religion, Churches and Moral Values. In P. Ester, L. Halman, and R. de Moor (eds). *The Individualising Society: Value Change in Europe and North America* (2nd edn). Tilburg: Tilburg University Press, 37–65.
Halman, Loek and Veerle Draulans. 2006. How Secular is Europe? *British Journal of Sociology* 57 (2): 263–88.

Hayes, Bernadette C. 2000. Religious Independents within Western Industrialised Nations: A Socio-Demographic Profile, *Sociology of Religion* 61 (2): 191–207.

Heelas, Paul and Linda Woodhead. 2005. *The Spiritual Revolution: Why Religion is Giving Way to Spirituality*. Oxford: Blackwell.

Hirschkind, Charles. 2010. Is There a Secular Body? The Immanent Frame. Available at <http://blogs.ssrc.org/tif/2010/11/15/secular-body/> [accessed 9 February 2015].

Hirschkind, Charles. 2011. Is There a Secular Body? *Cultural Anthropology* 26 (4): 633–47. DOI: 10.1111/j.1548-1360.2011.01116.x.

Houtman, Dick and Stef Aupers. 2007. The Spiritual Turn and the Decline of Tradition: The Spread of Post-Christian Spirituality in 14 Western Countries, 1981–2000. *Journal for the Scientific Study of Religion* 46 (3): 305–20.

Houtman, Dick and Peter Mascini. 2002. Why Do Churches Become Empty, While New Age Grows? Secularization and Religious Change in the Netherlands. *Journal for the Scientific Study of Religion* 41 (3): 455–73.

Hunsberger, Bruce and Bob Altemeyer. 2006. *Atheists: A Groundbreaking Study of America's Nonbelievers*. Amherst, NY: Prometheus Press.

Hunter, Ian. 2009. The Shallow Legitimacy of Secular Liberal Orders: The Case of Early Modern Brandenburg-Prussia. In G. Brahm Levey and T. Modood (eds). *Secularism, Religion and Multicultural Citizenship*. Cambridge: Cambridge University Press, 27–55.

Hyman, Gavin. 2010. *A Short History of Atheism*. London: I. B. Tauris.

James, William. 2008. *The Varieties of Religious Experience: A Study in Human Nature*. London: Routledge.

Keysar, Ariela. 2007. Who Are America's Atheists and Agnostics? In B. A. Kosmin and A. Keysar (eds). *Secularism and Secularity: Contemporary International Perspective*. Hartford, CA: ISSSC, 33–9.

Keysar, Ariela and Barry A. Kosmin. 2007. Freethinkers in a Free Market of Religion. In B. A. Kosmin and A. Keysar (eds). *Secularism and Secularity: Contemporary International Perspectives*. Hartford, CA: ISSSC, 17–26.

Keysar, Ariela and Juhem Navarro-Rivera. 2013. A World of Atheism: Global Demographics. In S. Bullivant and M. Ruse (eds). *The Oxford Handbook of Atheism*. Oxford: Oxford University Press, 553–86.

Kitson Clark, George. 1965. *The Making of Victorian England*. London: Routledge.

Knott, Kim. 2005. *The Location of Religion: A Spatial Analysis*. London: Equinox.

Knott, Kim. 2014. Interrogating the Secular: A Spatial Approach. In R. van den Breemer, J. Casanova, and T. Wyller (eds). *Secular and Sacred? The Scandinavian Case of Religion in Human Rights, Law and Public Space*. Göttingen: Vandenhoeck and Ruprecht, 34–55.

Knott, Kim, Elizabeth Poole, and Taira Teemu. 2013. *Media Portrayals of Religion and the Secular Sacred: Representation and Change*. Farnham: Ashgate.

Kosmin, Barry A. 2007. Introduction: Contemporary Secularity and Secularism. In B. A. Kosmin and A. Keysar (eds). *Secularity and Secularism: Contemporary International Perspective*. Hartford, CT: ISSSC, 1–13.

Kuper, Adam. 1999. *Culture: The Anthropologists' Account*. Cambridge, MA: Harvard University Press.

Laborde, Cécile. 2014a. Equal Liberty, Nonestablishment, and Religious Freedom. *Legal Theory* 20 (1): 52–77. DOI: 10.1017/S1352325213000141.

Laborde, Cécile. 2014b. Three Approaches to Religion. Immanent Frame. Available at <http://blogs.ssrc.org/tif/2014/02/05/three-approaches-to-the-study-of-religion/> [accessed 29 March 2014].

Lanman, Jonathan. 2011. Thou Shalt Believe–or Not. *New Scientist*, 26 March 2011, 38–9.

Lanman, Jonathan A. 2012. The Importance of Religious Displays for Belief Acquisition and Secularization. *Journal of Contemporary Religion* 27 (1): 49–65.

Lave, Jean and Etienne Wenger. 1991. *Situated Learning: Legitimate Peripheral Participation*. New York, NY: Cambridge University Press.

Lee, Lois. 2006. The Secular Individual in Britain: Toward a Sociology of (Ir)religion. Unpublished MPhil dissertation, University of Cambridge.

Lee, Lois. 2011. From Neutrality to Dialogue: Constructing the Religious Other in British Non-religious Discourses. In M. Behrensen, L. Lee, and A. S. Tekelioglu (eds). *Modernities Revisited*. Vienna: IWM Junior Visiting Fellows' Conferences 2011, 29. Available at <www.iwm.at> [accessed 23 June 2011].

Lee, Lois. 2014. Secular or Nonreligious? Investigating and Interpreting Generic 'Not Religious' Categories and Populations. *Religion* 44 (3): 466–82. DOI:10.1080/0048721X.2014.904035.

Lee, Lois. Forthcoming. Vehicles of New Atheism: The Atheist Bus Campaign, Nonreligious Representations and Material Culture. In C. Cotter and P. Quadrio (eds). *New Atheism's Legacy: Critical Perspectives from Philosophy and the Social Sciences*. Dordrecht: Springer.

Lee, Lucy. 2012. Religion: Losing Faith? In A. Park, E. Clery, J. Curtice, M. Phillips, and D. Utting (eds). *British Social Attitudes 28*. London: SAGE, 173–84.

Lehmann, David. 2010. Rational Choice and the Sociology of Religion. In B. S. Turner (ed.). *The New Blackwell Companion to the Sociology of Religion*. Chichester: Wiley-Blackwell, 181–200.

Lim, Chaeyoon, Carol Ann and Robert D. Putnam. 2010. Secular and Liminal: Discovering Heterogeneity Among Religious Nones. *Journal for the Scientific Study of Religion* 49 (4): 596–618.

Lüchau, Peter. 2010. Atheism and Secularity: The Scandinavian Paradox. In P. Zuckerman (ed.). *Atheism and Secularity: Volume 2: Global Expressions*. Santa Barbara, CA: Praeger, 177–98.
Luckmann, Thomas. 1967. *The Invisible Religion: The Problem of Religion in Modern Society*. New York, NY: Macmillan.
Lynch, Gordon. 2012a. Living with Two Cultural Turns: The Case of the Study of Religion. In S. Roseneil and S. Frosh (eds). *Social Research After the Cultural Turn*. Basingstoke: Palgrave MacMillan, 73–92.
Lynch, Gordon. 2012b. *The Sacred in the Modern World: A Cultural Sociological Approach*. Oxford: Oxford University Press.
Maclure, Jocelyn and Charles Taylor. 2011. *Secularism and Freedom of Concience*. Trans. Jane Marie Todd. Cambridge, MA: Harvard University Press.
Martin, Michael. 1990. *Appendix: Atheism Defined and Contrasted. Atheism: A Philosophical Justification*. Philadelphia, PA: Temple University Press, 463–76.
Martin, Michael (ed.). 2007. *The Cambridge Companion to Atheism*. Cambridge: Cambridge University Press.
McCrea, Ronan. 2013. How to Hobble Religion. *Aeon* 18 June 2013. Available at <http://aeon.co/magazine/society/ronan-mccrea-secular-europe/> [accessed 30 September 2014].
McCutcheon, Russell T. 2007. 'They Licked the Platter Clean': On the Co-Dependency of the Religious and the Secular. *Method and Theory in the Study of Religion* 19: 173–99.
McGuire, Meredith B. (2008). *Lived Religion: Faith and Practice in Everyday Life*. New York, NY: Oxford University Press.
McLennan, Gregor. 2010. The Postsecular Turn. *Theory Culture Society* 27 (3): 3–20.
McLoughlin, Seán. 2005. Religion and Diaspora. In J. R. Hinnells (ed.). *The Routledge Companion to the Study of Religion*. London: Routledge, 526–49.
Meek, James. 2011. In Broadway Market. *London Review of Books* (online). 9 August 2011. Available at <http://www.lrb.co.uk/blog/2011/08/09/james-meek/in-broadway-market/> [accessed 9 August 2011].
Mellor, Philip A. and Chris Shilling. 1997. *Re-forming the Body*. London: SAGE.
Mellor, Philip A. and Chris Shilling. 2010. The Religious Habitus: Embodiment, Religion, and Sociological Theory. In B. S. Turner (ed.). *The New Blackwell Companion to the Sociology of Religion*. Malden, MA: Wiley Blackwell, 201–20.
Merino, Stephen M. 2012. Irreligious Socialization? The Adult Religious Preferences of Individuals Raised with No Religion. *Secularism and Nonreligion* 1: 1–16.

Modood, Tariq. 2009. Muslims, Religious Equality and Secularism. In G. Brahm Levey and T. Modood (eds). *Secularism, Religion and Multicultural Citizenship*. Cambridge: Cambridge University Press, 164–85.

Modood, Tariq. 2010. Moderate Secularism, Religion as Identity and Respect for Religion. *The Political Quarterly*, 81 (1): 4–14.

Norris, Pippa and Ronald Inglehart. 2004. *Sacred and Secular: Religion and Politics Worldwide*. Cambridge: Cambridge University Press.

O'Reilly, Karen. 2009. *Key Concepts in Ethnography*. Los Angeles, CA: SAGE.

Pahl, Ray and Liz Spencer. 2004. Personal Communities: Not Simply Families of 'Fate' or 'Choice'. *Current Sociology*, 52 (2): 199–221.

Pasquale, Frank L. 2007. Empirical Study and Neglect of Unbelief and Irreligion. In T. Flynn (ed.). *The New Encyclopaedia of Unbelief*. Amherst, NY: Prometheus Books, 760–6.

Phillipson, Heather. 2009. *Faber New Poets 3*. London: Faber & Faber.

Pink, Sarah. 2006. *The Future of Visual Anthropology: Engaging the Senses*. London: Routledge.

Porter, Roy. 2000. *Enlightenment: Britain and the Creation of the Modern World*. London: Penguin.

Putnam, Robert D. 2000. *Bowling Alone: The Collapse and Revival of American Community*. New York, NY: Simon and Schuster.

Quack, Johannes. 2011. *Disenchanting India: Organized Rationalism and Criticism of Religion in India*. New York, NY: Oxford University Press.

Quack, Johannes. 2014. Outline of a Relational Approach to 'Nonreligion', *Method and Theory in the Study of Religion* 26 (4–5): 439–69.

Riis, Ole Preben. 2008. Methodology in the Sociology of Religion. In P. B. Clarke (ed.). *The Oxford Handbook of the Sociology of Religion*. Oxford: Oxford University Press, 229–44.

Riis, Ole and Linda Woodhead. 2010. *A Sociology of Religious Emotion*. Oxford: Oxford University Press.

Schielke, Samuli. 2013. The Islamic World. In S. Bullivant and M. Ruse (eds). *The Oxford Handbook of Atheism*. Oxford: Oxford University Press, 638–59.

Schnell, Tatjana. 2010. Existential Indifference: Another Quality of Meaning in Life. *Journal of Humanistic Psychology* 50 (3): 351–73. DOI: 10.1177/0022167809360259.

Schnell, Tatjana and William J. F. Keenan. 2011. Meaning-Making in an Atheist World. *Archive for the Psychology of Religion* 33: 55–78. DOI: 10.1163/157361211X564611.

Schofield Clark, Lynn. 2003. *From Angels to Aliens: Teenagers, the Media, and the Supernatural*. Oxford: Oxford University Press.

Sherine, Ariane. 2008a. Atheists–Gimme Five. *Guardian* (online), 20 June 2008. <http://www.guardian.co.uk/commentisfree/2008/jun/20/transport.religion> [accessed 21 February 2011].

Sherine, Ariane, 2008b. Dawkin 'Bout A Revolution. *Guardian* (online), 6 August 2008. <http://www.guardian.co.uk/commentisfree/2008/aug/06/richarddawkins.religion> [accessed 21 Feb 2011].

Shilling, Chris. 2008. *Changing Bodies: Habits, Crisis and Creativity*. London: SAGE.

Shilling, Chris and Philip A. Mellor, 2007. Cultures of Embodied Experience: Technology, Religion and Body Pedagogics. *Sociolgcial Review*, 55 (3): 531–49.

Siegers, Pascale. 2010. A Multiple Group Latent Class Analysis of Religious Orientations in Europe. In E. Davidov, P. Schmidt, and J. Billet (eds). *Cross-Cultural Analysis: Methods and Applications*. New York, NY: Routledge, 387–413.

Singler, B. V. L. 2014. 'SEE MOM IT IS REAL': The UK Census, Jediism and Social Media. *Journal of Religion in Europe* 7: 150–68. DOI: 10.1163/18748929-00702005.

Smith, Jesse M. 2011. Becoming an Atheist in America: Constructing Identity and Meaning from the Rejection of Theism. *Sociology of Religion* 72 (2): 215–37.

Something for the Weekend, Series, Princess Productions. TV, BBC2, 17 January 2010, 10 am.

Spencer, Liz and Ray Pahl. 2006. *Rethinking Friendship: Hidden Solidarities Today*. Princeton, NJ: Princeton University Press.

Stark, Rodney and William Sims Bainbridge. 1996. *A Theory of Religion*. New Brunswick, NJ: Rutgers University Press.

Stark, Rodney and Roger Finke. 2000. *Acts of Faith: Explaining the Human Side of Religion*. London: University of California Press.

Strhan, Anna. 2014. What Do We Do When We 'Do Life'? Studying Relations Between Religious and Non-religious Cultures. Nonreligion and Secularity, Nonreligion and Secularity Research Network. Available at <http://blog.nsrn.net/tag/anna-strhan/.>

Taves, Ann. 2009. *Religious Experience Reconsidered: A Building-Block Approach to the Study of Religion and Other Special Things*. Princeton, NJ: Princeton University Press.

Taylor, Charles. 2007. *A Secular Age*. Cambridge, MA: Belknap Press of Harvard University Press.

Taylor, Charles. 2009. Foreword: What is Secularism? In G. Brahm Levey and T. Modood (eds). *Secularism, Religion and Multicultura/Citizenship*. Cambridge: Cambridge University Press, xi–xxii.

Thompson, John B. 1995. *Media and Modernity: A Social Theory of the Media*. Stanford, CA: Stanford University Press.

Towler, Robert. 1984. *The Need for Certainty: A Sociological Study of Conventional Religion*. London: Routledge and Kegan Paul.

Turner, Bryan S. 2010. Religion in a Post-Secular Society. In B. S. Turner (ed.). *The New Blackwell Companion to the Sociology of Religion.* Chichester: Wiley-Blackwell, 649–67.

Vernon, Glenn M. 1968. The Religious 'Nones': A Neglected Category. *Journal for the Scientific Study of Religion,* 7 (2): 219–29.

Voas, David. 2009a. The Rise and Fall of Fuzzy Fidelity in Europe. *European Sociological Review,* 25 (2): 155–68.

Voas, David. 2009b. Who are the Non-religious in Britain and Where Do They Come From? Paper presented at the first conference of the Nonreligion and Secularity Research Network, Oxford, 11 December 2009.

Voas, David and Alistair Crockett. 2005. Religion in Britain: Neither Believing nor Belonging. *Sociology* 39 (1): 11.

Voas, David and Abby Day. 2007. Secularity in Great Britain. In B. A. Kosmin and A. Keysar (eds). *Secularism and Secularity: Contemporary International Perspectives.* Hartford, CA: ISSSC, 95–110.

Voas, David and Rodney Ling. 2010. Religion in Britain and the United States. *British Social Attitudes: The 26th Report.* London: SAGE/National Centre for Social Research: 67–87.

Voas, David and Siobhan McAndrew. 2012. Three Puzzles of Non-religion in Britain. *Journal of Contemporary Religion* 27 (1): 29–48.

Ware, Vron and Les Back. 2002. *Out of Whiteness: Color, Politics, and Culture.* Chicago, IL: Chicago University Press.

Weber, Max. 1993. *The Sociology of Religion.* Boston, MA: Beacon Press.

Weber, Max. 2003. *The Protestant Ethic and the Spirit of Capitalism.* New York, NY: Dover Publications.

Wohlrab-Sahr, Monika and Marian Burchardt. 2012. Multiple Secularities: Toward a Cultural Sociology of Secular Modernities. *Comparative Sociology* 11 (2012): 875–909.

Wood, Matthew. 2007. *Possession, Power and the New Age: Ambiguities of Authority in Neoliberal Societies.* Aldershot: Ashgate.

Woodhead, Linda. 2010. Real Religion, Fuzzy Spirituality. In D. Houtman and S. Aupers (eds). *Religions of Modernity: Relocating the Sacred to the Self and the Digital.* Leiden: Brill.

Woodhead, Linda. 2011. Five Concepts of Religion. *International Review of Sociology,* 21 (1): 121–43.

Woodhead, Linda. 2012a. Introduction. In L. Woodhead and R. Catto (eds). *Religion and Change in Modern Britain.* Aldershot: Ashgate, 1–33.

Woodhead, Linda. 2012b. Mind, Body and Spirit: It's the De-reformation of Religion. *Guardian,* 7 May 2012. Available at <http://www.theguardian.com/commentisfree/belief/2012/may/07/mind-body-spirit-dereformation-religion> [accessed 9 February 2015].

Woodhead, Linda. 2014. A Signal of What Really Matters. *Church Times,* 26 September 2014. Available at <http://www.churchtimes.co.uk/articles/

2014/26-september/comment/opinion/a-signal-of-what-really-matters> [accessed 9 February 2015].

Zuckerman, Phil. 2007. Atheism: Contemporary Numbers and Patterns. In M. Martin (ed.). *The Cambridge Companion to Atheism.* Cambridge: Cambridge University Press, 47–65.

Zuckerman, Phil. 2008. *Society without God: What the Least Religious Nations Can Tell Us about Contentment.* New York: New York University Press.

Zuckerman, Phil (ed.). 2010a. *Atheism and Secularity: Issues, Concepts and Definitions—Volume I.* Santa Barbara, CA: Praeger.

Zuckerman, Phil (ed.). 2010b. *Atheism and Secularity: Global Expressions–Volume II.* Santa Barbara, CA: Praeger.

Zuckerman, Phil. 2010c. Introduction. In P. Zuckerman (ed.). *Atheism and Secularity—Volume I: Issues, Concepts and Definitions.* Santa Barbara, CA: Praeger, vii–xii.

Zuckerman, Phil. 2012. *Faith No More: Why People Reject Religion.* New York, NY: Oxford University Press.

Index

Abrahamic religion 51
absence 18, 54, 55, 104, 113, 167
Advertising Standards Authority
   (ASA) 79
afterlife 45, 55, 96, 125, 160, 163
agnosticism 163, 164–5, 166, 172–5, 176
   relativism 164
   in religious culture 54
   and scientific knowledge 163
   and self-identification 152, 154,
      164, 172–5
Alpha course 83
alternative religion 37
alternative spirituality
   existential 160, 166
   individualization 56
   and religion 26, 47, 67, 194, 197
   and secularity 16, 36, 41
anthropology of religion 16, 29, 81, 87,
   187, 188
anti-existential 165, 169–71, 172,
   175, 177–8
anti-religion 9–10, 28–9, 37, 39, 46, 47,
   49, 60–1, 62, 64, 68–9, 76–9, 85, 87,
   106, 116, 118–19, 136, 147–8, 179,
   186, 190, 203gl
anti-spirituality 119
anti-theism 37, 38, 63, 203gl
areligion 203gl
   and non-religion 33, 47
   and post-secularity 45
   and secularity 53, 67, 80, 85,
      189, 190
   term 29, 30, 32, 37, 145
   use of church buildings 104
Asad, Talal
   and genealogical approach 46
   and postcolonial approach 58
   on 'religion' 23
   on religious basis of secularity 191
   on secular embodiment 88, 102
   on secularism 43, 57
Aston, Katie 77, 89
atheism 37–9, 62–3, 64, 203gl
   as affiliation 132

as 'aggressive' 135–6, 140
associations with elite 137–40
'British Atheism' 133–41
categories 165
in concept of secularity 10, 12
'convinced atheism' 136
as indication of religion 54
'militant atheism' 62
popular conceptions of 133, 134–6
positive or negative 8, 37
prevalence of 6
and relationship with god(s) 39
self-identification 24
use of term 48, 134
as Western concept 38
'Atheist Bus Campaign' 71n1, 81–4, 143
'atheist shoes' 89, 90–1
'atheocracy' 191
atomism and insufficient
   solidarity 123–5, 126
Attenborough, David 176, 177, 178

Bagg, Samuel and Voas, David 53, 142
Bailey, Edward 8, 56, 94
Baker, Joseph O'Brian and Smith,
   Buster 65
banality 70–85
   domestic non-religion 72–4
   identity markers 91, 101
   indifference 78, 79–81
   irreverence 80
   material non-religion 77–8, 88
   official non-religion 81–4
   public non-religion 74, 75–7
   self-identification 158
'banal nationalism' 70, 71, 82
Bauman, Zygmunt 54, 121, 128
Beck, Ulrich and Beck-Gernsheim,
   Elisabeth 54, 66
Becker, Howard 14
Beckford, James A. 23, 46, 157
Beit-Hallahmi, Benjamin 54
Bellah, Robert N. 82
Bender, Courtney and Taves, Ann 16
bereavement 54, 96, 112, 182

Berger, Peter 56, 184, 191
Berger, Peter, Davie, Grace and Fokas, Ellie 60, 61, 179
Berman, Morris 56
Berns, Steph 33, 34, 45, 98, 148
Bhargava, Rajeev 16
Billig, Michael 70, 71, 80, 82, 85, 170, 187
binary approaches 15, 16, 40, 41–2
body, human 18, 86–105
  badges and barriers 99–101, 102
  Christian 97
  humanist 102
  non-religious 94–6, 97–9
  secular 102–3
  secularist 45, 97–98
  statement clothing 88–91
  understatement clothing 92–4
Bourdieu, Pierre 32, 95, 101, 200
Brazil 1
'Bright' 151
Brigstocke, Marcus 106, 113, 147, 148
British Humanist Association (BHA) 35, 71n1, 82, 93, 123, 125, 144
  'Census Campaign' 143
British Museum 34, 45, 98, 148
British Social Attitudes survey 5, 24, 154, 155
Bruce, Steve 7, 53, 54, 85, 136, 156
Budd, Susan 63
Bullivant, Stephen 4, 36, 98, 139, 157
Burchardt, Marian 16, 47n6

Cambridge 10, 11
Campbell, Colin
  on ethics and religion 124
  on irreligion 24, 31, 32, 33, 63
  and non-religion 13, 15, 59, 64, 97, 137, 186, 187
  relational view 58, 67
  on terminology 28, 48
Cannell, Fenella 59
Casanova, José 9, 60, 117, 198
Casserley, Langmead 171
Census for England and Wales
  2001 142, 143, 153, 154, 156, 198
  2011 153, 154
Christianity
  anti-Christian graffiti 78
  ceremonies 117, 181
  embodiment 97
  ethnicization of 155, 156
  imagery 78, 79, 80, 91
  New Atheist attitude towards 86
  references in packaging 73–4
  secularism and 40, 43
  self-identification as 109, 114, 155, 156
  surveys and 51
Christmas, non-theist celebration of 126
church buildings, secular use 104
Church census 1851 29, 57
civil religion 82
cognitive research 29, 51, 97
collectivism 66
'communal secularism' 127
compensators 55
Congregational Year Book 57, 171
Connolly, William E. 45, 179
Copeman, Jacob and Quack, Johannes 96
Copson, Andrew 143
Corporale, Rocco and Grumelli, Antonio 63
Cox, Brian 176
Cultural Anthropology 87
cultural diversity 60
cultural icons 82

Dant, Tim 83, 88
Darwin, Charles 63, 77
Davie, Grace 8, 56, 65, 94, 97, 187
Dawkins, Richard
  'Atheist Bus Campaign' 71n1
  humanism 168, 176, 177
  New Atheism 63, 118, 134, 137, 198
  on the religious 86
Day, Abby 6, 13, 155
de Botton, Alain 129, 139
Denmark 6
Dennett, Daniel 63
Descartes, René 176
desecularization 2, 4, 31, 41, 56
digital media 83–4
disaffiliation 132, 152, 157; *See also* non-affiliation
dress, non-religious 89, 94–6
Durkheim, Émile 6, 7, 108, 126, 129, 148, 159

Eagleton, Terry 159
educational institutions, and non-religion 114

Index

Eisenstadt, Shmuel N. 43
embodiment, *See* body, human
Engelke, Matthew 77, 87, 89, 93, 187
Enlightenment 9, 46, 61, 176
ethics
  agnosticism 164
  anti-existential 169, 170
  existential 160, 172, 184
  'Golden Rule, the' 125
  humanism 144, 162
  and religion 66, 124, 125
ethnographic data 11
Europe 6, 56, 60, 192
evangelicalism 56
Evans, Pippa 129
evolutionary theory 63
exclusion 118
existential cultures 19, 159–84
  agnosticism 163, 164–5, 166, 176, 180
  anti-existential 169–71, 172
  binary approaches 168
  humanism 162–3, 164, 165, 166, 176, 180
  intellectualist 178
  in practice 172–5
  public and private 178–9
  in public life 175–8
  religion and non-religion 180–3
'existential indifference' 169
'existential security' 53

family, and non-religion 114
Fitzgerald, Timothy 23, 26, 57, 184, 200
Foucauldian approach 23
Foundation for Reason and Science 134
'four horsemen' 63
'freethinker' 151
friendship 108–9, 110
functionalism 159
fundamentalism 56
funerals 123, 124, 181
'fuzzy religiosity' 6

Gane, Nicholas 56
Geertz, Armin W. and Markússon, Guðmundur Ingi 38
Gellner, Ernest 184
gender 76, 165
genealogical approach 23, 40, 46, 57
Gibson, Nicholas 4
Gibson, Nicholas and Barnes, Kirsten 157

Giddens, Anthony 54, 55, 182
godlessness 38, 53, 54, 90, 136
'Golden Rule, the' 125
graffiti 76, 77–8, 84
Grayling, A. C. 86, 134
Guardian, the 134, 150, 175, 176, 178
Gutkowksi, Stacey 4, 32, 101

Haas, Peter M. 126
Habermas, Jürgen 60, 121
habitus 99, 101
Halman, Loek and Moor, Ruud de 56
Harris, Sam 63
Hawking, Stephen 176
Hayes, Bernadette C. 137
Heelas, Paul and Woodhead, Linda 119, 166
hidden solidarities 18, 19
  consolidation 126–8
  and friendship 108–9, 110
  intimacy and religion 110
  networks 121, 122
  non-religious socialization 111–12, 113
  taken-for-granted 113–15
Hirschkind, Charles 87, 88, 102
Hitchens, Christopher 63, 198
humanism 162–3, 180; *See also* British Humanist Association
  and agnosticism 163, 164, 165
  and the body 102
  ceremonies 95
  and non-religion 34, 35
  public discourse 175, 176
  'secular humanism' 35
  self-identification 151–2, 174, 175, 183
  and theism 166
Huxley, T. H. 63, 164
hypocrisy, religious 119
hypotheses for research 65–9

ideal-typical secularity, as non-entity 9
identification 131–58
  atheism 133, 134–41
  as contradistinction to religion 132
  indifference and indifferentism 144, 145–50
  in-group 115
  markers 99–101, 102
  multiple 13
  negative 133, 136, 141, 149, 151, 157
  nones and nothingness 153–6
  public 74, 75

immanence 99, 167, 169, 170
implicit religion 56, 94
inclusion 195–7
India 1
indifference 29–30, 144, 145–9, 185, 203gl
   as disaffiliation 132, 133
   British Social Attitudes Survey 154
   and irreligion 31
   irreverence and 78, 79–84
   secularity and 53, 54
indifferentism 90, 141, 149–50, 198
individualization 66, 67
industrial modernity 1, 6, 7
Institute for the Study of Secularism in Society and Culture (ISSSC) 4
insubstantial secularity
   Bruce on 53
   and categorization 157
   impact of 106, 132
   negative concepts 131
   non-religious encounters 59
   post-structuralism and 57
   relationship to religion 19
   and secularization theory 55, 56, 61
   theory of 55
interactions 5
irreligion 31–7, 203gl
   intellectual concept 9, 10, 171
   as middle class 171
   rejection of religion 31, 97
   sociology of 63
irreverence and indifference 78, 79–81
Islam 38, 45, 76, 80
Islamophobia 71, 77, 78, 80
isolation 122, 123
Institute for the Study of Secularism (ISSC) 4

James, William 36
Jesussaid.org 81, 83
Jones, Sanderson 129

Keysar, Ariela 4
Keysar, Ariela and Navarro-Rivera, Juhem 137
Kitson Clark, George 29, 57
Knott, Kim 27, 40, 42, 75, 93
Kosmin, Barry 4, 8, 16, 30, 44
Kuper, Adam 34

Laborde, Cécile 170, 183
'Land of Hope and Glory' (Elgar) 73

Lave, Jean and Wenger, Etienne 63
Lehmann, David 56
liberalism 40
life-cycle rituals 181, 182, 184
London 10, 11, 76, 138
London, University of 134
London Review of Books 138
Luckmann, Thomas 166
Lynch, Gordon 62

Maclure, Jocelyn and Taylor, Charles 170, 184
Maffesoli, Michel 66
Martin, Michael 35, 39, 163
Marx, Karl 55
material culture, non-religious 75, 77–8, 83, 96
McCrae, Ronan 192
McCutcheon, Russell 23, 26
McGuire, Meredith B. 91
McLennan, Gregor 61, 62
McLoughlin, Seán 200
media 77, 83, 99
mediated quasi-interaction 113
Meek, James 138
Mellor, Philip A. and Shilling, Chris 98, 99
'militant atheism' 62
modernist 9–10, 46, 64, 66, 101, 102, 106, 163, 176
modernity 1, 2, 6–9, 43, 54–7, 66–7, 102, 185, 189
modernization 1, 7, 54, 182
Modood, Tariq 8, 16, 136
morality, and religion 124–5
Muhammad, representations of 80
mysticism 179, 180

nationalism 70
National Secular Society (NSS) 35
naturalism 35
networks 108, 121–2, 128, 129
neutrality 53, 57, 58, 144, 145, 150, 198
New Atheism 63, 203gl
   centrality of 134
   in domestic spaces 73
   as elite 139
   influence of 198
   material form 71
   media representation 178
   negativity towards 136, 137
   reception studies 118

and solidarity 67
view of the religious 86
Nine Lessons and Carols for Godless People 12, 126, 148
nominal religion and non-religion 6, 155
non-affiliation 2, 133, 155
nones and nothingness 131, 132, 143, 153–6
non-religion 12–14, 31–5, 69, 203gl
　as affiliation 132, 143
　anti-social 118–21
　and celebration 128
　commitment to 154
　contradistinction to religion 32
　cultures 49, 50, 141–4
　and difference 34
　domestic 72–4
　as elite 137–40
　ethnography 17
　everyday forms 70–85
　existential 19
　images 72–4
　intellectualization 62–4, 113, 114, 137, 138, 139, 140
　and lack of visibility 125
　material 17, 18, 70
　multiculturalist approach 34
　multiple identities 153
　narratives 86–8
　and national identification 82
　non-institutionalization 109, 123, 124, 175, 193
　official 81–4
　organized 18, 187
　perceived openness of 141, 142
　prevalence 5
　public 74, 75–7
　in public life 131–58
　and rejection 34
　and religion 18, 19, 32, 97
　and religious others 119–20, 125
　research 65
　pro-social 115–18
　and secularity 14, 15–16, 20, 44–5, 62–4
　socialization 111–12, 113, 126–7
　social aspects of 67, 106–20, 128, 129
　as term 25, 144, 145
Nonreligion and Secularity Research Network (NSRN) 4
non-religionization 105, 133

non-theism 204gl
　articulation of 118
　movements 139
　public discourse 63
　self-identification 113, 114
　term 37, 38, 39
　toiletry packaging 73–4, 75
Norris, Pippa and Inglehart, Ronald 53, 55, 171
nostalgia 74
'not religious' 5, 143, 152

organic solidarity 108
organized relationships 106, 107
'othering' 87
otherness 100, 148
　embodiment of 97, 100
　enactment of 30
　and engagement 34, 58
　and indifference 148
　and relationships 120–1
　shared 117
　terminology 38
Oxford English Dictionary (OED) 31, 32

Pahl, Ray and Spencer, Liz 18
Pasquale, Frank L. 131
'peg communities' 128
Phillipson, Heather 177, 178
Pink, Sarah 75, 83
plurality and pluralism 186
Poland 6
political secularism 34, 35, 44, 45, 87
post-colonialism 40, 58, 64, 150
postmodernism 85
post-religion 30, 31, 53, 58, 79, 85, 130, 204gl
post-secular 45, 46, 59, 60, 67, 68, 69, 117, 192, 204gl
post-structuralism 23, 40, 57, 64
public life, non-religious 131–58
　'British Atheism' 133–41
　identification 150, 151–3
　indifference and indifferentism 144, 145–50
　'nones' 153–6
　secularity 49
　substantive 'non-religious' cultures 141–4
public spaces 45

Quack, Johannes 28, 31, 32, 47n6, 187, 199
Qur'an 38

rational choice theory 55, 56, 67
rationalism 35, 36, 118, 119, 151, 152, 163
reception studies 118
religion 25–7, 204gl
 as analytical category 27
 archaeology 63
 as comfort for disadvantaged 53
 communality 107
 conceptions of 26–7, 65–6
 critique as active choice 120
 egalitarian approaches 170–1
 institutions 29
 as irrelevant 9
 marginalization of 34, 46, 52, 53
 as other 76
 prevalence 5
 privatization 111, 116
 pluralism 44, 49
 and secularity 39–47
 separation from politics 52
 sociology of 23–4
 as substantial 50
 traditional 51, 52
 uses of images in non-religion 75
Religion for Atheists (de Botton) 129, 139
'religionization' 41
religious affiliation 51
religious and theological approaches 57, 58
religious communities, departure from 111, 112, 123
religious habitus 99
representation, social, political and legal 197–200
research methodology 10–11, 12
'resurgent religion' 41
Riis, Ole 38
Riis, Ole and Woodhead, Linda 98
rites of passage 54, 55, 95, 117
rituals 4, 55, 123
romantic relationships 110
Russell, Bertrand 86

'scepticism' 21, 57, 64, 151
Schielke, Samuli 38
Schnell, Tatjana 169, 171

Schnell, Tatjana and Keenan, William J. F. 165, 184
School of Life 129, 139
science 63, 64, 89, 176
secular 204gl
 body 102, 103
 consciousness 61
 'secular field' 11
 secular-in-relation 58–9
Secular Age, A (Taylor) 49, 50
'secular humanism' 35
secularism 42–3, 44, 151, 204gl
 as anti-religious 9
 hard and soft 30
 ideological nature 59
 modernist 64
 and non-religious embodiment 97, 98
 'radical secularism' 136
 and secularity 43
secularity 14–16, 39–42, 204gl
 Bruce on 85
 concept of religion 26, 66
 contradistinction 25
 as default position 53
 ethnography 17
 exclusion of religious 118
 heterogeneity of 51
 identification of self with religion 143
 insubstantial and substantial 17, 21, 49, 50–2
 literature on 8–10
 and non-religion 44–5
 pluralist 167
 and post-secularity 45
 prevalence 152–3
 as recent 6
 and religion 25
 seen in negative terms 53
 use of term 50
 as Western, Protestant concept 40
secularization 46–7, 63, 105, 191
secularization paradigm 7, 14, 50, 53, 54, 69
secularization theory 9, 52–4, 55, 61, 67
 and banality 70, 74
 critics of 55–6, 57
 and insubstantial secularity 52
 and non-religion 14, 15
 and post-religion 31
 and secularity 40
 subtraction account 51
secular liberalism 44

Index

secular modernity 7, 54, 189; *See also* modernity
self-identification 19, 24, 132, 157
Sherine, Ariane 81, 83
Siegers, Pascale 6, 29, 155
slogans, non-religion 89
Smith, Jesse 38
Soap and Glory 73–4, 75
social cohesion 6, 7
sociology of irreligion 63
Sociology of Religion, The (Weber) 23
solidarity, networked 122–3
Something for the Weekend 106, 113
Spencer, Liz and Pahl, Ray 66, 121, 122, 126, 150
spirituality 26, 36, 204gl
spiritualization of society thesis 67
Stark, Rodney 55
Stark, Rodney and Bainbridge, William Sims 55
Stark, Rodney and Finke, Roger 56
state atheism 191
state churches 187
statement clothing 88–91
state secularity 31
Stephen, Leslie 63
Stik 76, 94
Strhan, Anna 187
'subjective secularity' 2
subjectivism 164, 166, 167, 169
substantial non-religion 69, 87, 112
substantial secularity 4, 58–64, 185
Sunday Assembly 104, 129, 139
symbols, religious 93

tattoos 89, 93
Taves, Ann 200
Taylor, Charles
  on existential 161
  on humanism 163
  pluralist approach 15, 49, 167, 186
  A Secular Age 49, 50
  and secularity 40, 42
  on secularization 191
  and subtraction 51, 53
  terms 21
theism 204gl
  as narrow concept 26
  as norm 38
  rejection of 10

related terms 37–9
and romanticism 164
and subjectivism 165, 166–8
theocracy 41, 42
Thompson, John B. 113
Time of Tribes: The Decline of Individualism in Mass Society (Maffesoli) 66
Towards a Sociology of Irreligion (Campbell) 31
Towler, Robert 10, 27
Trinity College, Hartford, Connecticut 4
Turner, Bryan S. 59, 66, 67, 128

unbelief 48, 50, 62, 63, 65, 115
understatement clothing 92–4
unreligious 6, 57, 64, 67
urban environment 76
United States (US) 6, 38, 106, 139, 187

Varieties of Unbelief: Atheists and Agnostics in English Society, 1850–1960 (Budd) 63
Vatican 63
vicarious religion 56, 94
Voas, David 6
Voas, David and Crockett, Alastair 56
Voas, David and Day, Abby 155, 156
Voas, David and Ling, Rodney 6, 24, 154
Voas, David and McAndrew, Siobhan 137, 188
vocabulary 21–48, 150, 151–3
  intellectualization 151
  'religion' 25–7
  religion-related terms 28, 29–37
  relational 28
  secular-related terms 39–47
  theism-related terms 37–9

Ware, Vron and Back, Les 195
Weber, Max 6, 7, 23, 24, 53, 160
weddings 95, 96
Wohlrab-Sahr, Monika 16, 47n6
Wohlrab-Sahr, Monika and Burchardt, Marian 16, 40, 42, 43, 61
Woodhead, Linda 23, 24, 75, 95, 123, 149, 168

Zuckerman, Phil 2, 53, 54, 112, 171

Printed and bound by CPI Group (UK) Ltd, Croydon, CR0 4YY